Cambodia

THE BRADT TRAVEL GUIDE

The Bradt Story

The first Bradt travel guide was written by Hilary and George Bradt in 1974 on a river barge floating down a tributary of the Amazon in Bolivia. From their base in Boston, Massachusetts, they went on to write and publish four other backpacking guides to the Americas and one to Africa.

In the 1980s Hilary continued to develop the Bradt list in England, and also established herself as a travel writer and tour leader. The company's publishing emphasis evolved towards broader-based guides to new destinations – usually the first to be published on those countries – complemented by hiking, rail and wildlife guides.

Since winning *The Sunday Times* Small Publisher of the Year Award in 1997, we have continued to fill the demand for detailed, well-written guides to unusual destinations, while maintaining the company's original ethos of low-impact travel.

Travel guides are by their nature continuously evolving. If you experience anything which you would like to share with us, or if you have any amendments to make to this guide, please write; all your letters are read and passed on to the author. Most importantly, do remember to travel with an open mind and to respect the customs of your hosts – it will add immeasurably to your enjoyment.

Happy travelling!

Hilary Bradt

Hilary Bradt

19 High Street, Chalfont St Peter, Bucks SL9 9QE, England
Tel: 01753 893444 Fax: 01753 892333
Email: info@bradt-travelguides.com
Web: www.bradt-travelguides.com

Cambodia

THE BRADT TRAVEL GUIDE

Anita Sach

Bradt Travel Guides, UK
The Globe Pequot Press Inc, USA

First published in 2001 by Bradt Travel Guides,
19 High Street, Chalfont St Peter, Bucks SL9 9QE, England
web: www.bradt-travelguides.com
Published in the USA by The Globe Pequot Press Inc, 246 Goose Lane,
PO Box 480, Guilford, Connecticut 06475-0480

British Library Cataloguing in Publication Data
A catalogue record for this book is available from the British Library
ISBN 1 84162 016 5

Library of Congress Cataloging-in-Publication Data
Sach, Anita.
    Cambodia : the Bradt travel guide / Anita Sach.
        p. cm
    Includes bibliographical references and index.
    ISBN 1-84162-016-5
        1. Cambodia—Guidebooks. I. Title.
DS554.25 S23 2001
915.9604'42—dc21

                                                                    00-056206

Photographs *Front cover* Royal palace, Phnom Penh (Anita Sach)
Text Jamie Marshall/www.tribaleye.com (JM), Anita Sach (AS)

Illustrations Jane Keay
Maps Alan Whitaker

Typeset from the author's disc by Wakewing
Printed and bound in Italy by Legoprint SpA, Trento

Author

Anita Sach has worked in the travel industry for 17 years, much of which was spent as a specialist on Southeast Asia for Regent Holidays in Bristol and then for an incoming tour operator in Vietnam. She has been travelling to the region regularly since the late 1980s and was thrilled finally to be able to have the chance to travel beyond Phnom Penh and Siem Reap. Despite being lucky enough to have travelled to over 50 countries she finds herself continually drawn back to Cambodia and Vietnam and relishes the prospect of one day returning to the area to live. She now works freelance, writing, proofreading and regularly leading tour groups to Vietnam and China.

THIS BOOK IS DEDICATED TO MY FAMILY

Contents

LIST OF MAPS

Acknowledgements

So many people have helped in some way, either small or large, with the creation of this book. My first thanks must go to Neil Taylor, director of Regent Holidays in Bristol, who was responsible for sending me to Cambodia in the first place and always encouraged any interest in the country. Despite my no longer being an employee of his company, his continued support and friendship are greatly valued. Within Cambodia I cannot thank Kim, my guide and interpreter, enough for his resourcefulness in getting us across country, whatever the state of the roads, his patience in answering my millions of questions and for being such good company. His job was not an easy one.

My travelling companion for part of the journey was Teresa Measures who had worked on the Thai border in the refugee camps for a long time and relished the chance to visit the country whose people she had done so much to help. Thanks to Teresa for her good company, her sense of humour and her bargaining skills in Khmer, a language which she thought she had forgotten. My only regret is that she did not get to see the temples of Angkor, but I know she will rectify this before long.

I feel privileged to have gained the support of the Ministry of Tourism in Phnom Penh with my venture and particular thanks must go to Sambo Chey, the Under Secretary of State, and to the Minister of Tourism, Veng Sereyvuth, who took the trouble to contribute the foreword to this book. In addition I must also thank John Clapham, a journalist who does much to promote Cambodia and who has developed a deep affection and great enthusiasm for the country and its people. Thank you for your time and for collecting information on your frequent visits to Cambodia.

Several other people helped in some way. Peter from Lolei Travel in Phnom Penh was instrumental in getting the go-ahead for this book following his initial report on the developments and prospects for tourism in Cambodia for the feasibility study. In Prach, the Chief of Tourism in Battambang, took time to show us the main sites of interest. My guide around Angkor, Bros, was impressive in his knowledge of the history. Dr Felicity Nicholson ensured that I travelled healthily with plenty of expert advice. Hun Socheat of Pich Tourist in Phnom Penh has checked information for me and its managing director, Meng Hieng, has shown a keen interest in the writing of this book. Nguyen Tuyet Mai and her staff at Vidotour in Saigon gave much assistance with the planning. Diana McCracken of Silk Steps, Neil Taylor of Regent Holidays,

Hung Nguyen of Visit Vietnam and Craig Burkinshaw of Asian Journeys ensured the research got off the ground. Thank you all.

Finally thanks must go to David who has always encouraged and supported me in any venture and who shares my enthusiasm for Cambodia. Thanks for being there.

Foreword

by His Excellency, Veng Sereyvuth, the Minister of Tourism, Phnom Penh, Cambodia

As Cambodia enters a new millenium it does so with a new confidence. We welcome visitors to our country in order to share with them our unparalleled cultural heritage and, with the arrival of peace and stability, we can now open up our heartlands to you.

We have long basked in the glory of the temples of Angkor and these, among the greatest treasures in the world, we continue to preserve to ensure our rich history is not lost. Previously unvisited temples are now accessible and each one is unique.

But there is so much more to Cambodia...

We wish to introduce you to our capital, Phnom Penh, with its modern facilities and colonial charm. Sihanoukville, our main coastal resort, has miles of white, sandy beaches and offshore tropical islands with coral reefs just waiting to be explored. Battambang, the second city, has a wealth of attractive colonial buildings and an easy-going ambience. Small towns situated along the mighty Mekong, Kompong Cham, Kratie and Stung Treng, still enjoy a relaxed lifestyle, untouched by modern pressures.

The little-visited provinces of Rattanakiri and Mondulkiri have seen little development and ecotourism is being encouraged here to responsibly open up the region to our guests. Cool, forested hills are dotted with numerous tribal villages, each with its own language and customs. National parks throughout the country are working to retain their unique ecosystems and maintain natural habitat so that our wildlife can flourish.

Our infrastructure is improving all the time, making all these places so much more accessible by car, bus, boat or air.

This is just a little of what Cambodia has to offer, but the Bradt guidebook will give you the full picture. Read it and be amazed and then come to see us. Seeing is believing.

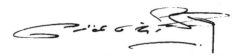

Veng Sereyvuth
Minister of Tourism

Introduction

The first Bradt guide to Cambodia in 1995 sadly had a section headed 'Restricted areas and restrictions on travel' in which foreign visitors were advised not to travel by bus, boat or train from Phnom Penh. There was a warning that foreigners attempting to buy train tickets were reported to the authorities and deported immediately. This followed the murder in 1994 of three Western tourists who were abducted from a train in Kampot province. In addition there was a strong warning that 'Under no circumstances should tourists enter zones known to be Khmer Rouge territory. These include Cambodia's Stung Treng Province bordering Laos, Preah Vihear, northern Siem Reap, Oddar Mean Chey, Battambang, Pursat, Kompong Speu and parts of Kampot'.

Happily I am able to report that, at the time of writing, all areas of Cambodia are now open and safe for visitors. I spent many weeks travelling around the country without incident and I never had any occasion to change my plans because of the security situation. In April 2000 the Ministry of Tourism announced that there had been a 41% increase of visitor arrivals by air in 1999, although this number will also include businessmen, aid workers and Cambodians returning to visit family. But it is still a very positive state of affairs.

I visited Cambodia for the first time in 1988 when, during a visit to neighbouring Vietnam, I was fortunate enough to be able to tag on to a small group of Americans who were flying to Phnom Penh and Siem Reap for a few days. Little did I know that this spontaneous visit would result in a long-lasting association with Cambodia and be the first of many more trips into the country.

In 1988 our small group of 14 people, including the Bradt author and photographer, John R Jones, were the only tourists in the country. Phnom Penh airport was a shell of a building with little inside apart from a regular flow of farm animals and dogs trooping through. The city itself looked as though families were camping in the ravaged apartment buildings and there were open sewers with a perfume all of their own in the oppressive heat. The best way to travel independently around the city was by cyclo and the drivers who waited outside the hotels all spoke reasonable English. Each one had a harrowing story to tell. So many young men and women, then only in their early twenties, were the solitary survivors of their family. I was struck by their cheerfulness and, coming from a society where any disaster is immediately followed up with a phalanx of counsellors to deal with the post-traumatic stress, I could only admire them for their positive, forward-looking attitude. They were delighted that tourists, albeit a very small trickle, were beginning to come to their country. Life was obviously improving.

The hotel accommodation in 1988 was fairly simple, with many being occupied by workers from non-governmental organisations (NGOs). Compared with life for the ordinary citizen it was more than adequate. There was a curfew in force and it was not yet possible to leave the city to venture into the countryside. For most members of the group the highlight was to be the flight up to Siem Reap for a one-day visit to the Angkor temples where we would be given a military escort. We were informed that there was a slight delay to our flight as our plane had to wait for a VIP jet to land first. The delay turned into hours, waiting in a building with only a few wooden benches where we were in danger of melting from the clammy heat. We never did make it to Angkor, there being a rumour that the Khmer Rouge were closing in on Phnom Penh and that their troops had set up an anti-aircraft gun to blow our plane out of the sky once it took off. It would have been quite a coup for the Khmer Rouge to have shot down a tourist plane. We reluctantly had to fly straight back to Ho Chi Minh City but at least we were safe.

I managed to get to Angkor for the first time in 1991 and the magic of the temples has remained with me ever since. At that time the trees had not been cleared away from the temples and the humidity of the jungle weighed heavily on us as we roamed the site, the air alive with the sound of insects. The Grand Hotel was very run down, with dingy rooms and rats scrambling around in the gloomy corridors. The only way to communicate with Siem Reap from Phnom Penh was by radio and the town had a distinct wild-west feel. By 1991 the road route between Ho Chi Minh City and Phnom Penh was deemed safe and was to be my first taste of the gentle countryside of Cambodia.

Subsequent visits to Cambodia throughout the 1990s were still restricted to Phnom Penh and Siem Reap although it was possible to take short visits out of the capital to Cheong Ek and Udong. But I always knew that there was a whole country out there waiting to be discovered. On each visit I noticed little changes – first of all bicycles and then motorbikes appeared on the streets, while now Phnom Penh experiences some pretty bad traffic jams as cars and bikes vie for the available space. Where once it had been a matter of survival to eat in one of the restaurants where it was difficult to identify exactly what you were eating, and probably best not to enquire too closely, there was now a choice of venues. Both Phnom Penh and Siem Reap were experiencing an increase in the number of visitor arrivals and canny locals realised that they needed to sleep somewhere as well as eat and drink and were keen to spend their dollars. Hotels, restaurants and bars mushroomed during 1992 and 1993 with the arrival of the UNTAC force, but many were to close once the thousands of men and women withdrew after the elections. UNTAC personnel were stationed throughout the country and small towns which had yet to see any tourists were quick to explore the earning potential of their arrival. Hotels and restaurants opened and in even the remote areas of

Cambodia it is not unusual to see 'hamburger' on the menu.

Post 1993 the countryside once again had a veil drawn over it, although temples within striking distance of the capital such as Tonle Bati, Phnom Chisor, Angkor Borei and Udong were generally safe to visit. Phnom Penh and Siem Reap prospered and even Sihanoukville began to welcome a few visitors who generally flew from Phnom Penh. Visitors began to travel by boat between Phnom Penh and Siem Reap, although initially this was not without incident. A few intrepid travellers did make their way to Kampot, Kompong Thom, Kompong Cham and remote places such as Rattanakiri and Mondulkiri, but the security situation was never certain. July 1994 saw a tragic event for tourism when three Westerners were abducted from a train near Kampot and subsequently murdered.

Fighting once again erupted on the streets of Phnom Penh when Hun Sen ousted Prince Ranariddh in a coup in 1997 with a short disruption in the number of tourist arrivals. It did not take long for visitors to return and once again Phnom Penh and Siem Reap continued to prosper. Still the rest of the country was seen to be off limits, but with the successful 1998 elections and the defection of the remaining Khmer Rouge troops to the government side the security situation stabilised.

1999 was a turning point for Cambodia. Overland routes which had previously been no-go areas for foreigners were finally safe and a few determined travellers began to put up with the discomfort of the poor road conditions to explore areas untouched by tourism. I count myself privileged to be among the few to have experienced something special. Cambodia can now be seen as a stand-alone country – one that can be visited on its own and not just a few days added on to the end of a holiday to Vietnam or Thailand. A week or more could be spent just experiencing the northeast of the country, with its small towns strung along the Mekong, and the sparsely populated provinces of Rattanakiri and Mondulkiri; another week is needed to do justice to the temples of Angkor; more time must be set aside to discover Phnom Penh and the temples and towns within reach of the capital; and finally, a few days need to be saved for relaxing on the beach at Sihanoukville. And now Cambodia has never been more accessible, with overland routes from Vietnam and Thailand open and international flights going into both Phnom Penh and Siem Reap.

Throughout this book I have attempted to show that there is already so much to be discovered in Cambodia and, as the infrastructure improves, so much more will become accessible. Do let me know of any new 'must-sees' which have opened up, places to stay or eat which deserve a mention or any tips in general which you feel should appear in future editions.

Part One

General Information

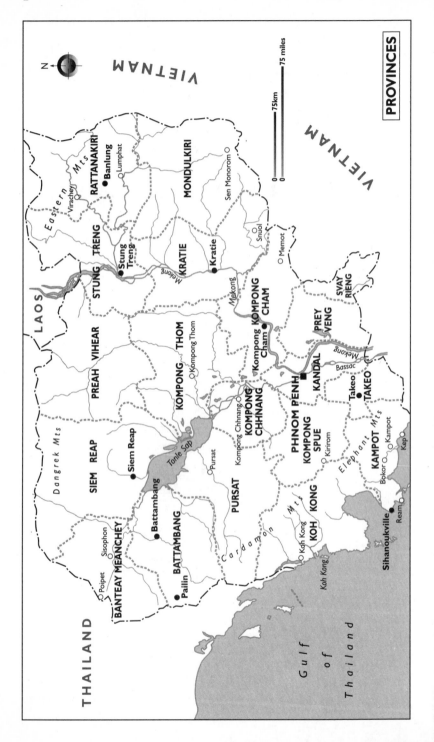

PROVINCES

Background and History

GEOGRAPHY

CAMBODIA, the capital of a kingdom of the same name in India, beyond the Ganges: E. long. 104°, N. lat. 12°30'.

The kingdom of Cambodia extends from 9° to 15° of N. lat. being bounded by the kingdom of Laos on the north, Cochin-china on the east, the Indian ocean on the south, and by the bay of Siam on the west.

Encyclopedia Britannica 1771

Cambodia borders Thailand to the west, Vietnam to the east and Laos to the north and covers an area of 181,035km² with three mountain ranges: the Cardamon Mountains in the southwest, the Dangrek Mountains in the north and the Eastern Mountains in the northeast. The mighty Mekong River flows through the country from Laos in the north to Vietnam in the south. In the north of Cambodia the river has several sections of rapids but becomes calm and constantly navigable as it approaches Vietnam. Phnom

FACTS AND FIGURES

Location	Southeast Asia, bordered by Thailand to the west, Laos to the north and Vietnam to the east.
Area	181,035km²
Population	11,700,000
Capital city	Phnom Penh
Other major towns	Siem Reap, Sihanoukville and Battambang
Currency	Riel
Language	Khmer – a Mon-Khmer language spoken by the majority of people
Religion	Predominantly Buddhist
Weights and measures	Metric system
Electricity	220 volts AC, 50Hz
National flag	Image of Angkor Wat on a red background bordered by two blue horizontal bands

Penh is situated at the confluence of three rivers, the Mekong, the Bassac and the Tonle Sap. The Tonle Sap (Great Lake), the largest freshwater lake in southeast Asia, in the centre of the country has an interesting annual occurrence. During the rainy season the waters of the Mekong rise causing the Tonle Sap River, leading to the Tonle Sap Lake, to swell and the lake to more than double in size. During the dry season water from the Tonle Sap drains back into the Mekong whose water level has fallen. It is at this time of year that Cambodians celebrate the annual Water Festival in Phnom Penh.

Much of the land is given over to rice production and rice paddies interspersed with sugar palms stretch for miles into the distance, especially in the west of the country, and are a wonderful patchwork of green. The phenomenon of the Tonle Sap means that when the waters recede in November, the soil that they leave behind is particularly fertile and therefore crucial to food production. Vast areas of Cambodia are forested but illegal logging is a serious problem and the politicians seem unwilling to put a stop to it. Income from legal logging should be an important source of foreign currency for Cambodia, but very little actually goes to government coffers

THE TONLE SAP

The Tonle Sap, or Great Lake, is at the heart of Cambodian life, irrigating around half of the country and supporting the economy with its abundance of fish. As the largest freshwater lake in South East Asia it has a unique ecosystem. The lake itself is home to many Cambodians who make their living from fishing. They live in extraordinary floating villages, in houses built on bamboo poles, where 90% of the population are fishermen. Absolutely everything floats including the police station, school, karaoke bars and the general store. Women and children selling fruit, vegetables, snacks and firewood float between the houses offering the ultimate in mobile shops for the housebound. Life in the floating villages is very simple but more and more aerials have appeared for televisions powered by batteries.

These villages are constantly on the move as the waters rise and recede with the seasons. The reason for this is that the waterways of Cambodia are truly unique. The waters of the Tonle Sap drain into the Tonle Sap River and then the Mekong River and eventually into the sea. During the rainy season, as the water level in the Mekong rises there is a build-up which forces the Tonle Sap River to reverse direction and flow back into the Tonle Sap Lake. The lake more than doubles in size and the villages literally go with the flow and find themselves nearer to main towns. In the dry season the reverse happens: the waters of the lake recede and the villages float further away. This is particularly noticeable at Siem Reap where visitors arriving by speedboat from Phnom Penh never know how long their journey into town will be.

from companies with official licences; most activity is carried on illegally with the cooperation of underpaid local government workers and the military.

CLIMATE AND WHEN TO GO

Cambodia lies within the tropics and has monsoon rains from the southwest between May and October. The heaviest rains in September and October can wash away already virtually impassable roads. Rainfall can be as much as 250mm per month in these two months alone. The dry season, from November to April, is generally hot and sunny, especially in March and April with temperatures around 35°C, although some areas, particularly in the north, can be quite cool from November to January. Humidity is at its lowest in January and highest in September.

It is possible to visit Cambodia at any time of year although if you are planning to travel overland extensively then avoid the rainy season, particularly September and October. The roads are virtually impassable at this time. The cool, dry season between November and January is ideal for sightseeing as it never gets hot enough to be uncomfortable. Overland travel is tolerable at this time, especially if you're planning to keep costs down and travel on the back of shared taxi pickups. However, at any time during the dry season you will find yourself covered in a layer of dust, whether you travel inside or on top of a vehicle. If you're travelling by boat and choose to sit on top rather than inside it is important to remember the dangerous effects of strong sunshine and wind. Cover up!

NATURE AND CONSERVATION
Flora

It was only in 1995 that the government in tandem with the United Nations Development Programme (UNDP) looked in detail at the state of the environment and published a report. This document gave a clear basic picture of the environmental situation and resulted in a legal framework to give power to the Ministry of Environment to manage protected areas and control pollution. A report published simultaneously on the unsustainable exploitation of the forests at that time showed that if illegal logging continued unchecked the forestry resources would be devastated within ten years. Proposals were put forward to introduce a system of logging concessions that would manage the forests. Cambodia's forests are a major natural resource and one which should be a long-term source of income and foreign exchange.

The UNDP has also initiated a project which would help the government to assemble a database on the extent and variety of its forestry resources. This information will ensure that the government is aware of the capacity of the forests and is able to develop a management programme.

Cambodia has a rich biodiversity but its lack of trained government personnel and the fact that there is no legal framework to protect the environment mean that conservation work is rather sketchy. Organisations such as the Worldwide Fund for Nature (WWF) and the World Resources Institute (WRI) are beginning to work together to implement projects to

ENDANGERED SPECIES

As hard as it may be to understand, the best method conservation charities such as Fauna and Flora International (FFI) has of ascertaining whether certain species of animal are thriving, close to extinction or even extinct is to visit the markets in small towns around the country. Much of Cambodia is still off limits and, although conservationists are beginning to explore remote regions of the country, it is still a lengthy and arduous task. Many locals hunt and poach in order to eke out a living; the skulls, horns and skins of their prey end up on market stalls. The skull of an animal, known to be on the verge of extinction, found hanging up in a market may be abhorrent to us, but it clearly indicates that it continues to survive. At the same time if a species of animal is not to be found in the market this may indicate that it has become extinct. Recent visits to provincial markets in Cambodia have revealed banteng and gaur skulls, tiger and leopard skins and bears' paws, a testimony to their healthy numbers. More interestingly, the skulls of Eld's deer (*Cervus eldi*), once thought to be extinct, and the horns of kouprey (*Bos sauveli*), now found only in Cambodia, have been sighted in the markets.

Twenty-five years of unrest in the country meant that certain areas were unsafe to live in for the general population, so, conversely, many species could thrive there, whereas elsewhere in the region they may have become very rare. In early 2000, the Cardamon Mountains in the southwest were the subject of a field trip and high numbers of elephant, Asiatic wild dog, pileated gibbon, various kinds of hornbill and green peafowl were recorded.

With the arrival of peace, people have returned to areas long uninhabited and timber companies are clearing the forests, both legally and illegally. The proximity of people close to an animal's habitat makes it susceptible to poaching, often to order, for collectors of trophies or for use in traditional medicine. Also, the presence of the loggers, clearing the forests at an alarming rate, means the destruction of their natural habitat. The Cambodian government understands that it needs to protect certain areas and species but they suffer from a serious lack of resources and the wildlife now faces its greatest threat in decades from poachers who see rich pickings in Cambodia.

Fauna and Flora International can be contacted in the UK on 01223 571000.

remedy this. Their activities include conservation training, protected area management and the introduction of a structured environmental policy together with legislation. They work closely with the Ministry of the Environment in Phnom Penh to formulate policies and environmental protection schemes are now under way.

The Tonle Sap Lake is a unique ecosystem which supports around 40% of the population as well as being home to a large quantity of water birds. In 1996 the UNDP introduced a management plan for the sustainable development of the lake as well as the Mekong River. The plan was designed to assist the government in the long-term conservation, resource management and development of the water system.

These optimistic plans may give the impression that Cambodia is now in a position to look at its natural resources and implement projects to preserve them for future generations. The reality is very different. Forested areas in the country continue to decline as a result of uncontrolled logging and the stark warning in 1995 that there would be no saleable timber left within ten years is beginning to appear frighteningly close. Illegal logging began with the Khmer Rouge who raised funds from the sale of timber to Thailand to fund their struggle against the government. This situation continued with the involvement of the military and civil servants, both poorly paid, who turn a blind eye to the activities of the loggers in return for bribes. The problem even extends to government ministers who line their pockets by negotiating the illegal export of timber to Vietnam. Big money is involved and it seems an impossible task to stem this tide. Some aid agencies and financial organisations have suspended aid payments to the government to try to force them to tackle the problem but with little result, and environmental organisations feel powerless to stop the inevitable.

Fauna

The conservation of the wildlife of Cambodia is being carefully monitored but as many of areas of the country were off limits up until 1999 the task of carrying out a 'head count' has been virtually impossible, although there are now ongoing camera-trap surveys being undertaken. Years of war meant that many animals were slaughtered, killed by land mines or fled into neighbouring countries. Deforestation poses a new threat. On the other hand the fighting meant that wide-scale hunting was impossible and some species may be abundant in remote areas, particularly in the northeast, where there may even be species that have become extinct elsewhere. Attempts are now being made to ascertain the types of wildlife within the country; the arrival of peace and the establishing of several national parks and protected areas will make this task easier. Once Cambodia was teeming with tigers, elephants, leopards, rhino and bears but most of these are now endangered. There are estimated to be around 100–200 tigers, although other reports put the figure nearer to 1000, mainly concentrated in the Cardamon Mountains and to a lesser extent in Mondulkiri. A 1995 estimate put banteng numbers at 700-1,000 spread at low densities over most of the northern half and western third of the country. The same report approximated 500-600 gaur, also in the same areas, with the largest population in Virachey National Park. The freshwater dolphins in the Mekong River close to Kratie are endangered because the local fishermen use dynamite to catch fish and now there are believed to be only around 60 left in the country.

Pollution

Pollution is not something normally associated with a non-industrialised society and, apart from the growing number of vehicles in Phnom Penh belching carbon monoxide into the air, it is not currently a significant factor. However, a serious situation developed through the greed of individuals who clearly did not understand the consequence of their actions. In December 1998, 3,000 tonnes of toxic waste was allowed to be dumped near Sihanoukville in a contract with a Taiwanese company, the Formosa Plastics Corporation. The waste contained mercury but subsequent tests revealed that the toxicity of this mercury was much higher than normally permitted. As a result several dock workers who had been involved in its handling either died or were taken seriously ill. The local population rioted in protest against the presence of the waste and the Cambodian army was brought in to load it into barrels. The Formosa Plastics Corporation then had to ship it back to Taiwan. This one incident shows how easy it is for unscrupulous companies to bribe individuals to accept consignments and to dump unsafe toxic waste, resulting in death or illness to local residents or unimaginable damage to the environment.

HISTORY

A guidebook cannot do justice to the long and rich history of a country such as Cambodia and this section aims simply to give an overview of the past millennium. Some periods of Cambodian history are particularly vague where there are few sources giving detailed information. If you have a particular interest in the history of Cambodia you should read the excellent *A History of Cambodia* by David Chandler. See *Appendix 3* for more details.

Early history

No one is certain exactly when the land known as Cambodia was first inhabited and there is still debate as to whether the first inhabitants came from China, India or elsewhere in southeast Asia. However, archaeological remains from northwest Cambodia suggest that as far back as 4000BC the caves in the area were inhabited. There is also evidence that from very early on houses were raised up on stilts, exactly as they are today.

At some stage – the exact date is still hotly debated – Cambodia became Indianised, with the introduction of written Sanskrit. Other aspects of Indian culture were also absorbed at different stages throughout about a thousand years, such as dress, dance and traditional livestock. There is even a myth of Indian origin which explains the founding of Cambodia. An Indian man, Kaundinya, sailed to the shores of Cambodia, a country mainly covered in water, carrying a magic bow. The princess of the realm went out in her canoe to meet him and Kaundinya shot an arrow into her boat, sinking it. The princess agreed to marry him and her father, the king, drank the water covering the country, so the young couple had more land, and named it Kambuja. A version of this story has also been found in Chinese historical documents.

THE GREAT KINGS OF ANGKOR

Jayavarman II	802– 850	Declared himself to be the first god-king at Phnom Kulen
Jayavarman III	850– 877	
Indravarman I	877– 889	Bakhon and Preah Ko
Yasovarman I	889– 910	Lolei, Phnom Bakheng and Phnom Krom temples
Harshavarman I	910– 925	
Isnavarman II	925– 928	
Jayavarman IV	928– 941	
Harshavarman II	941– 944	
Rajendravarman II	944– 968	Temples of East Mebon and Pre Rup
Jayavarman V	968–1001	Takeo and Banteay Srei temples
Udayadityavarman I	1001–1002	
Suryavarman I	1002–1050	
Udayadityavarman II	1050–1066	Baphuon
Harshavarman III	1066–1080	
Jayavarman VI	1080–1107	
Dharanindravarman I	1107–1113	
Suryavarman II	1113–1150	Angkor Wat and Banteay Samre
Dharanindravarman II	1150–1160	
Yasovarman II	1160–1165	
Tribhuvanadityavarman	1167–1177	
Jayavarman VII	1181–1218	Angkor Thom, the Bayon, Ta Prohm, Banteay Kdei, Ta Som and Preah Khan
Indravarman II	1218–1243	
Jayavarman VIII	1243–1296	
Indravarman III	1296–1308	
Indrajayavarman	1308–1327	

The names and dates of the kings that followed are obscure and there are no texts remaining that give accurate information for the remainder of the time that Angkor remained the capital.

Jayavarman Paramesvara	1327–?
Nippean-bat	1405–1409
Lampang Paramaja	1409–1416
Sorijovong or Lambang	1416–1425
Barom Racha or Gamkhat Ramadhapati	1425–1429
Thommo-Soccorach or Dharmasoka	1429–1431

Funan

Evidence has been uncovered that there was an important kingdom, known to the Chinese as Funan, stretching from the Mekong Delta into present-day Cambodia. It is believed that this was an important trading port for goods between India and China from the 3rd century AD because of its situation at the crossroads of all the great sea trading routes. The capital of the state of Funan was believed to be at Oc Eo in southern Vietnam and here strong evidence has been found of the extensive trading links, such as Roman coins and jewellery from India. Within two hundred years the power of Funan stretched far and wide, even down into the Malay Peninsula. During this period society began to absorb some influences from India, such as the religion and the alphabet.

At around the same time another state had been established in northern Cambodia and southern Laos called Chenla and this was widely acknowledged as a vassal state of Funan. The son of the last king of Funan, Rudravarman, had married a Chenla princess and when the king died, Prince Bhavavarman attacked Funan and subdued it.

Pre Angkor period (Chenla)

The first capital of Chenla, following the annexation of Funan, was established at Sambor Prei Kuk by King Isnavarman I in the beginning of the 7th century, close to present-day Kompong Thom (see *Chapter 7* for further details). Successive kings established the power of Chenla which became widespread, in particular through strategic marriages. Chenla dominated the region for around two hundred years until internal rivalry split the kingdom into two parts, Land Chenla and Water Chenla. Land Chenla in the north, comprising northern Cambodia and southern Laos, corresponded to the area making up the original kingdom of Chenla. Water Chenla towards the south comprised the area east of the Tonle Sap, including Sambor Prei Kuk, and along the Mekong towards the sea. Toward the end of the 8th century the powerful Sailendra dynasty from Java overran Water Chenla, having already taken over the neighbouring kingdoms of Annam and Champa. Members of the Water Chenla royal family were taken back to Java and little is known until the next ruler of the Khmer Empire, Jayavarman II, returned at the end of the 8th or beginning of the 9th century to establish what is now known as the Angkor period.

Angkor period

Jayavarman II was probably born in Java but returned to the land of his ancestors, gained control militarily and declared independence from Java. He installed himself as monarch in 802AD, declaring himself to be god-king, the first of the cult of the *devaraja* god-kings. Power was said to come from Siva himself and the symbol of authority of Siva and the *devaraja* was the royal lingam. Subsequent god-kings tried to outdo each other by building larger and more impressive temples to house the royal lingams, using their subjects, over whom they had absolute power, to carry out the work.

Jayavarman II established his first capital at Indrapura, east of Kompong Cham. During his 48-year reign he moved his capital another three times. His first move was to Hariharalya (the Roluos site) then to Mahendraparvata, on a mountain top (present-day Phnom Kulen), where he proclaimed himself god-king and finally back to Hariharalya where he reigned until his death in 850.

Little is known about his successor, his son Jayavarman III, but he reigned for 27 years until he was succeeded by his cousin Indravarman I in 877. He began the grand tradition of building temples to honour ancestors (Preah Ko) and instigated some major irrigation works. He died in 889 when his son Yasovarman I (889–910) moved the Khmer capital from Roluos to Angkor, which he named Yasodharapura, where it was to remain for over 500 years. He then began the building work (Phnom Bakheng and Phnom Krom) which was added to over the centuries, and which is now the incredible Angkor complex we know today. There was a period of 30 years when King Jayavarman IV, a northern provincial governor who declared himself king, established a rival capital at Koh Ker, but this was moved back to Angkor in 944 by his nephew Rajendravarman II. He continued the building tradition by adding the temples of East Mebon and Pre Rup until he was succeeded in 968 by his son, Jayavarman V, who instigated the wonderful Banteay Srei and Takeo.

A major period of expansion came under King Suryavarman I (1002–50) who, through military achievements, extended the Khmer territory into Thailand and Laos. A period of unrest followed during the reigns of Udayadityavarman II (1050–1066), Harshavarman III (1066–1080), Jayavarman VI (1080–1107) and Dharanindravarman I (1107–1113).

The glories of Angkor reached their peak under King Suryavarman II whose reign from 1113 to 1150 brought us Angkor Wat. He was also successful in conquering the Champa kingdom in 1145 but lost it again in 1149. Little of note happened during the following thirty years, until 1181, when the last great king, Jayavarman VII, came to the throne. Prior to this in 1177 the Champa kingdom had surprised the Khmers and attacked and successfully conquered Angkor. Cambodia was occupied until 1181 when Jayavarman VII retaliated and succeeded in overrunning the Champa capital, Vijaya, some years later. The annexation of Champa lasted until 1220 and the battle to win control of Champa is depicted in the bas-reliefs in the Bayon. Despite being in his fifties when he became king he reigned until 1218. He was a very religious man and undertook a massive building programme including the impressive Angkor Thom. He achieved much during his long reign including developing the social fabric by building hospitals, schools and roads. However, this enormous building programme meant using all available manpower, taking it away from agricultural work and causing great resentment. At the same time Jayavarman introduced Buddhism which slowly began to replace Hinduism. Statues of Buddha began to replace the royal lingam and appeared in the Bayon and it is thought that some of the Hindu temples were neglected or attempts were made to convert them to Buddhist worship.

The decline of Angkor

Despite being one of the instigators of some of the great architectural pieces at Angkor and developing the social infrastructure, it was under Jayavarman VII that the decline of Angkor began. So much money was being poured into building work that economic problems followed. It is even feasible that the workers were reluctant to continue carrying out the king's ambitious plans and went back to work in their neglected fields. At the same time the cult of the god-kings became undermined by the introduction of Buddhism and their authority weakened. There are few records of the kings that reigned after Jayavarman VII and during the last two hundred years of the empire of Angkor its power declined significantly. The kings were weaker, the economy was in a bad shape and the temples began to decline. At this time the Siamese, from Ayutthaya, were beginning to rattle their sabres and throughout the 14th century they were constantly battling with the Khmers. Khmer land was continually being taken and after a long siege in 1431 Angkor was left to the Siamese.

The next few hundred years were a difficult time for Cambodia. In 1432 King Ponhea Yat moved the capital to the Phnom Penh area. It was an ideal location to control trade to Laos and to the sea, being based at the confluence of three rivers, the Tonle Sap, the Mekong and the Bassac. However, a succession of weak kings were unable to stand up to the warring Siamese and Vietnamese; Cambodia found itself either the vassal of Siam and asking the Vietnamese for help or vassal of Vietnam and asking the Siamese for help. Land in the west was lost to Siam and in the east to Vietnam. This meant that the Khmers lost access to the South China Sea and an important trading route.

This period of Cambodian history is the least recorded of any and very few inscriptions have been found within the country. What is known comes from uncorroborated chronicles from China or Siam. Around twenty years after Angkor was left to the Siamese the Khmers successfully ousted the Siamese from Angkor, although they made no attempt to reestablish their capital there or even to administer the region. In the 16th century the Siamese kingdom had been severely weakened, in particular by the sacking of Ayutthaya by the Burmese, and the Khmers took advantage of this to attack several times. By the end of the century the Siamese once again had the upper hand and successfully invaded the territory of Cambodia. It was during the 17th century that Cambodia began to lurch from the Vietnamese to the Siamese asking each for protection from the other, depending on who was in control at the time. In 1618 the capital was moved to Udong where it stayed until 1866, after the arrival of the French. There followed an unsettled period with several internal disputes over who should be ruling. Vietnam was particularly dominant in the 19th century and after a long power struggle Ang Duong became king in 1847. He decided that Cambodia needed help from another quarter to stop the territorial threat of both the Vietnamese and the Siamese and he approached the French in 1854, the start of the process which resulted in Cambodia becoming a French colony.

Colonial times

Having spent the previous 400 years or more being governed by either Thailand or Vietnam, a weakened Cambodia welcomed the approach from the French government, which had already taken control of southern Vietnam. In 1863 King Norodom signed a treaty establishing Cambodia as a French Protectorate to stop Siam and Vietnam carving up Cambodia between them. He was not prepared for the fact that the French would recognise the claims of the Siamese over the provinces of Siem Reap, Sisophon and Battambang. The French control over Cambodia caused deep resentment amongst the people and there were several periods of unrest. Despite these problems Cambodia became a French colony in 1884. Effectively control of the country passed to the French Résident Supérieur with a purely symbolic role for the king. In 1887 the country became a member of French Indochina which included Laos and the protectorates of Vietnam, Cochin-China, Annam and Tonkin. At the end of the 19th century French troops began an attempt to take back the provinces they had given to Siam a few decades earlier. However it took until 1907 for the provinces to be finally restored to Cambodia and once again Angkor was in the hands of the Khmers.

King Norodom died in 1904 and was succeeded by his half-brother Sisowath, rather than by one of his sons. This was engineered by the French as Sisowath was an ally and therefore would be a cooperative king. French control of Cambodia was consolidated and they began to put up grand buildings in Phnom Penh and villas for themselves by the coast and cooler inland sites. Later they also started to build the railroad. Sisowath was followed in 1927 by his son King Monivong who continued in the same vein as his father. His cooperativeness with the French guaranteed a period of political stability under colonial rule. However, the economy, which had seen boom times in the 1920s with an international market for rice and the development of rubber plantations, began to suffer. The ordinary Cambodian saw little benefit from such successes and the profits were diverted into building works in the capital, electrification of towns around the country, road construction and the opening of beach resorts and hill stations. Cambodia was affected by the world depression in the 1930s and the price of rice dropped dramatically. Of course it was the peasants that suffered but even this did not provoke an uprising. There was very little organised antagonism against the French during this period but the seeds of discontent were being sown against the colonists and the good-living royal family.

The Kingdom of Cambodia

Life was to change dramatically for both the French and the Khmers with the outbreak of World War II. France had been occupied by Nazi Germany in 1940 and, shortly after, French Indochina was taken over by the Japanese. However, the colony was nominally still controlled by Vichy France. In 1941 Monivong died and Sihanouk was installed on the throne, rather than one of the king's own sons. Sihanouk was only a teenager at the time and the French thought they would be able to mould him to their way of thinking. In the same year Thailand

(Siam changed its name in 1939), with the connivance of the Japanese, again took control of the provinces of Battambang and Siem Reap although they were returned to Cambodia in 1946. During the war, the first rumblings for independence began, encouraged by the weakened state of the French government. In March 1945, following the liberation of France, the French administration in Cambodia was removed by the Japanese and King Sihanouk declared independence. Within months Japan had surrendered and in August 1945 France attempted to reestablish control of its Indochina colonies.

Most anti-colonial fighting took place in Vietnam, although there was a limited struggle within Cambodia. By political manoeuvring and by Sihanouk going into self-imposed exile in 1952, France, under pressure from Vietminh forces in Vietnam, caved in and granted independence to Cambodia on November 9 1953. Two years later the king abdicated in favour of his father Suramarit. By doing this he freed himself from the restrictions of the role of king and was able to form a political party in order to carry out his plans. He was to dominate politics within Cambodia until 1966 with his party winning every seat at every election. He steered the path of neutrality for many years and attracted aid from both the USA and the Soviet Union. In 1960 his father died and rather than become king again he became head of state.

The 1960s were volatile years for Asia and Cambodia was pulled in different directions. Sihanouk's neutral stance came under severe strain when full-scale fighting broke out in Vietnam and he was forced to take sides. He sided with the communist forces of North Vietnam and allowed them to use Cambodia as a military sanctuary and part of the Ho Chi Minh trail supply line. At this time Sihanouk refused aid from America and then broke off diplomatic relations with the US government for a few years. In 1969 America began to drop bombs within Cambodia to disrupt the movement of supplies from North to South Vietnam. Meanwhile there were also internal problems. The refusal of aid from America caused hardship amongst the people and the gap between city-dwellers and peasants grew significantly. In China the Cultural Revolution was under way and the influence of this was being absorbed by poor rural Cambodians. The seeds of the Khmer Rouge were being sown.

Following peasant riots in 1967 and 1968, Sihanouk reestablished diplomatic relations with the US to try to stem his domestic problems and to retain his neutrality. However, by allowing the North Vietnamese troops to use Cambodia he aggravated the American government who did nothing to intervene when Sihanouk was overthrown by his right-wing army chief, Lon Nol, in 1970 while he was on a state visit to Moscow.

The Khmer Republic

Lon Nol immediately abolished the monarchy and declared Cambodia a republic. Sihanouk did not return to the country and chose self-imposed exile in Beijing at the head of a government in exile. Lon Nol wanted the communist North Vietnamese soldiers out of Cambodia and allowed the American government to bomb the east of the country officially, despite the fact that this had already been going on for some time. Once again the peasants were suffering, thousands were killed and thousands more were forced to flee to Phnom Penh to escape the bombing. As a result of the carnage and the suffering of the Cambodian peasants a group of left-wing fighters began to grow in strength driven on by what was happening in their country. The leaders were well educated and their rhetoric encouraged young people to join them and become fiercely loyal. This fighting force was to become known as the Khmer Rouge and it was this group that linked up with Sihanouk and became part of his Beijing-backed government in exile. The Khmer Rouge gradually took control of more and more provinces throughout Cambodia in a bloody civil war, despite fierce opposition from Lon Nol troops, and there is much evidence of this throughout the country to this day. Once the Americans withdrew their support from the Lon Nol government, following its decision to pull out of Vietnam, it was only a matter of time before the Khmer Rouge took control. This happened on April 17 1975.

POL POT

Pol Pot is ranked alongside Hitler as one of the most infamous mass murderers of the 20th century. His name struck fear into the hearts of Cambodians from the 1970s right through until his death in 1998.

He was originally known as Saloth Sar and was born in Kompong Thom in 1928. He won a scholarship to Paris but his growing associations with communism resulted in his being sent back to Cambodia. He became a schoolteacher in Phnom Penh but continued his involvement with the communists, eventually becoming their leader in 1962. Shortly afterwards he fled to the countryside and the Khmer Rouge was formed to fight against the Sihanouk government using guerrilla tactics.

Pol Pot's troops overthrew the troops of Lon Nol, establishing the Democratic Republic of Kampuchea, with him as prime minister. Under his leadership Cambodia was transformed into an agrarian 'utopia' with all institutions being dismantled, 'enemies' of the state murdered and the population turned into slaves.

When the country was liberated by Vietnamese forces in 1979, Pol Pot returned to his former role as a guerrilla leader. Rumours abounded concerning his whereabouts, many consistently placing him on the Thai-Cambodian border. Several times his death was reported in the media, but no body was ever seen to prove it. Gradually divisions began to appear in the ranks of the Khmer Rouge and eventually the members began to turn on Pol Pot. In 1997 he was put on trial in the jungle at Anlong Veng where he was given a life sentence. He died on April 15 1998 and this time his body was on view for the world to see. It is claimed that he died of a heart attack, but rumours persist to this day that he actually committed suicide. Interestingly enough Pol Pot's death was not featured on Cambodian television news.

Democratic Republic of Kampuchea

The Khmer Rouge period of Cambodian history has been well documented during the past two decades and a few short paragraphs in a guidebook cannot adequately describe the horrors of this time.

Years of fighting and hardship had driven around a million people into Phnom Penh. When the government troops finally put down their arms and Pol Pot's guerrilla fighters entered Phnom Penh, wearing sandals made of old rubber tyres commonly known as Ho Chi Minh sandals, the population was relieved and welcomed them as heroes. Within hours the population was being instructed to leave the city, ostensibly because the Americans were said to be planning a full-scale offensive against it. They were assured that they would be able to return in a few days. As we now know many were never to return.

The Khmer Rouge troops had been emptying the cities and towns of the country as they gained control and Phnom Penh was the last city to come under their control. People were forced into the countryside where they were organised into groups working in the fields. Year Zero had begun. Anybody connected with the old regime such as government ministers and soldiers was hunted down and killed. Then the attentions of the Khmer Rouge turned to the educated people who they felt had not supported their revolution.

CHRONOLOGY OF EVENTS SINCE THE 19th CENTURY

1863 Cambodia becomes a French protectorate under King Norodom to prevent it from being divided up by Siam and Vietnam

1884 Cambodia formally becomes a colony of France

1887 Cambodia becomes a member of Indochina with Laos and the protectorates of Vietnam, Cochin-China, Tonkin and Amman

1904 King Norodom dies and is succeeded by his half-brother, Sisowath

1907 The temples of Angkor are restored to Cambodia from Siam

1927 King Sisowath dies and is succeeded by his son, Monivong

1940 Cambodia is occupied by the Japanese but still nominally run by Vichy France

1941 Monivong dies and is succeeded by Sihanouk

1941 The Japanese allow the Thais to reclaim the provinces of Battambang and Siem Reap including the temples of Angkor

1945 Following the liberation of France in March, the Japanese take control of Cambodia and Sihanouk declares independence. The French attempt to reclaim their colony upon the surrender of the Japanese in August

1946 The provinces of Battambang and Siem Reap are once again returned to Cambodia

1952 Sihanouk goes into self-imposed exile in an attempt to win independence from France

1953 Cambodia gains independence

Knowledge of a foreign language or the wearing of glasses was enough to ensure certain death at the hands of the young cadres of the Khmer Rouge. Thousands of teachers, doctors, monks and professional people suffered the same fate.

The aim of the Khmer Rouge was to start again, ie: Year Zero. The borders of the country were closed in order to prevent any interference from other countries. At the same time all institutions were dismantled, money was abolished, temples were destroyed and the citizens were put into collectivised units in the countryside. Families were torn apart and anybody who objected was clubbed to death – to use ammunition to shoot them was wasteful. People who had lived in the cities were known as New People and were treated very brutally. Those who had lived in Khmer Rouge liberated zones during the civil war were known as Old People, and fared slightly better. Everybody was put to hard manual work in order to create the planned agrarian utopia but the Old People found it easier than the New People as they were mainly used to working in the fields. However, the long hours, appalling living conditions, lack of food and rampant disease were equally hard for all.

Under Pol Pot's reign of terror it is estimated that around two million Cambodians died or were killed. Somehow a few managed to escape across the border into Thailand where they told of unimaginable atrocities. Still the

1955	Sihanouk abdicates in favour of his father, Suramarit, to be able to carry out his political ambitions
1960	Suramarit dies and Sihanouk becomes head of state
1969	America begins bombing campaign of Cambodia
1970	Sihanouk is overthrown by his right-wing army chief, Lon Nol. Sihanouk goes into self-imposed exile in Beijing and establishes a government in exile
1975	The left-wing fighting force known as the Khmer Rouge take over Phnom Penh on April 17 and Cambodia returns to Year Zero. There follows a period of unimaginable brutality against the people
1979	Vietnamese troops liberate Cambodia on January 7
1989	Vietnam withdraws its troops from Cambodia
1991	Paris Peace Accord is signed
1993	Democratic elections are held under the supervision of the UNTAC and Sihanouk is once again crowned king in August
1996	Death blow is dealt to the Khmer Rouge when one of their leaders, Ieng Sary, defects to the government side bringing thousands of his troops with him
1997	Infighting between the two prime ministers, Hun Sen and Prince Ranariddh, culminates in a violent coup instigated by Hun Sen
1998	Pol Pot dies in the jungle
1998	Democratic elections take place in July
1999	Cambodia is admitted to ASEAN

outside world did nothing, maybe unable to believe such horrendous things could really be happening. However, it is difficult to accept that no government wanted to find out why Cambodia had closed its borders and what was going on there. Possibly the Khmer Rouge could have sustained its brutal regime longer if Pol Pot had not wanted to reclaim land in the south of Vietnam for Cambodia. His troops made several incursions into the Mekong Delta area of Vietnam, killing many innocent Vietnamese in the process. Eventually the Hanoi government had had enough and on December 25 1978 they began to push into Cambodia and it fell very quickly, being liberated on January 7 1979. Regretfully most of the leaders of the Khmer Rouge were never caught.

People's Republic of Kampuchea

Vietnam should have been seen as a liberator in the true sense of the word, saving the Cambodian people from incredible hardship and certain death. Tens of thousands of Cambodians fled the country, crossing the border into Thailand where many of them lived in refugee camps for years. Only then did the true story emerge of the horrors experienced. The Vietnamese installed a government with Heng Samrin at its head. He had been a former Khmer Rouge member, but had fled Cambodia in 1978. The government faced the difficult task of reconstructing a country and its institutions which had effectively been dismantled. The infrastructure, communications system, electricity network and factories had been virtually destroyed. In addition many skilled and educated people had died or had fled the country and others who had survived and stayed were busy trying to find family members and reclaim their homes. This was an enormous task for any government, but the Vietnamese-backed one also had the problem that it was not recognised by the West, mainly because of antagonism led by the US, still smarting at being defeated in Vietnam.

Donors worldwide gave millions of dollars to assist Cambodia and the aid agencies began to help to rebuild the country through the provision of rice, seeds and medicines. However, this was too little without the support of Western governments and the task was made even harder by the fact that fighting still continued in the countryside. The new government was up against the combined forces of the Khmer Rouge, backed by China, Sihanouk supporters (the National Front for an Independent, Neutral, Peaceful and Cooperative Cambodia – FUNCINPEC) and the Khmer People's National Liberation Front (KPNLF) under Son Sann, a former Prime Minister, both backed by the US and other Western countries. It was this coalition (Coalition Government of Democratic Kampuchea – CGDK) that was recognised by the West as the legitimate government and allowed to take its seat at the United Nations. Thailand allowed the fighters to operate from the refugee camps on the Thai border. The fighting caused more Cambodians to flee the country and many areas were heavily mined, causing thousands of injuries and deaths among the farmers trying to rebuild their lives and feed their families.

Many saw the Vietnamese troops in Cambodia as more of an occupation force than a liberating one. The Vietnamese felt that they were there to ensure against the return of Pol Pot. However, they began to question their role with the arrival of Gorbachev in the Soviet Union. It was clear that great changes were taking place there and although Vietnam had been supported by Soviet government aid, it was isolated from the rest of the world. By the mid 1980s Vietnam was beginning to feel the effects of this isolation and in 1989 withdrew its troops. The country was renamed the State of Cambodia.

The State of Cambodia/Kingdom of Cambodia

Coalition forces continued to fight the government, whose army was seriously weakened without the support of the Vietnamese as well as by the withdrawal of aid from the Soviet bloc. Cambodia then came under intense international pressure for the warring factions to come together to hammer out a peace agreement. Negotiations took place, although it was October 1991 before a peace accord was signed in Paris. It was also agreed to hold elections in 1993 and prior to that the UN sent in a huge peacekeeping force. In the meantime Prince Sihanouk returned to Phnom Penh in November 1991 to an enthusiastic welcome. It had been 13 years since he had left Cambodia, having returned from Beijing in 1975 to become head of state when the Khmer Rouge took control. He had resigned in 1976 and was held under house arrest until he left the country in 1978. The UN force named UNTAC (UN Transitional Authority in Cambodia) arrived in early 1992 to keep the peace, supervise free elections and help with the resettlement of Cambodians returning from the refugee camps in Thailand.

Despite signing the peace accord the Khmer Rouge refused to hand over their arms and demobilise. They resumed their campaign from within Cambodia, trying to consolidate their position, refusing permission for UN peacekeepers to enter territories held under their control and even taking them hostage. The UN mission was a success with elections being held in May 1993 despite the boycott of the Khmer Rouge. They had tried to intimidate the population into not voting but in fact over 90% turned out to vote. Sihanouk's FUNCINPEC party, led by his son Prince Ranariddh, won a narrow victory over the Cambodian People's Party (CPP) led by Hun Sen, who had been Prime Minister in the Vietnamese-backed government. An uneasy coalition was established with Ranariddh and Hun Sun sharing the post of Prime Minister. Once again Sihanouk was crowned king in August 1993 and the UN forces had left the country by the end of the same year. The future for Cambodia still did not look certain as the coalition government was distinctly shaky and the Khmer Rouge continued to launch attacks across the country. They even went as far as to start kidnapping foreigners resident in or visiting Cambodia; this made world headlines in 1994 when three foreigners were taken from a train in Kampot province and subsequently killed.

In order to destabilise the forces of the Khmer Rouge an amnesty was offered to them which swiftly attracted a few thousand. By 1996 the death blow was dealt to the remaining fighters when Ieng Sary, one of the leading

TRIAL OF THE KHMER ROUGE

April 17 2000 saw the 25th anniversary of the occupation of Phnom Penh by the Khmer Rouge whose brutal regime was responsible for the deaths of between one and two million people. The anniversary itself passed virtually unnoticed in Cambodia as the Phnom Penh government wished to focus on reconciliation rather than stir up feelings again.

The fact is that within Cambodia now many former Khmer Rouge officials occupy high positions in government or commerce. However, the prime minister Hun Sen is working towards holding trials of the former Khmer Rouge leaders, many of whom defected to the government side between 1996 and 1998. Although many years have passed since Cambodia was returned to Year Zero by the Khmer Rouge, it was the arrest of Duch, the chief of Tuol Sleng interrogation centre in Phnom Penh, and his revelations which led to a call for the prosecution of Khmer Rouge leaders. Duch had implicated the whole of the leadership in the genocide including many members who were now working for the government.

The extent of Hun Sen's commitment to bring these men to trial is unclear and it is felt that many leading figures will be immune from prosecution because of the amnesties they have already received from the government. Khieu Samphan, Ieng Sary and Nuon Chea, key men who worked closely with Pol Pot and who now live securely in Pailin, near the Thai border, have been reassured by Hun Sen that they will not be tried in Cambodia. However, other leaders such as Nuon Paet, a former Khmer Rouge commander, was convicted in 1999 for his involvement in the kidnapping and murder of three foreign tourists in 1994. He was given life imprisonment in a trial which lasted only one day. Ta Mok, a former Khmer Rouge chief of staff, was captured in March 1999 and charged with genocide a few months later as was Duch.

Plans for trials began as far back as 1997 when the Cambodian government asked the United Nations for assistance. Legal experts from the UN felt that the courts in Cambodia were not able to hold fair and unbiased trials, especially as many officials were once linked to the Khmer Rouge. A plan to hold international trials, like those being carried out for war-crime suspects from the Yugoslavian conflict, was rejected by the government. A proposal was put forward where the court would consist of both international and Cambodian judges. There still seemed to be an impasse at the beginning of 2000 as the UN wanted the majority of judges to be international and the government wanted the majority to be Cambodian. Hun Sun felt that this would have compromised the sovereignty of Cambodia. Finally it has been agreed that three judges would be Cambodian and two would be international, appointed by the UN, and any decision would require the agreement of at least four of the court's members.

lights under Pol Pot, defected to the government side. He had several lucrative interests in logging and gem mining along the Thai border around Pailin and had lost the desire to overthrow the government. Incredibly, despite the knowledge that he had been involved in the deaths of many Cambodians, he was granted a pardon by the king. The Khmer Rouge went into terminal decline and infighting resulted in the capture of Pol Pot, previously proclaimed dead on several occasions, who was put on trial in one of their former strongholds, remote Anlong Veng. Journalists were invited to the show trial in the jungle and found an old man who clearly did not comprehend the genocide he had instigated, claiming that he had done it for the benefit of the Cambodian people. On April 15 1998 Pol Pot died of a heart attack and his body was put on view to prove that this time he really was dead.

Infighting was also rife in the government with the two prime ministers continually struggling for power. Neither trusted the other. All this was to come to a head in 1997 when Hun Sen ousted Ranariddh in a violent coup which saw fighting on the streets of Phnom Penh and the deaths of many civilians. Sympathisers of Ranariddh and the FUNCINPEC Party went into the countryside and once again began a struggle against the troops of Hun Sen's Cambodian People's Party. Elections had been planned for 1998 and it was feared that these would not take place. Hun Sen bowed to international pressure following the refusal of the Association of South East Asian Nations (ASEAN) to allow Cambodia membership and aid agencies stating that they would discontinue funding if the elections were not held. These took place in July 1998, to the satisfaction of international observers, when the CPP won a narrow majority. Several months of discussions took place between the CPP and FUNCINPEC and eventually, in November, a coalition was agreed with Hun Sen at the head. Political life in Cambodia was finally beginning to settle down, as was corroborated in April 1999 when Cambodia was admitted to ASEAN.

The last few months of the 20th century saw progress in moves to bring former leaders of the Khmer Rouge to trial. Developments began back in 1997 with the arrest of Pol Pot by Ta Mok (himself later arrested and charged with genocide), although the nation was cheated out of a trial by his death in April 1998. By early 2000 the United Nations and Cambodian government had agreed a format for conducting any trials with a combination of three Cambodian judges together with two international judges appointed by the UN. It still remains to be seen if many of the key players such as Khieu Samphan and Ieng Sary, who were given an amnesty when they defected to the government side, will be brought to trial for crimes against humanity.

POLITICS

The political picture within Cambodia has been one of chaos for most of the second half of the 20th century. Cambodia has long been a pawn in the struggles between the superpowers, starting with the Vietnam War, when Cambodia was drawn into the conflict first on the side of the communist north and then, belatedly, with the American-backed south Vietnamese.

Following the liberation of Cambodia in 1979 by Vietnamese forces, who were allied to the Soviet Union, the country should have been given all the support the world could muster. However, it allowed the Americans the perfect opportunity to punish the Vietnamese for defeating them by refusing to recognise the government in Phnom Penh. China was also angry at Vietnam's occupation of Cambodia and its support from the Soviet Union and allied itself with the United States. Both countries allowed the Coalition Government of Democratic Kampuchea (CGDK), which included an uneasy combination of the Khmer Rouge, Sihanouk's supporters, the National Front for an Independent, Neutral, Peaceful and Cooperative Cambodia (FUNCINPEC) and the Khmer People's National Liberation Front (KPNLF) under Son Sann, a former Prime Minister, to take Cambodia's seat at the United Nations in 1982. Other countries such as Britain, Thailand and Singapore joined China and the United States in their support for the CGDK as they felt it was more important to ally themselves with the superpowers.

The eighties

The early 1980s were a time when Thailand, and China in particular, cemented their support for the military struggle of the CGDK against the forces of the People's Republic of Kampuchea (PRK). Many soldiers used the refugee camps on the Thai border as their base of operations and the Thai government even supplied them with arms and ammunition. Thailand also allowed Chinese munitions to be supplied to the fighters in their camps on the Thai/Cambodian border. Many of the border camps were run by United Nations agencies who were effectively feeding and housing the families of the CGDK soldiers. The same agencies were not allowed to enter and help the devastated people still within Cambodia because the United Nations did not recognise the government and the PRK had to struggle on with only help from the Soviet bloc and non-governmental humanitarian organisations.

Despite the isolation of the PRK, the government did a fairly creditable job of reestablishing a constitution, although one modelled on Vietnam. It brought some organisation to a country of displaced people whose first priority, upon liberation, had been to try to find living relatives. Famine was a serious problem initially because nobody had harvested the 1979 crop and planting was haphazard in subsequent years, much of this due to the fact that so many people had fled to the refugee camps and those who remained were in a poor state of health. During the early years the PRK government attempted to reestablish some of the institutions which had been dismantled by the Khmer Rouge such as schools and banks and to help the people to work together to grow food.

Vietnam felt itself to be surrounded by enemies: China to its north, which had attacked towns close to Vietnam's border with China in February 1979 killing thousands of people and destroying several Vietnamese towns, as well as Thailand which had allied itself with China. Vietnam was determined to stay in Cambodia and this period for most Cambodians was definitely preferable to the unmitigated suffering experienced by all citizens in the

THE UNITED NATIONS TRANSITIONAL AUTHORITY IN CAMBODIA (UNTAC)

The Paris Peace Accord, signed in October 1991, brought an end (in theory) to the fighting in Cambodia and the warring factions joined together to form a Supreme National Council presided over by Prince Sihanouk. It was agreed that the United Nations would send in a peacekeeping force to oversee the run-up to democratic elections, the disarmament of the troops of the various parties and the repatriation of the refugees still in the Thai border camps. During 1992 around 20,000 troops, officials and volunteers arrived in Cambodia to form UNTAC.

Their task was a difficult one, not helped by the fact that the Khmer Rouge refused to be disarmed and even expanded their areas of control and refused to allow UN workers into them, holding UN soldiers as hostage at times. Supporters of the various parties continually tried to intimidate opposition party backers with violence and the UN were continually asked to negotiate with various factions. UN workers were more successful in repatriating the hundreds of thousands of Cambodians still living in the refugee camps on the Thai border. They also succeeded in registering well over 90% of the population eligible to vote. The elections themselves, held in May 1993, were peaceful and free, even though they were boycotted by the Khmer Rouge. Around 90% of the registered voters turned out to vote despite being threatened with reprisals from the Khmer Rouge if they did.

The UNTAC operation cost an estimated US$2 billion, making it the most expensive to date for the UN. At any one time the UN has a number of peacekeeping operations ongoing around the world but usually the cost of these is only a fraction of that spent on Cambodia.

preceding years. From the outset there was opposition within the country from the educated people who had survived the excesses of the Khmer Rouge years. As far as they were concerned the Khmer Rouge had been communists and the Vietnamese/Soviet-backed PRK government was also communist. Many chose to flee to Thailand and their loss to Cambodia was a problem.

As the eighties progressed Cambodians in general feared that Vietnam intended to dominate politics there indefinitely or even to annex it. However, there was no effective alternative other than the CGDK which had little support within Cambodia. Vietnamese troops and Cambodian soldiers trained by the Vietnamese endured many battles with the forces of the CGDK and were successful in driving them back into Thailand. Following the collapse of the Soviet Union aid to Vietnam decreased dramatically and this made it impossible for the Vietnamese government to keep a standing army in Cambodia. Repatriation to Vietnam began and the last troops left in

September 1989. Very soon the forces of the CGDK occupied areas within Cambodia, particularly the gem-mining area around Pailin and the remote provinces to the northwest. At night much of the countryside belonged to these forces who planted landmines killing and maiming many Cambodians. Now the Vietnamese had gone the fighting was once again Khmer against Khmer.

The nineties

The early 1990s were once again difficult times for Cambodia as the much-needed aid from the Soviet bloc dried up. However, unexpectedly in July 1990 the American government indicated that it was prepared to halt its support for the CGDK. China responded by scaling down its support for the Khmer Rouge fighters. A major stumbling block to peace and prosperity within Cambodia had begun to be removed. In October 1991 a conference took place in Paris to reach an agreement with all interested parties in Cambodia. A temporary government was established including the current government, the Khmer Rouge, FUNCINPEC and the KPLF with Prince Sihanouk. The United States formally withdrew support from the CGDK and China ceased support for the Khmer Rouge. The temporary arrangement was to be overseen by a contingent from the United Nations who would also assist with the repatriation of hundreds of thousands of refugees, disarm the troops of each faction, oversee the preparations for national elections and monitor the election itself. Despite the agreement signed in Paris by all sides the Khmer Rouge refused to take part in any election or to disarm.

The elections held in May 1993 were a great success with over 90% of registered voters turning out. However, the results were not decisive and within a few months an uneasy coalition was established between the FUNCINPEC party headed by Prince Ranariddh, the son of Sihanouk, and Hun Sen, the head of the government installed by the Vietnamese. Strangely the agreement allowed for two prime ministers, Ranariddh and Hun Sen. Sihanouk was crowned king once again in August 1993, but the new constitution effectively gave him very little power.

The Khmer Rouge were still refusing to 'come in from the cold' and continued their struggle from the countryside where large areas were still under their control. Most of their funding came from their illegal exploitation of timber and gems which were sold to unscrupulous Thai entrepreneurs (the Khmer Rouge no longer had the support of the Thai government). An amnesty was offered to members of the Khmer Rouge which immediately brought several thousand over to the government side, probably aware that they had no chance of regaining power. The leadership became desperate and even started to kidnap and murder foreigners in an attempt to regain control by terror. When Ieng Sary, one of the leaders under Pol Pot, also defected, the Khmer Rouge were effectively a spent force. Ieng Sary was given an amnesty and his group a degree of autonomy over the area they controlled in the west of the country, around the gem-rich town of Pailin.

NON-GOVERNMENTAL ORGANISATIONS (NGOS)

Hundreds of non-governmental organisations (NGOs) are working in Cambodia and covering a whole range of needs. Their work is sponsored by donations from their home countries and their task appears to be an endless one.

Most NGO workers are volunteers and they find themselves working in remote areas of the country, wherever the need is greatest. Various organisations work in the same small towns and their presence is evident from the ubiquitous white landcruisers, each flying the flag of its organisation, 4WD vehicles being essential because of the appalling state of the roads.

The NGOs were pivotal in helping Cambodians in the 1980s when there was no aid coming from such organisations as the United Nations or large donor countries like the United States. The Vietnamese-backed government was not recognised by the UN or the USA and Britain so no formal development funding was forthcoming. The NGOs did what little they could to get farmers farming again, establishing basic medical care, helping amputees, providing clean water and setting up cottage industries.

Their work remains as important as before even though organisations such as the World Bank and the International Monetary Fund (IMF) are now helping the economy. An ongoing problem is the clearing of the landmines and the treatment and rehabilitation of the victims of these gruesome weapons.

For information on the various NGOs working in Cambodia contact the office of the Cooperation Committee for Cambodia in Phnom Penh at PO Box 855, Phnom Penh; tel/fax: 023 26009; email: ccc@pactok.peg.apc.org.

The demise of the Khmer Rouge did little to unite the two prime ministers who were continually at loggerheads. The situation boiled over in 1997 when Hun Sen ousted Ranariddh in a violent coup which saw fighting in the streets of Phnom Penh; supporters of FUNCINPEC fled to the countryside and started an armed struggle against Hun Sen's Cambodian People's Party. The situation was so desperate that many Cambodians fled back into Thailand and expat workers were flown out of the country. The election scheduled for July 1998 appeared to be under threat and it was feared Hun Sen would carry on without allowing it to take place. However, international pressure from aid donors, who threatened to withdraw funding, ensured that it did take place although the run-up to polling day was a disturbed time with sporadic fighting in the countryside. The CPP won a narrow victory over FUNCINPEC but it was many weeks before the two parties settled their differences and formed a coalition government with just one prime minister, Hun Sen.

Since the elections in 1998, political life in Cambodia has settled down to a certain extent with the CPP and FUNCINPEC coalition attempting to

THE RESTORATION OF ANGKOR

Although the temples of Angkor were rediscovered at the end of the 19th century it was only at the very beginning of the 20th that work began to document and then to restore them. In 1898, the Ecole Française d'Extrême Orient (EFEO) was established in Cambodia to carry out this work, which continued through much of the 20th century. The EFEO began to clear the jungle away from the temples, to document the temples in great detail and to compile maps of the area. Earlier expeditions had already taken place such as that by Ernest Doudart de Lagrée who in 1866, while attempting to see if there was a route via the Mekong into China, took the opportunity to visit Angkor; his findings were published in *Voyage d'exploration en Indo-Chine*. A member of the team was the French archaeologist and artist, Louis Delaporte, who later published *Les documents du Cambodge*, an extensive inventory of the temples.

The temples had suffered for many centuries from successive lootings by the Siamese and Vietnamese (Chams), the encroachment of the jungle and the humidity. Work to clear the growth of vegetation from the temples proved a thankless task as it tended to grow back very quickly. Roots of enormous trees had grown around and through some of the temples and it was quickly realised that most were actually holding the structures together. Removing them would effect the collapse of the walls. To this day many tree roots are still in place, precariously supporting such temples as Ta Prohm. A technique known as anastylosis was introduced by the French curator at Angkor, Henri Marchal, who had learned from the Dutch working at Borobudur in Indonesia. The method was to dismantle a temple, recording each block of stone and its location, and then to reconstruct the building. This painstaking method can currently be seen in action at the temple of Baphuon.

The French continued to work on the temples until 1972 when the civil war made their position untenable. Once again the jungle reclaimed the temples and it was only in the mid-1980s that the Cambodian government invited a team of archaeologists from India to clean and restore Angkor Wat. Their methods have been much criticised as they used unskilled Cambodian labourers to clean the delicate bas-reliefs with chemicals which may have caused untold damage. However, they were working under very difficult conditions, constantly under threat from attack by the Khmer Rouge. Following the signing of the Paris Peace Accord in 1991, international agencies were able to continue restoration work. A number of countries are now working to preserve this unique site. The greatest threat for the temples of Angkor today comes from the looters who continue to plunder the treasures, generally to order, lured by the vast sums of money to be made on the international market. Such is the value of Angkor.

improve all aspects of Cambodian life under the guise of a democracy. Peace and stability appear to have arrived. However, the actions of the government are far from transparent and corruption is rife, intimidation commonplace, bickering between the coalition partners continual and political assassinations not unknown. Much debate within political circles is now given over to whether or not to put on trial former leaders of the Khmer Rouge. Most Cambodians feel that these men should stand trial for their crimes but some in power feel that it would stir up old feelings and antagonisms and, if the country is to move on from its current, more settled position, then bygones should be allowed to be bygones. The United Nations currently appears to have the cooperation of Hun Sen in working out a satisfactory formula for holding such trials and early in 2000 an agreement was hammered out for them to take place in Cambodia (not outside the country as the UN originally wanted) with five judges, three of which would be Cambodian and two international, appointed by the UN. However, dates are yet to be fixed and it is still not clear whether key players such as Ieng Sary and Khieu Samphan would stand trial. Hun Sen may choose to allow matters to drift on and without pressure from the United States, who may prefer trials not to happen, they may never take place. If the Khmer Rouge leaders do face a court of law, countries such as America, China and even Britain may have an uncomfortable time when the world is reminded that they supported the Khmer Rouge and failed to recognise the sitting government from 1979 until the early nineties: not a period that any government leaders can be proud of and not one about which they will want to be reminded. Once again the Cambodian people may find themselves the pawns of the superpowers and their wishes may be ignored. Hopefully by the time this book is published trial dates will have been set.

ECONOMY

Considering the extent of Cambodia's natural resources, in theory it should be a rich country. It has large areas of forests, very productive gem mines and fertile land thanks to the seasonal fluctuations of the Tonle Sap. However, the decades of political instability have prevented the country's economic potential from being realised.

The Khmer Rouge successfully destroyed the economy between 1975 and 1979 with their return to 'Year Zero'. Prior to that the country had suffered from years of fighting and this was to happen once again, with the Vietnamese invasion and the struggle which continued through much of the 1980s. The situation was aggravated when the Vietnamese withdrew in 1989 and the Soviet Union, which had been a major player in aid to Cambodia, collapsed. Western governments refused to support the Vietnamese-backed government and had introduced an embargo on trade and aid. Throughout the last two decades of the 20th century Cambodia relied heavily on foreign aid, much of which came (and still comes) from humanitarian aid groups such as CARE International, the International Committee of the Red Cross, Caritas, Oxfam, Médecins sans Frontières and Save the Children Fund. Without these organisations the farmers would not have been able to buy seed or even the basic tools needed to tend the paddies; hospitals would not have been able to treat patients and education would have been a non-starter. Farmers were hampered by the thousands of mines that had been laid across the country and many continue to be maimed or even lose their lives as a result. Help came from groups such as the Mines Advisory Group and the Halo Trust who continue painstakingly to demine areas of the country. All this was carried on against the backdrop of yet another civil war which was a drain on the government's coffers.

The early '90s were a time when the so-called 'tiger' economies of southeast Asia were booming and this encouraged entrepreneurs to look to Cambodia for short-term profits. Illegal logging became a serious problem and corrupt government employees, soldiers and even the Khmer Rouge raked in thousands of dollars from their activities. Many soldiers, doctors, teachers and civil servants survived on ridiculously low salaries of less than US$10 per month, if they were paid at all, so they became involved in the illegal exportation of gems as well as timber and many made huge fortunes, particularly if they lived close to the borders with Thailand and Vietnam. The economy was in a real mess as the government was receiving no income at all from this illicit trade. High inflation, combined with the arrival of the United National Transitional Authority in Cambodia (UNTAC), encouraged workers from the countryside to come into the cities to seek new employment opportunities in the hotels, restaurants, bars and clubs which were springing up. Many women also joined the flood and most ended up working as prostitutes, as their choices were limited and their families back home relied on them for money. The boom continued until 1996, following the successful elections in 1993. Tourist arrivals increased dramatically and businessmen from the region came to look at the prospects for this fledgling economy and began to invest heavily, in particular in the service industry. Inflation had decreased massively and for the first time the economy was showing significant growth. Optimism was high.

Financial crisis hit the 'tiger' economies of southeast Asia in 1997. The region in general had been producing staggering growth rates for most of the 1990s and was seen as the most dynamic part of the world economy. For many years the European and American markets had been pouring in money and setting up joint ventures just to get a slice of the action. What they didn't perceive was that at some stage the bubble would burst; this started with the collapse of the Thai baht and then other currencies around the region, in particular South Korea, Indonesia and Malaysia, went into free fall. Many of the problems stemmed from corruption, bad investments, disinformation by governments to attract loans and uneconomic trading practices. The West stepped in to help, mainly because it feared a knock-on effect worldwide, and the crisis was averted. However, the West insisted that the Asian economies most affected should change their operations, with more open finances and better information on business.

Although a very small player in southeast Asian economics, Cambodia was still adversely affected. The public sector was hit by a reduction in aid from overseas, vital to much of Cambodian society. Investment projects were terminated, construction was halted and there was a noticeable drop in the number of tourist arrivals from other Asian countries. The 1997 Asian crisis coincided with unrest in Cambodia prior to the 1998 elections, and these political events combined to exacerbate the situation. The agricultural sector was virtually unaffected because it is not touched by external economic uncertainty. The Cambodian riel depreciated only 25% compared with between 60% and 80% for other major Asian currencies. Analysts put this down to the fact that the economy relies largely on US dollars rather than Cambodian riels for most transactions.

A major result of the crisis in southeast Asia was that countries which had previously not been considered viable by foreign investors because their wages bill was too high were now more attractive. Currency depreciation and unemployment had put downward pressure on wages resulting in cheap labour, a strong selling point for Cambodia. Now it had competition from neighbouring countries and investment was diverted to these countries. At the same time imports from these countries were cheaper, which was a threat to domestic industries. The government's response was to raise tariffs on several products to protect certain industries. Opponents argue that as the decrease in the prices of imported goods is likely to be temporary the country should enjoy the lower rates because the government's action may result in a retaliatory increase in tariffs on Cambodian exports. Likewise an increase on tariffs will make smuggled goods, already a big problem for the government, more attractive.

April 1999 saw Cambodia's admittance into ASEAN (Association of South East Asian Nations), two years later than planned. Cambodia was on the point of joining the association in 1997 when Hun Sen ousted Ranariddh and the membership decision was put on hold until events settled down. It is an important time for Cambodia to be a member of ASEAN: now all the member countries must pull together to develop the region clear in the understanding that all the Asian economies are interdependent upon each other. Much work has to be done within Cambodia to bring their practices into line with those of other ASEAN members but the current settled period in its turbulent history gives the country the opportunity it needs to move forward.

Cambodia is still very reliant on the international community for assistance and a large proportion of its national budget comes from overseas aid. An important slice of revenue comes from logging, but there is evidence that most of the money never reaches the government as most logging is carried on illegally, often with connivance of individuals within authority. Rubber also used to be a major earner of foreign currency but the trees are old now, having not been replaced, and the yield is minimal. Gem mining in Rattanakiri and particularly around Pailin should bring in significant revenue for the government but it is controlled by former members of the Khmer Rouge who siphon off most of the profits. The government must now be seen to be attacking corruption and ensuring that the country as a whole, not just a few well-connected individuals, benefits from the few natural resources that the country does have. There is still much to do to improve health, education and the infrastructure for all Cambodians, 70% of whom still work in agriculture. Without significant improvements in the lives of all inhabitants, not just those in the cities, the country could find itself once again facing unrest from the 'have-nots'. In theory, history could repeat itself – but this time the world is watching to ensure it does not.

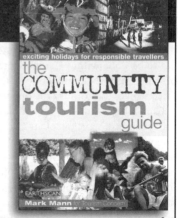

People and Culture

2

THE PEOPLE

The population of Cambodia is currently around 11.7 million of whom approximately 90% are ethnic Khmers who began to colonise the area around the 2nd century AD. The remaining 10% are divided between several minorities including Chams, Vietnamese, Chinese and the hill tribes or *chunchiet*, meaning nationalities.

The **Chams** are Muslims who live mainly in southern Cambodia particularly along the banks of the Tonle Sap and Mekong Rivers and on the coast. This ethnic group, which dominated central Vietnam from the 2nd to the 15th century, migrated when they were conquered by the Viets. Official estimates indicate that there are around 500,000 Chams in Cambodia, despite their having been particularly targeted by the Khmer Rouge.

It is very difficult to establish the true number of **ethnic Vietnamese** living in Cambodia, as many of them are there unofficially. Many Vietnamese are fishermen so live in the numerous floating villages. There has long been mutual distrust between the Cambodians and Vietnamese and this does not ease with the passing of years and mutual suffering. Hundreds of thousands of Vietnamese fled into Vietnam during the Khmer Rouge time (those that remained were systematically slaughtered) but a high percentage of these returned in the 1980s. Many Vietnamese have lived in Cambodia for generations but still do not have Cambodian citizenship nor have they any right to live in Vietnam. Trouble erupted once again in 1993 when members of the Khmer Rouge attacked families of Vietnamese origin and killed many of them. As a result around 20,000 fled to Vietnam.

The **ethnic Chinese** are very active businesspersons, as they are in all countries, and contribute a great deal to the urban economy. Their presence generally appears to be a welcome one in Cambodia and there are frequent occurrences of intermarriage between Khmer and Chinese people. Like the Vietnamese, ethnic Chinese suffered greatly at the hands of the Khmer Rouge and the situation did not improve for them when the Vietnamese troops liberated the country. Relations were at an all-time low between Vietnam and China at that time so many Chinese fled. The official estimate is that there are 100,000 Chinese but the true figure is believed to be higher.

The **hill tribes**, or *chunchiet*, live mainly in the mountainous region in the northeast of the country near the borders with Laos and Vietnam. They generally have a lifestyle distinct from the Khmers with their own languages, animistic worship and slash-and-burn agriculture. Their mode of dress is similar to that of the Khmers and not particularly colourful, unlike the hill tribes of Vietnam or Thailand, but many older women have tattoos on their faces as well as stretched and pierced earlobes. Very little is, in fact, known about them although there are believed to be around 30 different ethnic groups whose situation has not always been an easy one. A UNTAC survey found that six groups each numbered around 10,000 people and the remainder contained fewer than 3,000 in each group. The largest groups are the Tumpuon, Kreung, Charai, Stieng, Kuay and Mnong, all of which practise slash-and-burn subsistence farming.

Various regimes have tried to assimilate the *chunchiet*. The French employed them when they introduced rubber plantations as well as using them on construction work such as the building of roads and bridges. They continued to work on the rubber plantations during the first Sihanouk era, following independence, but their plight worsened as they were made to work longer hours and were generally harassed by government workers.

Their dilemma did not improve under the Khmer Rouge who took shelter in the remote provinces of the northeast. The government believed that the *chunchiet* were sheltering them, although in reality they had little choice. As a result government troops burnt down their villages and consequently the villagers did turn to the Khmer Rouge and even joined the fighters. The ferocity of the US bombing of the eastern provinces of Cambodia also encouraged the *chunchiet* to link up with the Khmer Rouge. However, recent studies have concluded that they did not actually understand the ideology of the Khmer Rouge but associated themselves with them as they felt persecuted by the government. Between 1975 and 1979 the *chunchiet* probably fared better than most Cambodians as they were already accustomed to a peasant existence and hard work. However, they were still used as slave labour and forbidden to speak their own language in an attempt to assimilate them into Khmer society. Many fled to Laos and Vietnam to evade persecution.

Subsequent governments have virtually left the *chunchiets* alone but subtle changes to their lifestyle are occurring all the time. They continue to use slash-and-burn techniques and this requires much land. As the Khmer population grows their numbers encroach on the land and the arrival of tourism and the subsequent need for accommodation will further absorb land which may cause tension. There is now a lot of contact with the Khmers following the development of a market economy and many young *chunchiets* have abandoned traditional dress. Their languages – particularly vulnerable because they are only spoken and not written – are in danger of disappearing completely as young people now learn Khmer.

LANGUAGE

Khmer is a Mon-Khmer language which is spoken by the majority of people in Cambodia. It has absorbed influences from many other languages over the centuries such as Sanskrit, Pali, Thai, Vietnamese and even French. Being a non-tonal language Khmer is easier to pick up than Vietnamese or Chinese which are notoriously difficult for Westerners. As a casual visitor you should attempt at least some basic phrases which will please your hosts, unless you plan to spend any length of time in Cambodia in which case a serious attempt should be made to learn the language. It is also worthwhile trying to master numbers to use when bargaining in markets and with moto drivers. Visitors to Cambodia will have no trouble in moving around the country as road signs and destination boards on buses appear in both Khmer and English. For some basic vocabulary, see *Appendix 1*.

French is still widely spoken among the older Khmers but English has overtaken it as the language of preference amongst young people. They realise that it is the language of opportunity and English language lessons are on offer everywhere throughout Phnom Penh and every town in the country. This has caused some upset in French circles, and as the government of France is one of the largest donors of aid to Cambodia, attempts are being made to promote the language there.

RELIGION

Hinduism was the prominent religion for much of the Angkorian period with most buildings dedicated to Siva, until the 12th century when Vishnu was more in favour. By the end of the 12th century Buddhism was introduced and coexisted with Hinduism until the 14th century when it became the state religion. Now over 90% of the population practise Theravada Buddhism and the remainder are divided between Muslims, Christians and animists.

Buddhism plays a large role in Cambodian life and many men spend time in a temple at some stage during their lives. In the countryside every village has a temple or *wat* around which daily life revolves. Most of the festivals that take place throughout the year are linked to Buddhism and the lunar calendar. Buddhist monks and the temples suffered particularly at the hands of the Khmer Rouge. They were determined to eradicate religion and to this end thousands of monks were murdered and temples and religious artefacts were severely damaged or destroyed.

The temples are once again beginning to flourish; many have been renovated and young boys are encouraged to become novices. The last few years have seen a steady increase in the number of orange-robed monks on the streets in the mornings with their bowls, collecting alms in the form of rice from the local population. The sight of nuns with shaved heads and white robes is also becoming more common. In the countryside new temples are beginning to be built in the villages, particularly along Route 5. All the work is undertaken by the villagers who also raise the money for materials.

Islam is practised by the Cham people who came to Cambodia from Vietnam at the end of the 15th century. Small mosques can be seen in many Cham communities and the women always have their heads covered. Despite being Sunni muslims, their practices are very relaxed, although financial and educational support from the Middle East may eventually introduce a shift to a more orthodox form of worship.

The only practising **Christians** in Cambodia are Vietnamese Catholics and members of the expatriate community. Some of the aid agencies in the country are Christian organisations who spread the word at the same time as helping the people so there may be a few new Christians around where these are based.

MUSIC AND LITERATURE
Music

Cambodian music dates back to the royal temples of Angkor where musicians are depicted on many of the bas-reliefs. There are two types of orchestra. A *Pin Peat* orchestra is purely sacred and is usually found in Buddhist temples especially playing for religious ceremonies, festivals and funerals as well as court music in front of the royal family. A *Mahouri* orchestra consists mainly of stringed instruments. The leader of the orchestra is the *Roneat Ek*, which is a bamboo xylophone. This is complimented by the *Roneat Thoung*, also a bamboo xylophone but with a lower, sweeter pitch, and the *Roneat Dek*, made with bronze and iron bars rather than bamboo. The *Kong Touc* is a set of sixteen small, copper gongs arranged horizontally in a circle on a bamboo

KHMER DANCE

Khmer classical dance dates back around 2,000 years and was originally influenced by Hinduism from India before adding its own movements during the great Angkor period. In the past classical dancing was only performed before royalty to honour the gods. The dancers, or *apsaras*, are depicted everywhere on the walls of the temples of Angkor where the style of dancing, the different headdresses and the costumes can be clearly seen. To the casual observer there are many similarities, in particular the hand movements and costumes worn, with Thai classical dance which shares the same cultural heritage.

Many of the dances reenact scenes from the *Ramayana*, the Hindu epic, and others depict ancient legends or recreate great battles. Women used to play all the roles in classical dance, but now men often play the monkey role which appears frequently. Classical dance was traditionally taught in the palace and girls began to train at a very early age, when their bones were still supple, in order to be able to perform the extraordinarily graceful hand gestures which are so symbolic.

Sadly, very few dancers, choreographers, dance teachers and costume designers survived the Khmer Rouge period and for a while it appeared that this ancient form of dancing would not survive. However, the few survivors got together and began to train young girls, drawing students from the many children who had been orphaned. Dance is once again well established and there is a Faculty of Choreographic Arts at the Royal University of Fine Arts which teaches classical dance as well as masked drama, shadow puppetry and traditional music. Performances are no longer for royal eyes only and can be seen in major hotels in Phnom Penh and Siem Reap and at Phnom Penh's Chatomuk Theatre.

frame. The *Kong Thom* is a set of sixteen larger gongs. The rhythm of the music is set by the *Samphor*, a drum made from treated cow hide, which is the most sacred instrument in the orchestra.

Literature

A civilisation which produced such wonderful architecture and sculpture would surely have been a prolific producer of various forms of literature. From evidence in carved inscriptions it appears that this was the case and tanned animal skins and dried palm leaves were used to write on. However, nothing survives to this day because of the effects of the climate on written texts and destruction during times of war. Many of the temples at Angkor had libraries which would have stored literary works, and it is strange that no attempt was made by scholars to copy any works which were in danger of being destroyed. The carved inscriptions tell us that literary works included the great Indian epics, such as the *Ramayana*, royal chronicles and descriptions of battles. They may even have recorded daily life, an aspect which can only be gleaned from the bas-reliefs on temples, such as the Bayon. However, most literature would have been of a religious nature and this fact is reflected in the carved inscriptions which still survive.

CULTURAL DOS AND DON'TS

As will become apparent soon after arrival, the Khmers are friendly, welcoming people with a terrific sense of humour. Despite the trauma the population has gone through and the difficulties of living in Cambodia today, the people always have a ready smile and will go out of their way to help you, a visitor to their country.

As Cambodia is a Buddhist country, the usual practices should be observed when visiting temples. Always remove shoes and hats when entering a temple and never wear shorts or sleeveless tops. Monks are often happy to talk with you, especially if it gives them a chance to practise their English. However, women should never touch a monk. Do not touch people on the top of the head and if sitting quietly in a temple, always kneel and never point your feet towards the Buddha.

Khmers greet people by placing both hands together as if praying. They are very hospitable people and may invite you into their homes. Always remove your shoes and take a small gift such as a memento of your home country, fruit, flowers or something small for the children.

The Khmer people believe in social harmony and you rarely hear voices raised in anger. If you have a problem always keep calm and do not get angry. You will get nowhere if you start shouting, but people will do everything they can to help you if you explain calmly what you want. You may find that when you are explaining your problem the Khmers may giggle. They are not laughing because they think it is funny, but because they are nervous. Finally, if trying to attract somebody's attention never point at them as this is extremely rude. Beckon them with the palm of your hand facing down and waggle your fingers.

Tipping is not expected but as salaries are very low in Cambodia it is much appreciated. Begging is commonplace throughout the country but it is not carried out aggressively. Most beggars are landmine victims, and it is important to remember that begging is likely to be their only source of income as they receive no assistance from the government. Keep a supply of small

CHARITIES WORKING IN CAMBODIA

The number of charities (non-governmental organisations) working within Cambodia is very extensive and many of the programmes overlap. Many of them went to the country initially to assist with emergency relief but the focus has changed now and most are helping the population to help themselves. Below is a small selection of the charities based in Cambodia with their contact details and objectives.

Action Against Hunger No 15, St 7, Chak Tomok, Daun Penh, Phnom Penh; tel: (023) 426934/363701; fax: (023) 361291; email: acfcambodge@bigpond.com.kh. Runs programmes covering nutrition, water and sanitation, food security and health.

American Red Cross Corner St 51/360, Boeung Keng Kang, Khan Chamcar Morn, Phnom Penh; tel: (023) 211996; fax: (023) 214105; email: gdixon@ bigpond.com.kh; web: www.redcross.org. Involved with health education, HIV/AIDS education, primary health and disaster preparedness and response.

CARE House 4-B, St 812, Boeung Keng Kang, Phnom Penh; tel: (023) 721115; email: care.cam@bigpond.com.kh; web: www.care.org. Operates a series of programmes including health, HIV/AIDS education, hygiene education and water projects.

Helen Keller International PO Box 168, Phnom Penh; tel(023) 210851; fax: (023) 210852; email: hki@bigpond.com.kh; web: www.hki.org. Runs programmes to prevent blindness, restore sight and rehabilitate the blind.

Jesuit Refugee Service PO Box 880, Phnom Penh; tel: (023) 880139; fax: (023) 880140; email: denise.coghlan@jesref.org; web: www.jesuit.org/jrs. Meets the short term and long term needs of refugees.

Medecins Sans Frontières No 8, St 211, Sangkat Veal Vong, Khan 7 Makara, Phnom Penh; tel: (023) 880334/5/6; fax: (023) 880338; web: www.dwb.org. Provides emergency medical relief to populations threated by war, civil strife, epidemics and natural disasters.

Oxfam America No 54, St 352, Boeung Keng Kang, Phnom Penh; tel: (023) 720928; fax: (023) 210357; email: OxfamAmerica@bigpond.com.kh; web: www.oxfamamerica.org. Funds disaster relief and self-help development projects.

Trickle Up Khum Sovan Sakor, Phoum Ta Eng, Kampot; tel: (033) 932999; email: ucc@forum.org.kh. Its mission is to reduce poverty by helping the population to start and expand businesses for land mine victims.

WHEELCHAIRS FOR CAMBODIA

The need for wheelchairs in Cambodia is great and for most victims of trauma, such as landmine amputees, there is no means of obtaining them. Any Cambodians injured by a landmine explosion must pay for their medical treatment and rarely have any money left over to afford a wheelchair.

Most Cambodians have to rely on obtaining wheelchairs from charitable organisations within the country. These charities have raised the funds to buy wheelchairs or receive donations of unwanted wheelchairs from overseas. However, it was apparent that many wheelchairs from the West were just not suitable for local conditions. In 1993 a UK charity called **Motivation** was asked to address the problem of wheelchairs for double, above-knee amputees. Motivation is the only charitable organisation dealing with the design of suitable wheelchairs using locally available materials for use in developing countries. For countries such as Cambodia, where there are no supplies of tubular steel, Motivation developed a chair using local wood and with only three wheels which enables the user to get over rough ground more easily. Three-wheeled wheelchairs are more stable and more manoeuvrable.

The work of Motivation is not only about the design of wheelchairs but extends to the training and education of the recipients to allow them to enjoy a more active life and help them to become independent. They also established production and distribution systems for their low-cost wheelchairs in Cambodia and made the chair into a flat-pack design so it is easier to transport around the country by the limited means available.

The work of Motivation continues within Cambodia through its local partner the Jesuit Refugee Service but it has many projects throughout the world in places such as Afghanistan, the former Soviet Union and Nicaragua where there is still a great need.

Motivation can be contacted at Brockley Academy, Brockley Lane, Backwell, Bristol BS48 4AQ; tel: 01275 464012; fax: 01275 464019; email: motivation@motivation.org.uk; web: www.motivation.org.uk

denomination notes to hand out if you wish. Obviously the choice is yours as to whether or not you give to the beggars. Around the temples at Angkor, and elsewhere, many children will offer their services as your guide or even just ask for money. It is better to reward them for a service such as guiding rather than just to give them money as this may encourage them to become dependent on begging into their adult life.

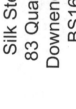

Practical Information

WHEN TO GO

Cambodia has two distinct seasons, the dry from November to April and the wet from May to October. The best time for a visit to Cambodia is in December and January when it is cooler and therefore pleasant to travel around. As the beginning of the wet season approaches the heat and humidity begin to build and it is wise to travel or sightsee in the early morning or late afternoon, avoiding the blistering heat at the middle of the day.

A visit during the rainy season is not out of the question as it does not necessarily rain every day and there are still many sunny days. Travel by boat is easier at that time as the rivers are higher and the larger boats can operate. Road travel, however, can be severely disrupted as there is often flooding on some of the major routes, many of the laterite roads turn into quagmires and vehicles regularly become stuck. Sightseeing around the towns and temples is still possible though, provided you dodge the downpours. Another bonus of travel during the rainy season is that many hotels reduce their rates in order to attract customers.

GETTING THERE AND AWAY

For many years the only way to reach Phnom Penh was by plane from Bangkok, Ho Chi Minh City or Vientiane. Now numerous international carriers fly into Phnom Penh and there are even direct flights from Bangkok to Siem Reap. The direct service to Siem Reap is often under threat as the Phnom Penh authorities feel that the city is being bypassed and that tourists are only visiting Siem Reap. However, the popularity of the flights is such that it would be difficult to justify any cancellation of the route.

To date the airlines flying into Cambodia have been regional carriers but it is hoped that a European airline may consider extending one of its asian routes into Phnom Penh. However, at the moment no serious contenders have come forward.

The land border with Vietnam has been open for several years and the Thai border has only been considered safe in recent years. As yet there is no official border crossing open with Laos although locals are allowed to use it.

By air

There are no direct flights from Europe, Australia or America yet and it is necessary to change planes somewhere in Asia. Several Asian carriers fly to and from Cambodia and an outline of their operation is given below. Phnom Penh Airport is 8km from the city and Siem Reap airport 7km from the town. There is an international departure tax of US$20.

Bangkok Airways 61A St 214, Phnom Penh; tel: 023 300409/426624; fax: 023 310409; email: www.bkkair.co.th. Daily flight to Bangkok and several flights per day from Siem Riep to Bangkok; Tuesday, Thursday and Saturday flight from Sukhotai to Siem Reap and Tuesday, Thursday and Saturday flight from Siem Reap to Phuket.
China Southern Airlines Regency Square, 168 Monireth Bd, Phnom Penh; tel: 023 424588; email: csa@camnet.com.kh. Monday and Friday flights to Guangzhou.
Dragon Air Regency Square, 168 Monireth Bd, Phnom Penh; tel: 023 217665. Monday, Tuesday, Thursday and Saturday flights to Hong Kong.
Lao Aviation 18B Sihanouk Bd, Phnom Penh; tel: 023 216563. Monday and Friday flight to Vientiane.
Malaysian Airlines Diamond Hotel, 172–184 Monivong Bd, Phnom Penh; tel: 023 426688. Shared daily (except Saturday) flight with Royal Air Cambodge to Kuala Lumpur.
President Airlines 50 Norodom Bd, Phnom Penh; tel: 023 212887, 210338/9; fax: 023 212992. Tuesday and Friday flights to Chongqing; Friday flight to Penang and Monday and Thursday flights to Taipei.
Royal Air Cambodge 206a Norodom Bd, Phnom Penh; tel: 023 811143; fax: 023 810274; email: flights@royalaircambodge.com.kh. Twice-daily flight to Bangkok and one flight per day from Siem Reap to Bangkok; Wednesday and Saturday flight to Guangzhou; Thursday and Sunday flight to Shanghai; daily flight to Ho Chi Minh City; Monday and Friday flight to Hong Kong; shared daily (except Saturday) flight with Malaysian Airlines to Kuala Lumpur; Tuesday, Friday and Sunday flights to Singapore.
Silk Air Pailin Hotel, 219B Monivong Bd, Phnom Penh; tel: 023 364443. Daily flight to Singapore.
Thai Airways International 19 St 106, Phnom Penh; tel: 023 722335; email: thaiair@bigpond.com.kh. Twice-daily flights to Bangkok.
Vietnam Air 41 St 214, Phnom Penh; tel: 023 363396. Three flights per day to Ho Chi Minh City; five flights per week from Ho Chi Minh City to Siem Reap.

By sea

Many visitors from Thailand now enter Cambodia through the port of Sihanoukville. The exit point from Thailand is on the coast at Hat Lek where a taxi has to be taken for the 15–20-minute journey to the port. Here a small boat crosses to Koh Kong in around five minutes (one-way fare 20 baht) to connect with the large speedboats to Sihanoukville. The boats operate every day but it is necessary to have a Cambodian visa issued in advance (see *Red Tape* section on page 39).

The border is open from 07.00 to 17.00 and the speedboat which connects Koh Kong with Sihanoukville has a one-way fare of US$15. The boat from Koh Kong leaves at 08.00, arriving at 11.30 and stopping at Koh Sdach en route. The return boat leaves Sihanoukville at 12.00 arriving at 15.30. The small boats between Koh Kong and Hat Lek meet the boats so journeys in both directions can be completed during the border opening hours provided the boats run on time. When travelling from Sihanoukville to Koh Kong get off the boat at Pak Klong, which is the stop before Koh Kong town, where the small boats then take you to Hat Lek.

By land

The land borders between Cambodia and both Vietnam and Thailand are open, but at the moment it is not possible for foreigners to cross into Laos, although Lao and Cambodian citizens can do so.

The border with Vietnam has been open for several years and is a popular and cheap option for entering the country. Until the beginning of 2000, when entering or leaving Vietnam, the Vietnamese visa stamped into your passport had to show the border crossing as Moc Bai. Now, although you have to advise the authorities of your plans, the actual crossing does not appear on the visa so there is no longer any need to alter the visa if your plans change. Entry into Cambodia will be refused if there is not a valid visa stamped into your passport.

There is a bus service operating between Phnom Penh and Ho Chi Minh City. The bus departs Phnom Penh from the Land Transportation Enterprise, St 182, Sangkat Vel Vong, Khan 7 Makara, Phnom Penh (tel: 012 846836/012 845550 – both mobile numbers). The bus makes the journey twice a week on Wednesday and Saturday leaving at 06.00 and arriving in Ho Chi Minh City at around 14.00. The arrival time varies as it depends how long the bus takes getting across the border. The one-way fare is US$20 per person.

The Capitol Guesthouse (tel: 023 724104) also operates a daily minibus service to Ho Chi Minh City departing Phnom Penh at around 06.45 and arriving at approximately 15.30 with a fare of US$6 one way. This bus is operated in conjunction with the Sinh Café in Ho Chi Minh City where the bus leaves at 08.30 and arrives in Phnom Penh at around 17.00. The Sinh Café is at 246–248 De Tham, Ho Chi Minh City; tel: 00 848 8367338; fax: 00 848 8369322.

It is also possible to take a taxi between Phnom Penh and Ho Chi Minh City. Taxis in either direction stop at the border and then it is necessary to cross on foot and pick up a shared taxi on the other side. Taxis from Phnom Penh to the border cost US$20–30 per car and from the border to Ho Chi Minh City US$40 per car. If you are going to the Vietnamese border shared taxis can be picked up from the Chhbar Ampov Market, across the Monivong Bridge in Phnom Penh. The total journey should take around six hours.

The Thai border is open at Aranyaprathet on the Thai side and Poipet on the Cambodian side. It is open from 07.00 to 18.00 and shared taxis can take you to Sisophon and then on to either Siem Reap or Battambang. Whichever route you choose the roads are bad (the journey can take 7–9 hours to Siem Reap) so it is necessary to enter Cambodia in the early morning in order to have time to reach your final destination. Aranyaprathet, close to the Thai border, can be reached from Bangkok by either bus or train and then taxi or moto to the border a few kilometres away.

TOUR OPERATORS

If you are starting your journey in the UK, Australia or the USA, the following companies are worth contacting as they all have considerable expertise in the area. Many put together tailor-made itineraries to suit your interests and budgets and some have small group departures on set dates. A trip can also be combined with a visit to another country in the vicinity such as Thailand, Vietnam or Laos.

Australia

Intrepid Travel 11–12 Spring St, Fitzroy, Vic, 3065; tel: 00 613 9473 2626; fax: 00 613 9419 4426; email: info@intrepidtravel.com.au; web: www.intrepidtravel.com.au. Emphasis on real adventure tours for small groups of all ages who want to discover and understand Cambodia.

Orbitours 3rd Floor, 73 Walker St, North Sydney, NSW 2060; tel: 00 612 9954 1399; fax: 00 612 9954 1655; email: orbitours@compuserve.com; web: www.orbitours.com.au. One of the first tour operators in the world to resume tours into Cambodia and always at the forefront of travel to the region.

Peregrine Adventures 258 Lonsdale St, Melbourne 3000; tel: 00 613 9663 8611; fax: 00 613 9663 8618; email: info@peregrine.net.au; web: www.peregrineadventures.co.uk. Small group tour operator which visits the main sights as well as those off the tourist trail. Their focus is on local lifestyles and customs.

Travel Indochina 403 George St, Sydney, NSW 2000; tel: 00 612 9244 2133; fax: 00 612 9244 2233; email: travindo@travelindochina.com.au; web: www.travelindochina.com.au. Specialist small group company helping participants to gain an insight into the country.

UK

Asian Journeys Ltd 6 Willows Gate, Stratton Audley, Oxfordshire OX27 9AU; tel: 01869 276200; fax: 01869 276214; email: mail@asianjourneys.com; web: www.asianjourneys.com. Excellent brochure and detailed dossiers and itineraries with staff who are skilled in putting together trips tailored to individual requirements.

Gateway to Asia Gateway House, Marchington, Uttoxeter, Staffs ST14 8LW; tel: 01283 821096; fax: 01283 820467; email: specialist-travel@gateway-to-india.co.uk; web: www.gateway-to-asia.co.uk; www.gateway-to-india.co.uk

Mekong Travel 16 Ledborough Wood, Beaconsfield, Bucks HP9 2DJ; tel: 01494 674456; fax: 01494 681631; web: www.mekongtravel.com

Regent Holidays (UK) Ltd 15 John St, Bristol BS1 2HR; tel: 0117 921 1711; fax: 0117 925 4866; email: regent@regent-holidays.co.uk; web: www.regent-holidays.co.uk. One of the first tour operators to develop a tour programme to Cambodia when it opened its doors to tourists once again in 1987. Knowledgeable staff skilled at putting together tailor-made itineraries.

Silk Steps Ltd 83 Quaker's Rd, Downend, Bristol BS16 6NH; tel: 0117 940 2800; fax: 0117 940 6900; email: info@silksteps.co.uk; web: www.silksteps.co.uk. Enthusiastic and knowledgeable specialists to the region. Can put together creative itineraries on request. Efficient service. Informative brochure.

SSbD Travel Elm Church, Trudoxhill, Frome, Somerset BA11 5DP; tel/fax: 01373 836013. Run by Beverley Palmer who has lived and worked in Cambodia so knows the country well. Offers small group tours as well as tailor-made arrangements.

Steppes East Ltd Castle Eaton, Cricklade, Wilts SN6 6JU; tel: 01285 810267; fax: 01285 810693; web: www.steppeseast.co.uk

Symbiosis Expedition Planning 205 St Johns Hill, London SW11 1TH; tel: 020 7924 5906; fax: 020 7924 5907; web: www.symbiosis-travel.co.uk

Tennyson Travel Ltd/Visit Vietnam Tennyson House, 30–32 Fulham High St, London SW6 3LQ; tel: 020 7736 4347; fax: 020 7736 5672; email: tennyson@visitvietnam.co.uk. Despite its name, Visit Vietnam also includes Cambodia in its tour programme. Friendly, knowledgeable service with excellent prices on its group tour programmes. Can also arrange tailor-made itineraries for individuals and groups.

USA

Absolute Asia 180 Varick St, New York, NY 10014; tel: 00 1 212 627 1950; fax: 00 1 212 627 4090; email: info@absoluteasia.com; web: www.absoluteasia.com. Knowledgeable staff design tailor-made itineraries to suit the budget and interests of individual travellers.

Global Spectrum 1901 Pennsylvania Av, NW Suite 204, Washington, DC 20006; tel: 00 1 202 293 2065; fax: 00 1 202 296 0815; email: gspectrum@gspectrum.com; web: www.vietnamspecialists.com. A leading Vietnam specialist whose programme has expanded to include Cambodia and other Southeast Asian countries.

InnovAsian Travel 40 Edgewood Rd, Hartsdale, NY 10530; tel: 00 1 914 674 0414; fax: 00 1 914 674 0708; email: InnovAsian@ibm.net; web: www.InnovAsian.com. Southeast Asian specialist travel company with creative itineraries for both individual travellers and small groups.

Vietnam

If you are travelling around Vietnam and looking for help in putting together a trip through Cambodia there are a few companies who are very knowledgeable about the country.

Vidotour 41 Dinh Tien Hoang, Ho Chi Minh City; tel: 00 848 829 1438; fax: 00 848 829 1435; email: vidotour@fmail.vnn.vn. Definitely the best in Ho Chi Minh City and possibly in Vietnam when it comes to understanding exactly what you want and putting your plans into practice.

Exotissimo Saigon Trade Centre, 37 Ton Duc Thang St, District 1, Ho Chi Minh City; tel: 00 848 825 1723; fax: 00 848 829 5800; email: info@exotissimo.com; web: www.exotissimo.com. Very professional with original ideas and informed staff.

RED TAPE
Arrival/departure by air
Visas

Cambodia is, surprisingly, easier to enter than both Laos and Vietnam as for several years it has granted visas on arrival at Phnom Penh and Siem Reap airports, valid for one month, to visitors arriving by air. The process is straightforward and quick although this could depend on the number of planes landing at any one time. A simple form has to be completed at the airport and given to the first official in a long line of them, together with passport and one photo and US$20 cash (or US$25 for a business visa). There are about ten officials behind the desk and your documents are passed from one to another, duly processed at each stage until the final official silently waves your passport in the air complete with a full-page stamp. It is an interesting process to watch as it is like an efficient assembly line.

Cambodian visas can be extended to a maximum of three months. This can be handled by a travel agent or by going direct to the Bureau des Etrangers on Street 200. A one-month extension costs US$30 and three months US$60. There is a fine of US$5 per day for overstaying the validity of the visa.

Customs

Customs officials are pretty casual at the airports. Even though a form is handed out by the airline they barely glance at it or just wave you through if you have lost the form, as I have done on two occasions. An entry/exit form also has to be completed; the exit form must be kept with your passport at all times and handed in at immigration on departure.

Departure tax

When flying out of Cambodia on an international flight there is a departure tax, payable in cash, of US$20 from Phnom Penh and Siem Reap.

Arrival/departure overland
From/to Vietnam

Vietnamese visas must be obtained in advance in Phnom Penh or Sihanoukville or before travelling at one of the embassies or consulates overseas. You need to specify the departure point from or entry point into Vietnam as Moc Bai but since January 2000 Vietnam embassies have been able to issue visas which no longer specify the departure or arrival point. Until now it has been a real chore to alter the entry or exit point on the visa if your plans change, or else pay a heavy 'fine' at the border to amend it. Cambodian visas must be obtained in advance from one of its embassies or consulates overseas (see overleaf). For business visas, see page 72. The visa process can take several days so apply well in advance.

From/to Thailand

The border crossing at Poipet has been open for a while but until the beginning of 2000 it was necessary to obtain a Cambodian visa in advance. Now tourist visas can be obtained at the border for 1,000 baht but at the moment these cannot be extended for a longer stay. Check before travelling if you envisage staying in Cambodia for any length of time. Thai visas can be obtained at the border, if required.

From/to Laos

The border crossing north of Stung Treng at Veun Kham has long been open to Lao and Cambodian citizens but at the moment it is not a formal crossing

BRITISH CONSULAR SERVICES ABROAD

Most travellers are not really clear as to the exact role of the British Embassy when it comes to helping British citizens in difficulty abroad. Here is an outline of what they can and will do.

- Issue emergency passports (this possibly has to be done through the Bangkok embassy for visitors to Cambodia, so may take some time)
- Contact relatives and friends and ask them to help you with money or tickets
- In an emergency, cash you a sterling cheque worth up to £100 if supported by a valid banker's card
- As a last resort, and as long as you meet certain strict rules, give you a loan to get back to the UK. This loan must be repaid. The embassy will only do this if they are sure there is no one else who can help you
- Help you get in touch with local lawyers, interpreters and doctors
- Arrange for next of kin to be told of an accident or a death and advise on procedures
- Visit you in prison. In certain circumstances they can arrange for messages to be sent to relatives or friends
- Give guidance on organisations who help trace missing persons Speak to the local authorities for you, in certain circumstances

The embassy cannot:

- Intervene in court cases
- Get you out of prison
- Give legal advice or start court proceedings for you
- Get you better treatment in hospital or prison than is given to local nationals
- Investigate a crime
- Pay your hotel, legal, medical or any other bills
- Pay your travel costs, except in special circumstances
- Do work normally done by travel agents, airlines, banks or motoring organisations
- Get you somewhere to live, a job or work permit
- Formally help you if you are a dual national in the country of your second nationality

point for other nationalities. There are often rumours that this border is about to open so check the current situation when you are in Phnom Penh.

EMBASSIES AND CONSULATES
Cambodian embassies and consulates

Australia 5 Canterbury Ct, Deakin ACT 2600, Canberra; tel: 00 61 26273 1259; fax: 00 61 26273 1053

China 9 Dong Zhi Men Wai Dajie, 100600 Beijing; tel: 00 86 1065322101; fax: 0086 1065323507

France 4 rue Adolphe Yvon, 75016 Paris; tel: 00 331 45 03 47 20; fax: 00331 45 03 47 40

Germany Gruner Weg 8, 53343 Wachtberg Pech, Bonn; tel/fax: 00 49 228 328572

Laos Bane Saphanthong Nou, ABP/34, Vientiane; tel/fax: 00 856 21314951

Thailand 185 Rajadamri Rd, 10330 Bangkok; tel: 00 66 2254 6630; fax: 00 66 2253 9859

USA 4500-16th St NW, 20011 Washington DC; tel: 00 1 202 726 7742; fax: 001 202 726 8381

Vietnam 71a Tran Hung Dao, Hanoi; tel: 00 844 825 3788; fax: 00 844 826 5225; Consulate 41 Phung Khac Khoan St, Ho Chi Minh City; tel: 00 848 829 2751; fax: 00 848 829 2744

Foreign embassies

Australia 11 St 254, Phnom Penh; tel: 023 426000

Canada (c/o Australian Embassy) 11 St 254, Phnom Penh; tel: 023 426000

China 256 Mao Tse Tung Bd, Phnom Penh; tel: 023 426971

Cuba 98 St 214, Phnom Penh; tel: 023 427428

France 1 Monivong Bd, Phnom Penh; tel: 023 430020

Germany 76–78 St 214, Phnom Penh; tel: 023 426381

Japan 75 Norodom Bd, Phnom Penh; tel: 023 427161

Laos 15–17 Mao Tse Tung Bd, Phnom Penh; tel: 023 426441

Malaysia 161 St 51, Phnom Penh; tel: 023 426176

Russia 213 Samdeach Sothearos Bd, Phnom Penh; tel: 023 722081

Singapore 92 Norodom Bd, Phnom Penh; tel: 023 360855

Thailand 4 Monivong Bd, Phnom Penh; tel: 023 426182

United Kingdom 27–29 St 75, Phnom Penh; tel: 023 427124; fax: 023 427125; email: BRITEMB@bigpond.com.kh (open Mon, Tue, Thu, Fri 08.00–12.00 and 13.30–17.00 and Wed 08.00–13.00).

USA 16 St 228, Phnom Penh; tel: 023 216436

Vietnam 436 Monivong Bd, Phnom Penh; tel: 023 725481

HEALTH

Dr Felicity Nicholson

This section deals with health topics particular to travel in Cambodia. All travellers, and especially those hiking in rural parts of this country, should be prepared to deal with the whole spectrum of common ailments and first aid crises.

Before you go
Immunisations

Preparations to ensure a healthy trip to Cambodia require checks on your immunisation status; you'll also need to pack lotions and long clothes to protect you from insect bites and the sun. It is wise to go, if you can, to a travel clinic at least a couple of months before departure to arrange immunisations. The only requirement for Cambodia is a yellow fever certificate if you are coming from a yellow fever infected area (certain countries in South America and sub-

Saharan Africa). However, for health the following vaccines are recommended. **Tetanus** immunity needs to be boosted every ten years, as does **diphtheria** and **polio**. The majority of travellers are advised to have immunisation against **hepatitis A** with hepatitis A vaccine (eg: Havrix Monodose, Avaxim). One dose of vaccine lasts for one year and can be boosted to give protection for up to ten years. The course of two injections costs about £100. It is now felt that the vaccine can be used even close to the time of departure. It is nearly always preferable to gamma globulin which gives immediate but partial protection for a couple of months. There is a theoretical risk of CJD (the human form of mad cow disease) with this latter blood-derived product.

The newer **typhoid** vaccines are about 85% effective and should be encouraged unless the traveller is leaving within a few days for a trip of a week or less when the vaccine would not be effective in time. It needs boosting every three years.

Immunisation against **cholera** is currently ineffective, but a cholera exemption certificate is not required in Cambodia.

Hepatitis B vaccination should be considered for extended trips or for those working in situations where contact with blood is increased. Three injections are ideal which can be given at 8, 4 and 0 weeks prior to travel or, if there is insufficient time, then on days 28–21, 14–7, then 0. The only vaccine licensed for the latter more rapid course at the time of printing is Engerix B. The longer course is always to be preferred as immunity is likely to be longer lasting.

Rabies vaccine should be considered for travellers likely to be more than 24 hours away from medical help or who are specifically going to handle animals. Ideally three doses of vaccine should be taken over a four-week period before departure, but two doses are better than one, and one is still better than nothing at all. Contrary to popular belief these vaccines are relatively painless!

Another vaccine that should be considered for travellers who are spending a month or more in rural parts of Cambodia is **Japanese encephalitis** vaccine (see page 52). The Japanese brand of this vaccine is still unlicensed in the UK, but has been licensed in the USA and Japan. This vaccine is not usually stocked by GPs but is more readily available in travel clinics where it is often cheaper anyway. Ideally three injections are required, taken on days 21–28, 7–14, and 0. The Department of Health recommends that the last dose should not be given less than ten days before a long-haul flight in case any severe side effects develop.

It is always wise to be up-to-date with BCG for tuberculosis (most people from the UK will have been vaccinated between the ages of 11 and 14). It is more important for trips of eight weeks or longer, but note that it can take this length of time for the vaccine to be given. Another good reason to plan your trip well in advance!

Travel clinics
UK
British Airways Travel Clinic and Immunisation Service 156 Regent St, London W1; tel: 020 7439 9584. This place also sells travellers' supplies and has a

branch of Stanford's travel book and map shop. There are now BA clinics all around Britain and four in South Africa. To find your nearest one, phone 01276 685040.

MASTA (Medical Advisory Service for Travellers Abroad) Keppel St, London WC1 7HT; tel: 09068 224100. This is a premium-line number, charged at 50p per minute.

Nomad Travel Pharmacy and Vaccination Centre 3–4 Wellington Terrace, Turnpike Lane, London N8 0PX; tel: 020 8889 7014.

Thames Medical 157 Waterloo Rd, London SE1 8US; tel: 020 7902 9000. Competitively priced, one-stop travel health service. All profits go to their affiliated company InterHealth which provides health care for overseas workers on Christian projects.

Trailfinders Immunisation Centre 194 Kensington High St, London W8 7RG; tel: 020 7938 3999. Also 254–284 Sauchiehall St, Glasgow G2 3EH; tel: 0141 353 0066.

USA

Centers for Disease Control 1600 Clifton Road, Atlanta, GA 30333; tel: 877 FYI TRIP; 800 311 3435; web: www.cdc.gov/travel. This organisation is the central source of travel information in the USA. Each summer they publish the invaluable *Health Information for International Travel* which is available from the Division of Quarantine at the above address.

Connaught Laboratories PO Box 187, Swiftwater, PA 18370; tel: 800 822 2463. They will send a free list of specialist tropical-medicine physicians in your state.

IAMAT (International Association for Medical Assistance to Travelers) 736 Center St, Lewiston, NY 14092. A non-profit organisation which provides lists of English-speaking doctors abroad.

Australia

TMVC tel: 1300 65 88 44; website: www.tmvc.com.au. TMVC has 20 clinics in Australia, New Zealand and Thailand, including:
Brisbane Dr Deborah Mills, Qantas Domestic Building, 6th floor, 247 Adelaide St, Brisbane, QLD 4000; tel: 7 3221 9066; fax: 7 3321 7076
Melbourne Dr Sonny Lau, 393 Little Bourke St, 2nd floor, Melbourne, VIC 3000; tel: 3 9602 5788; fax: 3 9670 8394.
Sydney Dr Mandy Hu, Dymocks Building, 7th floor, 428 George St, Sydney, NSW 2000; tel: 2 221 7133; fax: 2 221 8401.

South Africa

There are four **British Airways travel clinics** in South Africa: *Johannesburg*, tel: (011) 807 3132; *Cape Town*, tel: (021) 419 3172; *Knysna*, tel: (044) 382 6366; *East London*, tel: (0431) 43 2359.

Insurance

Before you travel make sure you have adequate medical insurance which has comprehensive cover for hospitalisation as well as repatriation in the case of an emergency. The choice of insurance policies is excellent nowadays so shop around for the best one to suit your plans when in Cambodia. This is particularly important if you are planning to hire a bicycle or motorbike; many policies do not cover this should you have an accident.

Local medical facilities

Medical facilities are rather limited around the country apart from in the capital, and for any emergencies or serious illnesses it is important to get back to Phnom Penh as soon as possible. Even then it may be necessary to continue to Bangkok. Occasionally NGO staff work in some of the provincial hospitals but they are unable to deal with more than routine problems.

SOS International 161 St 51, Phnom Penh; tel: 023 216911; fax: 023 215811. Well-equipped clinic that can deal with routine problems as well as emergencies.
Calmette Hospital 3 Monivong Bd, Phnom Penh; tel: 023 426948. The main hospital in Phnom Penh.
Tropical & Travellers Medical Centre 88 St 108, Phnom Penh; tel/fax: 023 366802. British-run practice covering general medical practice through to tropical medicine.
European Dental Clinic 195a Norodom Bd, Phnom Penh; tel: 023 362656

There is no shortage of pharmacies throughout Cambodia and it is possible to obtain medicines over the counter that you can only get on prescription in the UK. It goes without saying that you should check the expiry date on the packet.

Water sterilisation

It is not safe to drink the tap water in Cambodia, and those that do, do so at their peril. If there is a shortage of bottled water then it is necessary to sterilise the local water. Hepatitis A, dysentery and giardiasis (amongst others) can all contaminate water. You can't tell by looking; the foulest swamp water may be perfectly safe, while that pristine, babbling mountain stream may harbour giardia.

Boiling water for five to ten minutes should destroy all viruses and bacteria, and is pretty failsafe. A second option is chemical treatment with iodine. Iodine tablets such as Potable-Aqua, Coughlan's or Globaline have been proven to deliver eight parts per million (8ppm) of iodine, which effectively kills all micro-organisms. Many medical professionals now advise you to let the treated water stand for at least two hours before using; that's much longer than the usual 30 minutes the manufacturers recommend. Iodine leaves an unmistakable taste; neutralising tablets are available, but are costly, so try either a pinch of sodium thiosulphate (available in pharmacies and photographic equipment shops) or powdered fruit drink to make the water palatable. Using iodine is safe in the short term, but is not recommended throughout a long trip and is contraindicated in pregnancy.

Chlorine tablets such as Halazone disintegrate within a week of opening the container, and few medical authorities still recommended them.

A number of water filters are available and more recently have undergone rigorous field-testing. Many experts advise a combination of filtration and chemical treatment. Take advice from a backpacking store or one of the travel clinics mentioned earlier.

Medical problems and diseases
Malaria

Malaria is potentially fatal and is by far the most serious health risk to travellers in tropical countries. Every year the disease kills between one and two million people worldwide. There is no vaccine against malaria, but using prophylactic drugs (even though none is 100% effective) and preventing mosquito bites will considerably reduce the risk of contracting it. Malaria is especially dangerous in pregnancy and not all tablets are suitable, so pregnant women should always seek advice before travelling.

Another reason why it is worth checking with a travel medicine specialist for up-to-date advice is that drug resistance is always changing and newer drugs may come on to the market. With the exception of the Phnom Penh area and close to Tonle Sap, malaria is widespread in Cambodia. Depending on which part of Cambodia you are visiting, one of two drugs will be recommended. At the time of writing, these are either mefloquine (Lariam) or doxycycline. Mefloquine is an effective prophylactic agent for most parts of Cambodia except the western provinces where the *Plasmodium falciparum* (the protozoan responsible for malaria in Cambodia) has developed resistance. Doxycycline is the drug of choice for this region. Mefloquine should be started at least two and a half weeks before departure to check that it suits you, unless you have already used this drug previously with no ill effect. Then it is safe to start one week before travel. Stop immediately if it seems to cause depression or anxiety, visual or hearing disturbances, severe headaches, changes in heart rhythm or fits. Anyone who is pregnant, has been treated for depression or psychiatric problems, has diabetes controlled by oral therapy or who is epileptic (or who has suffered fits in the past) or has a close blood relative who has epilepsy should not take mefloquine.

The antibiotic doxycycline (100mg daily) is the alternative prophylactic agent and need only be started one day before arrival. Many people use doxycycline in preference to mefloquine in any part of Cambodia, because of the largely unwarranted bad press that the latter drug has received. Doxycycline may also be used in travellers with epilepsy, unlike the other regimes, although the antiepileptic therapy may make it less effective. Users should be warned about the possibility of allergic skin reactions developing in sunlight; these can occur in about 5% of people. The drug should be stopped if this happens. Women using oral contraceptives should use an additional method of protection for the first four weeks when using doxycycline. Remember that it is unwise to rely on the 'pill' as the sole means of contraception on any trip abroad, as an episode of diarrhoea can render it ineffective!

All malaria tablets are best taken with food and plenty of fluid in the evening to reduce side effects like indigestion and nausea. Since no drug is totally effective, you should be vigilant for symptoms of malaria that can develop from seven days into your trip up to one year after your return. You should go immediately to a doctor if you develop a temperature of over 38°C, regardless of any other symptoms (eg: headaches, abdominal pain, joint pains, jaundice etc) that may be present.

Some travellers who know they will be far away from medical help may wish to carry a **treatment** for malaria. The current recommended regime for Cambodia is Malarone (atovaquone and proguanil), but specific up-to-date advice should be taken, and the drugs purchased preferably before travel. You may hear about a drug called *artesunate* or *artemether* in relation to the treatment of malaria. These compounds are related to *qinghaosu*, an ancient remedy that has recently enjoyed a return to favour. It is unrelated to other antimalarials and appears to be safe and effective for the treatment of highly resistant malaria in Cambodia (and Thailand). It has been currently restricted to these areas to prevent resistance developing and should not be used as a prophylactic agent.

Traveller's diarrhoea (TD)

Many authorities claim that TD is due to faecally contaminated food or water, while a growing number suggest that the cause could be a simple change in diet, heat and humidity, and the stress of a foreign land. (Witness the fact that visitors from developing countries frequently get sick when they visit our own, spotlessly hygienic nations.) Realistically it is more likely to be a combination of the two. There is no doubt, however, that everyone agrees on one point – sooner or later, you're bound to get a case of TD. Besides diarrhoea itself, symptoms may include stomach cramps, nausea, bloating, fever and a general malaise. It's not the end of the world and the problem usually resolves itself without specific treatment within a few days. But to lessen the risks, doctors recommend that you follow these guidelines:

PEEL IT, BOIL IT, COOK IT OR FORGET IT!

Don't drink tap water or even brush your teeth with it unless it's chlorinated and considered safe. When in doubt use bottled water or even mouthwash. Likewise, avoid ice cubes, iced drinks, ice-cream and dairy products. Don't eat uncooked or warmed-over food. Don't eat raw vegetables, especially unwashed salads, or any fruit you haven't peeled yourself. The prejudice against street vendors may well be unwarranted since their food is often freshly cooked, sells fast, and is visible at all times. Common sense tells you to avoid stalls that are surrounded by flies and stray dogs. Restaurant meals, on the other hand, are prepared out of sight, and are often reheated. Reject any meal that is not piping hot when it is brought to the table. Bottled water is readily available throughout Cambodia, but be vigilant and check the seal. It has been known for vendors to refill the bottles with tap water.

Remedies for TD abound. The trend nowadays is away from the old 'quick cures' like Lomotil, Imodium, Kaopectate, Enterovioform, kaolin and a host of other medicines. Most of these may prolong the problem and therefore make things worse. Enterovioform can have serious side effects, and kaolin apparently interferes with the absorption of the anti-malarial chloroquine. Only resort to Lomotil or Imodium if you really need a short-term 'cork', such as during a long overland trip.

Most doctors now recommend the simple regimen of rest, and fluid and salt replacement. Always drink something even if you're not thirsty. Sachets of oral rehydration salts (eg: Electrolade or Dioralyte) give the perfect biochemical mix to replace all that is pouring out of your bottom! However, any dilute mixture of sugar and salt in water will do you good, so if you like Coke or orange squash, drink that with a three-finger pinch of salt added to each glass. Otherwise make a solution of a four-finger scoop of sugar with a three-finger pinch of salt in a glass of water. Alternatively add eight level teaspoons of sugar (18g) and one level teaspoon of salt (3g) to one litre (five cups) of safe water. A squeeze of lemon or orange juice improves the taste and adds potassium, which is also lost during a bout of diarrhoea. Drink two large glasses after every bowel action and more if you are thirsty. You need to drink three litres a day plus the equivalent of whatever is pouring into the toilet.

It is best to avoid food for 24–48 hours, then eat bland, non-fatty foods for the next two or three days. If the diarrhoea is bad, or you are passing blood or slime or you have a fever, you will probably need antibiotics in addition to the fluid replacement. Try to seek medical advice before starting antibiotics. If this is not possible then a three-day course of ciprofloxacin (500mg twice a day) or norfloxacin is appropriate. If the diarrhoea is greasy and bulky and is accompanied by sulphurous ('eggy') burps the likely cause is giardia. This is best treated with tinidazole (2g in one dose repeated seven days later if symptoms persist). Be careful about what you take from local pharmacies: drugs like chloramphenicol (sold as Chloromycetin, Catilan or Enteromycetin) and the sulpha antibiotics, (eg: streptomagma) have too many serious side effects to be worth the risk in treating simple diarrhoea. Do not take them.

Rabies

Rabies may be carried by all mammals and is passed on to man through a bite or a lick of an open wound. You must always assume any animal is rabid (unless personally known to you) and seek medical help as soon as possible if you are bitten. In the interim, scrub the wound with soap and bottled/boiled water for a few minutes, then pour on a strong iodine or alcohol solution. This helps stop the rabies virus entering the body and will guard against wound infections including tetanus.

If you are exposed as described, then treatment should be given as soon as possible, but it is never too late to seek help as the incubation period for rabies can be very long. Those who have not been immunised will need a full course of injections together with rabies immunoglobulin (RIG), but this product is expensive (approximately US$800) and may be hard to come by. Another reason why pre-exposure vaccination should be encouraged in travellers who are planning to visit more remote areas.

Tell the doctor if you have had pre-exposure vaccination as this will change the treatment you receive. Remember if you contract rabies, mortality is 100% and death from rabies is probably one of the worst ways to go!

Insects and insect-borne diseases

Malaria, dengue fever and probably even Japanese encephalitis are quite common in Cambodia especially among residents. All these diseases are rarer among Western travellers, but still should be taken seriously. Both malaria and Japanese encephalitis can kill, whilst dengue fever is unlikely to do so, especially if it is a first attack. These diseases are all transmitted by mosquitoes. The protozoal disease, malaria, is transmitted via the bite of an infected female *Anopheles* mosquito. This mosquito emerges from dusk till dawn, flying low to the ground. Dengue fever is a viral disease that is increasingly common worldwide, and is transmitted by the day biting *Aedes aegypti* mosquito. *Aedes* is an urban insect, favouring towns and cities, but all the mosquitoes live in a variety of habitats. First-time attacks of dengue are likened to a severe form of flu, with pain behind the eyes and a rash. Japanese encephalitis, another viral disease, is spread by various species of *Culex* mosquito, which bite mostly at night and need the pig as a vector. As its name suggests, this disease affects the brain and has a mortality rate of around 15%. The disease is most prevalent during the rainy season (May to October) when the mosquitoes breed in and around paddy fields.

Avoiding contact with host insects is the most obvious way to stay healthy. Repellent with at least 50% DEET is best throughout Cambodia. People who are especially prone to being bitten or who are unable or unwilling to take malaria tablets should consider 100% DEET (eg: Repel 100). You should cover up, particularly at night, with long-sleeved shirts and long trousers. Mosquito coils, if you can stand the smell, work well in unscreened hotel rooms. The free-standing type is the most practical and can also be used in hotel rooms that do not have insect screens. If the electricity supply is reliable, small plug-in devices which burn repellent tablets are effective and easy to pack. During the evenings, wear long-sleeved shirts, long trousers, and try tucking your trouser legs into your socks.

The Macaw or warble fly lays her eggs on mosquitoes so that when the mosquito feeds the warble infants can burrow into the victim's skin. Here they grow, feasting happily until they mature to cause a boil-like inflammation that will need surgical removal. Now there's another reason to avoid mosquito bites!

Bilharzia

Bilharzia or schistosomiasis is a common debilitating disease afflicting perhaps 200 million people worldwide. Those most affected are the rural poor who repeatedly acquire infections. Infected travellers and expatriates generally suffer fewer problems because symptoms will encourage them to seek prompt treatment and they are also exposed to fewer parasites. But it is still an unpleasant problem, and worth avoiding.

When someone with bilharzia excretes into fresh water, the eggs hatch and swim off to find a pond snail to infest. They develop inside the snail to emerge as torpedo-shaped cercariae, barely visible to the naked eye but able to digest and burrow through human or animal skin. This is the stage that attacks people as they wade, bathe or shower in infested water. The snails which harbour bilharzia are a centimetre or more long and live in still or slow-moving fresh water which is well oxygenated and contains edible vegetation (water-weed, reeds). The risk is greatest where local people use the water, bearing in mind that wind can disperse cercariae a few hundred metres from where they entered the water. Wading in slow-moving, reed-fringed water near a village thus carries a very high risk of acquiring bilharzia, while swimming in a rocky pool below a waterfall in a forest carries a negligible one. Some protection is afforded by applying an oily insect repellent like DEET to your skin before swimming or paddling.

Water which has been filtered or stored snail-free for two days is safe to drink, as is water which has been boiled or treated with Cresol or Dettol.

Cercariae live for up to 30 hours after they have been shed by snails, but the older they are, the less vigorous they are and the less capable they are of penetrating skin. Cercariae are shed in the greatest numbers between 11.00 and 15.00. If water to be used for bathing is pumped early in the morning from deep in the lake (cercariae are sun-loving) or from a site far from where people excrete, there will be less risk of infestation. Swimming in the afternoon is riskier than in the early morning. Since cercariae take perhaps ten to 15 minutes to penetrate, a quick shower or a splash across a river followed by thorough rubbing dry with a towel should be safe. Even if you are in risky water longer, towelling off vigorously after bathing will kill any cercariae in the process of penetrating your skin. Only a proportion of those cercariae which penetrate the skin survive to cause disease. The absence of early symptoms does not necessarily mean there is no infection, but symptoms usually appear two or more weeks after penetration: typically a fever and wheezy cough. A blood test, which should be taken six weeks or more after likely exposure, will determine whether or not parasites are going to cause problems. Treatment is generally effective, but failures occur and re-treatment is often necessary for reasons that aren't fully understood, but which may imply some drug resistance. Since bilharzia can be a nasty illness, avoidance is better than waiting to be cured and it is wise to avoid bathing in high-risk areas.

Flukes

These trematode parasites have a similar life cycle to bilharzia also involving freshwater snails. The reservoirs for these flukes are most commonly humans and pigs. Dogs and cats may also be infected as may wild carnivores. It takes about six to ten weeks for the ingested flukes to mature and start to lay eggs in man, completing the cycle when the eggs are excreted in the faeces.

They can infect the liver, lung or intestine of man depending on the species and where they settle. Flukes are common in Southeast Asia, and are most likely to be acquired from eating raw freshwater fish or crustaceans or uncooked water plants. You can also acquire them from eating dishes that are contaminated by infected water. Symptoms from the disease are related to the dose of the inoculum (how much of the organism gets into your body): the greater the dose the more the symptoms.

Liver flukes can cause fever, with tenderness over the liver and jaundice (turning yellow). It is possible to develop long-term liver problems including cancer. Lung flukes not surprisingly cause chest symptoms including a cough (with or without rusty sputum), fever and chest pain.

Other sites that may get infected include the intestine (diarrhoea/ constipation, vomiting and anorexia), the eye (blindness) and the brain (mimicking a tumour). Diagnosis is made from examining the stool for eggs or flukes. Treatment is the same for all the flukes: praziquantel 20–30mg/kg twice daily for three days.

AIDS

Travel is a time when we may enjoy sexual adventures, especially when alcohol reduces inhibitions. Remember that the risks of sexually transmitted infection are high, whether you sleep with fellow travellers or with locals.

About half of HIV infections in British heterosexuals are acquired abroad. Use condoms or femidoms and buy them before you leave to ensure they are of a high standard. If you notice any genital ulcers or discharge get treatment promptly; sexually transmitted infections increase the risk of acquiring HIV.

Skin infections

Skin infections set in remarkably easily in warm climates and any mosquito bite or small skin-nick is a potential entry point for bacteria. It is essential, therefore, to clean and cover even the slightest wound.

Creams are not as effective as a good drying antiseptic such as dilute iodine, potassium permanganate (a few crystals in half a cup of water) or crystal (or gentian) violet. If the wound starts to throb, or becomes red and the redness starts to spread or the wound oozes, and especially if you develop a fever, five days of antibiotics will probably be needed: flucloxacillin (250mg capsules four times a day) or Augmentin (375mg three times a day). For those allergic to penicillin, erythromycin (500mg twice a day) should help. See a doctor if it does not start to improve within 36–48 hours of starting treatment. Fungal infections also get a hold easily in hot moist climates so wear 100% cotton socks and underwear and shower frequently. An itchy rash in the groin or flaking or soreness between the toes is likely to be a fungal infection. This needs treatment with an antifungal cream such as Canesten (clotrimazole) or if this is not available try Whitfield's ointment (compound benzoic acid ointment) or crystal violet (although this will turn you purple!).

Ticks and mites

Ticks and mites are common worldwide and inhabit woodland, scrub and long grass, residing on the local fauna. They are responsible for a wide selection of odd diseases, through either their bite, their body fluids or inhaling their faeces in dust. It is good to know that despite their prevalence it is uncommon to become infected. However, some of the diseases they transmit can be serious so it is wise to take precautions to avoid being bitten (see box page 56). Most tick-borne diseases cause a skin rash, recurrent fever, headaches, vomiting, aching muscles and joints. Seek medical advice if you suspect you have been infected. Tick paralysis is rare but if you experience difficulty in breathing it should be taken seriously. Some diseases spread by ticks can be treated with antibiotics.

PRECAUTIONS AGAINST TICK BITES
- Seek local advice on areas to avoid (usually long grass or scrubland)
- Wear long trousers tucked into boots
- Use insect repellents containing DEET on any exposed areas and consider soaking clothes in permethrin (another insect repellent) if you are trekking in rural parts
- Every time you have finished walking in an infected area check your body for ticks
- If you are sleeping in such an area, make sure you use a net and sleep high off the ground
- Avoid close contact with animals – they may be the source of ticks

If you discover a tick on you then you need to encourage it to let go. Resist the temptation to just pull it off with your bare hands as the tick body fluids can also transmit disease. If you can remove the tick whole there is less chance of transmitting disease. See box below.

Sun and heat
Prickly heat
A fine pimply rash on the trunk is likely to be heat rash; cool showers, dabbing (not rubbing) dry and talc will help; if it's bad you may need to check into an air-conditioned hotel room for a while. Slowing down to a relaxed schedule, wearing only loose baggy 100% cotton clothes and sleeping naked under a fan will reduce the problem.

Protection from the sun
The incidence of skin cancer is rocketing as Caucasians travel more and spend more time exposing themselves to the sun. Sun exposure also ages the skin, making people prematurely wrinkly. Cover up with long loose clothes, put on plenty of suncream and wear a hat when you can. Keep out of the sun during

QUICK TICK REMOVAL
Using a pair of tweezers, or failing that finger and thumb, pinch the tick's mouthparts as close to your skin as possible and slowly and steadily pull away at right angles to your skin. This often hurts. Jerking or twisting will increase the chances of damaging the tick which in turn increases the chances of disease transmission. Once the tick is off, dowse the little wound with alcohol (local spirit, pisco etc, is excellent) or iodine. An area of spreading redness around the bite site or a rash or fever coming on a few days or more after the bite should stimulate a trip to a doctor. Remember if you have used your hands to wash them thoroughly afterwards.

the middle of the day and, if you must expose yourself, build up gradually from 20 minutes per day.

Heat stroke

This is most likely within the first week or ten days of arriving in a hotter, more humid climate. It is important to slow down and drink plenty and avoid hard physical exercise in the middle of the day, particularly at first. Treatment for heat exhaustion is rest in the shade and sponging, plus lots to drink.

Snakebite

Cambodia has its fair share of venomous snakes, for example cobras, vipers and kraits. On the whole snakes don't bite unless they are provoked, so don't be tempted to poke or prod one, even from a distance. An apparently somnolent reptile can strike with alarming speed if annoyed! If you do get bitten, don't panic. Remember that there are plenty of non-venomous snakes that will bite too. Remember also that even the venomous species don't always inject poison with every bite; after feeding, for example, venom sacs are often depleted. In short, you need to be careful about venomous snakes, but don't let unwarranted paranoia keep you from enjoying your trip. Encounters with snakes are rare, and most naturalists count themselves lucky when they've seen one.

Watch your step in the forest, especially near tree falls and large piles of leaf litter beneath trees. Be particularly cautious at night. If bitten, try to stay calm, remembering that most snakebite victims recover without treatment. Cleanse the wound, try to note the snake's characteristics for identification, and attempt to get to a doctor. Try to immobilise the affected area with a sling or splint, and keep it below the level of the heart. Do not apply a tourniquet or open the wound with a razor – both can do far more harm than the bite itself. Many authorities now recommend the syringe-like suction devices (such as the X-Tractor). If used soon after the bite occurs, they help in removing some of the venom.

Drugs

Drugs are widely available in Cambodia for those who are determined to find them but the unsuspecting may come across them anyhow. Many pizza restaurants in Phnom Penh have 'happy herb' in their name or refer to them on the menu. They are referring to marijuana which is a special topping to regular pizzas. Beware the specials! However, in mid-2000 the government clamped down on this activity, so marijuana may no longer be on the menu.

SAFETY

Sadly there has been an increase in crime over the years, often linked with the situation at the time or purely opportunistic where foreign visitors are involved. Most crime occurs in Phnom Penh and often at night. Be careful if using motorbike taxis (motos or *motodops*) at night and do make sure that the driver knows where you want to go. Carry only enough money for the particular outing and do not wear jewellery or expensive watches. Never

CAMBODIA'S LANDMINE PROBLEM

In 1992 and 1993 the UN Transitional Authority in Cambodia (UNTAC) carried out a survey and estimated that there were between eight and ten million mines throughout the country, making it one of the most heavily mined countries on earth. More than 1,900 areas were believed to be mined and more are being discovered all the time. Landmines have been used extensively in most conflicts throughout the world during the last 40 years. Records of where they have been laid are rarely kept so the task of clearing them is interminable.

The effect landmines have on people is significant. The presence of mines (suspected or actual) denies the community access to economic resources and makes water sources, agricultural land, roads and bridges unusable. Local people constantly live in fear of being injured or killed by treading on a mine, or of losing precious farm animals to landmines laid on grazing land. Mines do not distinguish between soldiers, civilians and children. People injured by mines usually have to have the lower leg or legs amputated. However, because of the nature of the blast, which pushes upwards driving fragments of the mine, earth and footwear into the tissue of the leg, many legs have to be amputated higher up to get rid of any metal or soil which could cause infection. There are frequently secondary injuries such as the loss of hands or sight and damage to the abdomen or chest.

The work of clearing the mines in Cambodia is carried out by organisations such as the Mines Advisory Group and the Halo Trust, both charitable organisations. Their aim is to clear landmines and to return the land to the local community. The work is painstakingly slow and deminers work in pairs in lanes a metre wide. One deminer uses a detector to locate metal in the ground while the other observes the work in progress to ensure safety at all stages. Any metal detected is carefully exposed to ascertain whether it is purely scrap metal or a mine. If it is a mine its location is marked so that it can be destroyed later in situ. It is much safer to destroy them where they are found and also ensures that they cannot be reused. When a mine is found the deminers then leave that lane and start work in another lane. The demining pair change roles every 30 minutes to ensure that concentration levels are maintained. Only at the end of the day are the mines destroyed in the various working lanes. Although the work is slow and manual it is the most effective method of clearing mines and making the land safe. Areas which have become overgrown with vegetation are particularly dangerous for the deminers to clear before they can start to detect any metal in the ground. Specially developed tractors are being trialled to make the clearance of vegetation both safer and faster.

carry your passport and air ticket around with you. Keep a firm grip on any shoulder bags and cameras. If you are travelling overland you should keep any valuables in security pouches around your waist and out of sight. I always feel that bumbags worn on the outside of clothes are advertising the fact that everything you have of value is stored in there. Try to use hotel safes where possible, making sure that you receive a receipt for your valuables. However, many of the smaller hotels do not have safes and I feel it is better to take responsibility for your own valuables than to entrust them to reception. This is no reflection on the hotel staff but personally I wouldn't wish to put temptation in their way, whether it be a town in Cambodia or one in Britain or America.

Women travelling on their own are no more or less targets than any other foreign visitor. As in any country, women should not walk down unlit streets at night or wear clothes that are likely to attract attention or cause offence to local sensibilities. If you use common sense and are aware of what is going on around you then you are unlikely to become a victim. You are in fact safer in Phnom Penh than you are in most Western capital cities and more so in provincial towns.

If the worst does happen there is a **telephone** number for the police, where English and French is spoken, on 023 724793. Other emergency numbers are:

Police hotline 117
Fire 118
Ambulance 119

When travelling outside of Phnom Penh, although the situation is generally safe now it is always wise to check at each overnight stop before moving on. By keeping well informed about local conditions you should never find yourself in a situation you are unable to handle. If travelling independently talk to other travellers and also the local long-distance taxi drivers. They travel the same route every day and will soon tell you if they are unwilling to take a foreign passenger. They would not want to draw attention to themselves if there were any bandits operating in the area.

Landmines are a constant problem for Cambodians and, although everywhere you travel you see the trucks of the Mines Advisory Group or the Halo Trust who are working valiantly to clear the mines, there are still many in the countryside. Never stray away from the path and always seek local advice.

WHAT TO TAKE
Clothes
There are never any extremes of temperature in Cambodia and cotton, loose-fitting clothing is fine year-round. However, it may be wise to take a sweater or jacket for the dry season, particularly November to January, when it can be cooler in certain areas, particularly in the early mornings. Waterproof jackets are useful during the rainy season, but they must be breathable because of the high humidity. An umbrella is always useful. Good walking shoes are a must

particularly when exploring the temples around the country as the ground is very uneven and there are often steps to climb. Cambodia is a very relaxed country so formal clothes are rarely required, unless you anticipate dining in one of the very upmarket hotels or have been invited to an official function.

Useful items

If travelling off the beaten track, you may wish to take a mosquito net as only a few guesthouses provide them. If you don't want to carry a mosquito net, coils are useful for keeping mozzies away at night and it goes without saying that an insect repellent should also be carried. Some guesthouses only have a small, light blanket for cover at night and it is always useful to carry a sheet sleeping bag. Although many guesthouses supply towels, I always take one of those highly absorbent towels, 'Wondertowel'. Torches are invaluable as power cuts occur from time to time. Batteries can be bought in main towns but it is a good idea to carry a spare. Bottled water is widely available so it is unnecessary to carry water filter kits or purification tablets unless you are staying in very remote areas.

It is very important to carry a first-aid kit at all times for minor problems and this should include plasters, paracetamol (or aspirin), diarrhoea remedies, rehydration sachets, eye drops, tubi-grips, antiseptic cream, personal prescription items, needle and syringe, antihistamine and suncream.

Luggage

If planning to travel around Cambodia by public transport, particularly buses, pickup truck taxis and boats, it is best to have a sturdy rucksack or holdall. You may find that your belongings will be crushed and items damaged if you use a soft and squashy bag, but rigid suitcases are too large and unwieldy to be stored on the back of pickups or under seats on boats. Whatever you use make sure that there is nothing valuable or breakable inside and that they are always padlocked.

MONEY
Currency

The Cambodian unit of currency is the riel which is divided into notes of 100, 200, 500, 1,000, 2,000, 5,000, 10,000, 20,000, 50,000 and 100,000. However, the higher-denomination notes are hard to come by. In reality US dollars are used extensively throughout the country. Most prices are given in US dollars so it is important to carry cash in that currency with you. Most small change is given in riels, so local currency quickly accumulates. However, it is not uncommon for change to be given in a combination of dollars and riels. The best place to exchange dollars for riels is in the markets at the jewellery stalls. Cash can also be exchanged in hotels and banks but the rate is not so attractive. Note that US dollars cash must be in pristine condition – torn and dirty notes will not be accepted. This is not the case for riel notes which are invariably tatty.

Thai baht are legal tender close to the Thailand border in towns such as Koh Kong, Battambang, Pailin, Poipet and Sisophon.

Exchange rates

The rate for the riel is pretty static at around 3,700–3,900 to one US dollar.

The current exchange rates for the riel against most currencies can be checked on www.oanda.com/converter/classic. In September 2000 the rates were:

UK£1	= 5,377 riels	US$1	= 3,850 riels
A$1	= 2,100 riels	Thai baht 1 =	91.81 riels

Travellers' cheques

US dollar travellers' cheques can only be exchanged in banks in Phnom Penh, Sihanoukville and Siem Reap and to a lesser extent in Kompong Cham, Battambang and Pailin. The commission charge is 1% in Phnom Penh and 2% elsewhere. They can be exchanged for dollars cash and then a small amount can be converted into riels. Banks in smaller towns are considering the introduction of travellers' cheques transactions during 2000 and this may well have happened by the time this book is published.

Credit cards

Cash advances on credit cards such as Visa, MasterCard and JCB are now possible in Phnom Penh and Siem Reap and there is a charge of 4%. Items such as hotel accommodation, restaurant meals, air tickets, tours in some travel agencies and purchases in a few shops can be made using credit cards in Phnom Penh, Siem Reap and Sihanoukville.

Banks are open from Monday to Friday, generally from 08.00 to 15.30. Some of the private banks also open on Saturday mornings. At the time of writing there are no ATMs in Cambodia.

GETTING AROUND

The infrastructure within Cambodia is very poor, with a few exceptions, especially at the end of the rainy season. There is plenty of transport around the country but travel times are slow and not always comfortable and patience is crucial.

The roads around Phnom Penh are generally in good condition but the further away you travel from the capital the more the roads deteriorate and land travel becomes a gruelling experience. Road travel only becomes tolerable once you have gone through the pain barrier and can no longer feel your backside. Note that in the rainy season even the excellent roads, such as Route 4 to Sihanoukville, can suffer disruption because of serious flooding.

By air

There is now serious competition in Cambodia on domestic routes as there are three airlines vying for passengers and flights are rarely full apart from on the Phnom Penh to Siem Reap route or during public holidays. By the time this book is published one of the two smaller airlines may have become a casualty of the intense competition. See also *Chapter 4*, page 78.

Royal Air Cambodge (VJ) has the most extensive timetable with flights from Phnom Penh to Siem Reap, Battambang, Mondulkiri, Rattanakiri and Stung Treng. Their fleet is relatively modern using mainly Boeing 737s and ATR72s.

Phnom Penh Airways (P1), the newest airline which started operating in October 1999, also flies to Siem Reap, Battambang, Rattanakiri, Koh Kong, Sihanoukville and Stung Treng and has plans to introduce flights to Mondulkiri. The fleet consists of Soviet Antonov 24s. This airline is privately owned by Prince Norodom Chakrapong. The third airline, also privately owned by Indonesians, is **President Airlines (TO)** which has flights to Siem Reap, Battambang, Rattanakiri and Stung Treng. They have Antonov 24s and Fokker 28s in their fleet.

Details of all the domestic flights are given in the relevant sections. Note that in the rainy season flights can be severely disrupted or unable to operate at all to the smaller airstrips.

By boat

Boat travel on the rivers has developed significantly in the last few years because of the poor state of the roads. By comparison the Soviet-built speedboats are an efficient way of moving around the country, are quite comfortable, generally run on time (with the exception of frequent breakdowns) and are a super way of seeing river life. During the rainy season when the water is high the boats have no trouble in reaching their destinations. However, as the water level drops, smaller, slower boats may have to be used and occasionally they cannot operate at all, particularly in the northeast. See also *Chapter 4*, page 79.

The large speedboats between Phnom Penh and Siem Reap carry 138 passengers and are quite spacious with plastic seats, fan, basic toilet and video. The engines are so noisy that even with the video blaring at full volume I do not understand how any passengers can enjoy the music or film being shown. It is possible to buy soft drinks on board. There are also smaller 90- and 100-seater boats which are used during the dry season. Travellers who are concerned about safety standards should not consider using the boats as maintenance is poor and there are no life jackets. However, the engineers do an excellent job with the tools and spares available and although these boats ply the rivers on a daily basis I have yet to hear of a massive disaster. Personally I prefer sitting on the roof to enjoy the scenery and get away from the noise of the video. A most surreal memory for me is when travelling from Kompong Cham to Kratie they played one of the recent James Bond films complete with English soundtrack and Khmer subtitles. What the locals thought of that I really don't know.

The Battambang to Siem Reap route only has the smaller boats and during the dry season these are replaced with tiny speedboats seating around 12 people. Usually I am quite relaxed about boat travel but I was a little concerned during the four-hour journey as the boat was very low in the water at the back when the two outboard motors weren't working. This was a regular occurrence as they frequently stalled when caught up in vegetation or would just putter to a stop for no reason. The mechanic sat by the motors and whenever he needed to attend to them the back three people, of which I was one, had to stand up, causing the boat to rock violently.

The main river routes are from Phnom Penh to Siem Reap, from Phnom Penh to Kompong Cham, Kratie and Stung Treng and from Siem Reap to Battambang. Until the roads are improved dramatically the river journeys are definitely preferable with the exception of the trip from Phnom Penh to Kompong Cham where there is an excellent road in place.

Luggage on the big boats can be stored inside under the seat or at the front of the boat. The small speedboats generally have space at the front beside the driver to store bags. It goes without saying that you should keep an eye on your luggage, but generally theft is not a problem.

By bus

The roads out of Phnom Penh are generally good and for this reason there is an extensive bus service from the capital to Sihanoukville, Kompong Cham, Kompong Chhnang, Takeo, Neak Leung, Wat Angkorchey, Kampong Speu, Udong, Takhmao and Rowkakong. These services are operated by the Ho Wah Genting Transport Company who were granted a licence in 1996 giving them exclusive rights to operate bus services from the capital for 25 years, except on the Sihanoukville route where two other bus companies, DH Cambodia Group Transport and GST Export Bus Company, also operate a timetable. Further afield there are no overland bus routes, but you may find very local services in towns such as Battambang and Rattanakiri, although the vehicles are definitely not roadworthy.

The Ho Wah Genting buses are a well-maintained, modern fleet of Malaysian buses with air conditioning. The DH and GST buses are more ramshackle but adequate for the relatively short journey to Sihanoukville. Bus stations throughout the country are very basic. There are rarely any facilities apart from a food stall for snacks and drinks. Tickets have to be bought in person at the ticket desk at the bus station. The buses are very frequent so it is rarely a problem getting a seat on a bus except during public holidays.

Luggage is carried with you inside the bus, if size permits, or may be tied on top. Make sure that luggage is waterproof if you anticipate that it may have to travel on the top of the bus.

See also *Chapter 4*, page 79.

By train

There are only two train routes in Cambodia, to Sihanoukville and Battambang. The trains are very slow and uncomfortable. At one stage foreigners could be deported for attempting to travel on the trains, but this is no longer the case. See also *Chapter 4*, page 80.

By taxi

Because of the lack of bus service in many parts of the country the only way to travel around is by shared long-distance taxi. Every town has one or more taxi stations where pickup trucks and occasionally cars wait for passengers. The pickup trucks are usually four-wheel drive and have room for passengers inside as well as on the back. It obviously costs more inside and the front seat is more comfortable than the narrow back seat which is fairly hard. Passengers on the back of the truck often have to share the available space with sacks of rice, baskets of vegetables and even motorbikes, and the nature of the road means that you are eating dirt for several hours. Because of the lack of space inside the pickups, luggage will always be carried on the back so make sure it is waterproof and that there is nothing breakable inside as you will often find other heavy items being piled on top or passengers using it as a seat or a back rest.

By car
It is possible to hire cars with drivers through travel agencies, at some cost, for overland journeys from Phnom Penh and Siem Reap but elsewhere cars can only be arranged through some enterprising hotels and then only for local journeys and sightseeing. Self-drive is not currently possible for visitors, although long-term residents are able to drive cars provided by their place of employment.

ACCOMMODATION
Following the arrival of the United Nations Transitional Authority in Cambodia in 1992 there was a flurry of activity with hotels appearing overnight in most towns and particularly in Phnom Penh and Siem Reap. Many closed once the UN personnel departed but a lot are still operating although it must have been a struggle since 1993. Up until then the standard of accommodation had been rather poor and most were often occupied by workers from NGOs. Phnom Penh, Siem Reap and Sihanoukville now have a glut of hotels and elsewhere there is usually a choice of accommodation, particularly in Battambang. In the more remote areas the hotels are all quite simple but Phnom Penh and Siem Reap have a selection ranging from tiny backpacker establishments right through to deluxe hotels. Deluxe hotels haven't yet arrived in Sihanoukville but there are a couple of first-class standard. At the end of each town section I have listed a few hotels and guesthouses with their current published rates.

EATING AND DRINKING
Cambodia does not enjoy the fine meals to be found in its neighbours Vietnam and Thailand but there are similarities with the cuisine of these two countries as well as Laos. Rice is at the heart of many dishes as is freshwater fish, which is cheap. Other meat is available but on the whole more expensive. Grilled fish or *trey ang* is very popular and appears on most menus. It is quite delicious dipped in *tek trey*, a fish sauce similar to the *nuoc mam* which is served with many dishes in Vietnam. Soups often appear as part of a meal and a great favourite is a sour soup, *samlo*, which contains fish and vegetables. Another delicious sour soup is *samlo machhu kreng sach ko chea muy tro khun* which is with beef and morning glory. Salads often appear on the menu such as *ngom trey*,

fish salad and *ngom mon*, chicken salad. Fruit often follows a meal and is to be recommended as it is so fresh, juicy and tasty.

The French colonial influence is very apparent with the abundance of *baguettes* for sale in the streets. The Cambodians were well taught as the bread is excellent and always fresh. Thai food often appears in the west of the country, particularly in Battambang and Siem Reap. In Phnom Penh it is possible to find restaurants serving food from many countries such as China, India, America, Thailand, Greece, Russia, Germany, France and Italy.

Bottled water is plentiful in Cambodia. The local stuff is as good as imported and a fraction of the price. Wherever it comes from do ensure that the bottle is sealed when you buy it otherwise you may end up drinking tap water which has been put into a 'recycled' bottle. Local beer is widely available, the most popular being Angkor which comes from a huge factory outside Sihanoukville. Bayon is another brand but is not always easy to find. There are many imported beers and arriving in a bar you may find yourself surrounded by girls wearing sashes advertising the brand they are promoting. These are most likely to be San Miguel, Fosters or Tiger but Carlsberg and Heineken are also generally on sale. Obviously imported beers are more expensive, as is wine. Locally made spirits are very cheap, unbelievably strong and probably best avoided unless you wish to ponder those missing hours of oblivion together with your missing wallet.

Fizzy soft drinks are plentiful in the form of lemonade and cola. Even more thirst quenching are fresh fruit drinks which are available in restaurants and on fruit stalls. Fresh coconut milk, drunk straight from the coconut, has to be tried as it is so delicious. Tea appears with meals in a restaurant and is often included in the price. It is served black and is very refreshing. You usually have to pay for coffee and it is very strong. If you ask for milk you are most likely to be given condensed milk which makes the drink very sweet. However, it is an acquired taste and one that I have come to enjoy despite never taking sugar in tea or coffee at home.

Tipping

Tipping is not customary in Cambodia, but good service should be rewarded especially when you know that wages are in most cases very low. Generally leave around 10% of the total bill. The larger restaurants may already include a service charge on the bill particularly in the towns where there are a number of foreign visitors.

NIGHTLIFE

Cambodia is not noted for its nightlife but there are a handful of nightclubs in Phnom Penh and many of the bars there as well as in Sihanoukville and Siem Reap are open until the early hours. These are listed in the restaurant/bars section under the relevant town section. In Phnom Penh the Sharaton Hotel has a nightclub called Casa, and the Manhattan Club is attached to the Holiday International Hotel. Both open late and are particularly popular with the young things of Phnom Penh, especially at the weekends. As to be expected drink prices are high. Martini on Mao Tse Tung, near the Intercontinental Hotel, has a large beer garden with open-air movies and a dance floor which is heaving at the weekends. Some of the smaller towns have karaoke bars and local clubs which open fairly late, but generally the music is not to the taste of the foreign visitor. Wherever you go, men will attract the attention of the bar girls who hang around ready to offer their services – a sad fact of life in such a poor country. As in any city or town, clubs and bars come and go so it is best to check around on arrival to find out which are the 'happening' bars and clubs at that time.

MEDIA AND COMMUNICATIONS
Mail
There is a main post office in every town and details of its location and opening hours are given for each town. Stamps can only be bought at the post offices and the price is the same around the country although the offices in smaller towns may not have the exact stamps available so you may have to pay a little more. It costs 1,800 riels to send postcards to Europe and Australia and 2,100 riels to the US. Letters are more expensive being 2,300 riels to Europe and Australia and 2,500 riels to the US. Within Asia postcards and letters cost 1,700 riels and 2,200 riels respectively. There are no post boxes in Cambodia so all mail to be posted has to be taken to the post office.

Telephone
International calls from Cambodia are very expensive and it is probably cheaper to ask friends and relatives to contact you, where possible. Hotel calls will probably cost in the region of US$3–5 per minute but it is cheaper to go to the main post office where international calls cost US$8.70 for three minutes during the week and US$2.90 for additional minutes. It is cheaper at the weekend at US$6.90 for three minutes and additional minutes US$2.30.

Phonecards for domestic and international calls can be purchased for either Mobitel or Camintel street phones with card prices ranging from US$2 up to US$50. The phones are dotted around many towns (although not all) and the phonecards can be bought from nearby shops.

Many of the provincial towns still use radios for communication, especially where there is no mobile phone coverage. Even in Siem Reap where mobile phones are commonplace radios are still used by many offices and hotels.

Mobile phones can be rented at Phnom Penh airport for a minimum of one day. Rates range from US$7 for one day to US$28 for a week and US$66 for a month. VAT is added at a rate of 10%. There is a refundable deposit of US$200. The phones work on a pay-as-you-go system and cellcards can be bought for US$10–50. The phones work in Phnom Penh, Siem Reap, Sihanoukville, Battambang and Kompong Cham for domestic and overseas calls.

Fax
The charge for sending a fax from Cambodia is per page. This can work out at around a rather expensive US$5 per page and can be done either at the post office or in one of the business centres of the larger hotels.

Email

The internet and email are now well established in Cambodia and there are numerous internet cafés in Phnom Penh with reasonable rates: generally around US$5 per hour. Siem Reap and Battambang also have a few internet venues and it is just starting in Sihanoukville. Elsewhere I only found an internet shop in Kompong Cham. Outside of the capital internet prices are very high and can be as much as US$2 per minute. Details of internet shops and charges are given in each chapter where there is access.

Newspapers

Cambodia Daily An English-language newspaper which is published six times a week in Phnom Penh. It is rather a serious paper but has good coverage of local events as well as some international news. The Friday edition has a good *What's On* section.

Phnom Penh Post Published fortnightly with well-written news and topical subjects. This is definitely the best English-language newspaper and it is a shame that it does not come out more regularly.

Bayon Pearnik A free tourism and information magazine which generally comes out every two months. Their style is rather irreverent and they describe themselves as a magazine dedicated to raising beer money and not to be taken seriously or while driving or operating heavy machinery. Great fun with some useful information amongst the rantings.

Principal Excellent city listings magazine with a wide range of articles, *What's On* section and city map. Good place to look for ideas of what to do when in Phnom Penh.

Other English-language papers such as the *International Herald Tribune* and the *Bangkok Post* are available in Phnom Penh.

Radio

The BBC World Service can be heard 24 hours a day in Phnom Penh on FM100. A free programme guide can be picked up from the Foreign Correspondents' Club of Cambodia on Sisowath Quay or schedules can be found on the internet on www.bbc.co.uk/worldservice/schedules for programmes on short-wave radio. The Voice of America and Radio Australia can also be picked up by short-wave radio.

Television

Many mid-range hotels have televisions with satellite channels; these are either in the rooms or in a lounge. Depending on what the hotel subscribes to, channels such as CNN, BBC World Service, Star TV, MTV and the Australian Broadcasting Corporation are available in English. The French satellite company, TV5, is also occasionally on offer.

SHOPPING

Cambodian artisans are very skilled and there is no shortage of articles to buy throughout the country with some regional variations. Most visitors to

Cambodia end up buying a *krama* – a checked scarf which has many uses such as keeping the sun off your head and protecting your eyes against dust when travelling on the back of pickup trucks. The krama is made from cotton or silk and each province has its own pattern and colour.

Silk is still handwoven in Cambodia and is always a favourite 'must buy'. It is possible to buy bags and purses made from silk as well as scarves or just lengths of material. If you are looking for mementoes of Cambodia make sure when purchasing silk material that it is Cambodian and not imported from Thailand or Laos.

Silver boxes are popular traditional souvenirs as they are copies of those which were used in ceremonies or to hold betel leaves. Many are shaped like animals and are particularly attractive.

When you enter the Central Market in Phnom Penh it positively glistens with thousands of cut gems in all colours. Most of these come from the west of Cambodia and in particular, Pailin. It is possible to buy some small stones for just a few dollars but if you are planning to spend hundreds or even thousands of dollars, do make sure you know what you are buying.

DISABLED CRAFTSMEN

Cambodia has a massive challenge coping with the tens of thousands of its citizens disabled by land mines or illness and each person has his or her own personal struggle to survive. Both the country and the individuals need help to overcome these obstacles and this is where the role of the non-governmental organisations (NGOs) is crucial.

The government, in particular the Ministry of Social Action, Labour and Veterans Affairs, works with NGOs to establish projects around the country to train disabled people in skills which will then enable them to earn a living and reintegrate within society. Established programmes help the poorest people to become craftsmen, skilled in fields such as silk weaving, carpentry, tailoring, carving and painting. At the same time they are given help with basic business skills, health education and literacy. When their training is finished they graduate to the programme workshops where they work for a further six months perfecting their new skills. Items that they produce are sold in various outlets, benefitting the craftsmen and ensuring the continued success of the programme.

When pupils return to their towns or villages they have enough skills to find work, with the help of the programme organisers, or the confidence to establish their own business, aided by a small loan. These programmes are proving highly successful as they help people to help themselves, which in a proud nation such as Cambodia is very important. At the same time, reintegrating the disabled into society and showing that they have something to offer helps to break down some of the barriers they otherwise face.

Small copies of statues from Angkor are particularly good and are made from a variety of materials such as ceramic, bronze and wood.

If you are travelling around Cambodia for any length of time and missing some familiar items from home, Phnom Penh has small supermarkets selling food items for the expat market. There is also a small supermarket in Siem Reap and two in Sihanoukville, but nothing elsewhere at the moment. There is never any problem buying toiletries, camera films and batteries unless specialist ones are required. In Phnom Penh there are a few bookshops selling books in English and French.

Bargaining is a way of life in the markets but to a lesser extent in the shops. You can guarantee that prices are always inflated as soon as they see you, but less so than in places such as Thailand. Generally you will find that the prices are very low and it is just a bit of fun to haggle over the price and quite satisfying at the same time. However, remember that the triumph you feel over saving a few thousand riels, quite often just small change to you, is at the expense of the vendor to whom the same sum can be a significant amount.

TOURIST INFORMATION

Visitors should not fail to get hold of the visitors' guides for Phnom Penh, Siem Reap and Sihanoukville which are free of charge and available from some travel agents and hotels. They are packed full of information with suggestions for places to eat and drink.

Each town has a tourist office which is open from Monday to Friday. However, there is rarely any tourist literature and they are rather depressing places with little sign of activity and staff who rarely speak English. The most dynamic offices I came across were in Rattanakiri and Battambang: the former was preparing a leaflet on tourist sites in the region and the latter had a map. In Rattanakiri a local guide can be hired who knows the local tribes and their languages but is unlikely to speak English, so you also need to have an English-speaking guide with you.

PHOTOGRAPHY

Both print and slide film are readily available in Phnom Penh and to a lesser extent in Siem Reap and Sihanoukville, although slide film may be harder to come by outside the capital. Films are generally very cheap as is the processing of prints, which is of a good standard. It is best to have slide film printed once you have returned from your trip. Video film is available in Phnom Penh but nowhere else. Regular camera batteries are sold throughout Phnom Penh but bring your own if you need more specialist ones. The X-ray machines at Phnom Penh and Siem Reap airports are film safe.

When taking photographs of people it is polite to ask permission first. Photography is generally allowed in the temples, although there may be a camera charge in some, but be sensitive about taking photos of people worshipping. Officials do not seem to be worried about photos being taken at airports but it is best not to take photos of any military personnel or equipment. For practical tips, see page 70.

MAKING THE BEST OF YOUR TRAVEL PHOTOGRAPHS
Subject, composition and lighting
If it doesn't look good through the viewfinder, it will never look good as a picture. Don't take photographs for the sake of taking them; film is far too expensive. Be patient and wait until the image looks right.

People
There's nothing like a wonderful face to stimulate interest. Travelling to remote corners of the world provides the opportunity for exotic photographs of colourful people and intriguing lifestyles which capture the very essence of a culture. A superb photograph should be capable of saying more than a thousand words.

Photographing people is never easy and more often than not it requires a fair share of luck plus sharp instinct, a conditioned photographic eye and the ability to handle light both aesthetically and technically.
* If you want to take a portrait shot, always ask first. Often the offer to send a copy of the photograph to the subject will break the ice – but do remember to send it!
* Focus on the eyes of your subject.
* The best portraits are obtained in early morning and late evening light. In harsh light, photograph without flash in the shadows.
* Respect people's wishes and customs. Remember that, in some countries, infringement can lead to serious trouble.
* Never photograph military subjects unless you have definite permission.
* Be prepared for the unexpected.

Wildlife
There is no mystique to good wildlife photography. The secret is getting into the right place at the right time and then knowing what to do when you are there. Look for striking poses, aspects of behaviour and distinctive features. Try to illustrate the species within the context of its environment. Alternatively, focus in close on a characteristic which can be emphasised.
* The eyes are all-important. Make sure they are sharp and try to ensure they contain a highlight.
* Get the surroundings right – there is nothing worse than a distracting twig or highlighted leaf lurking in the background.
* A powerful flashgun can transform a dreary picture by lifting the subject out of its surroundings and putting the all-important highlights into the eyes. Artificial light is no substitute for natural light, so use judiciously.
* Getting close to the subject correspondingly reduces the depth of field; for distances of less than a metre, apertures between f16 and f32 are necessary. This means using flash to provide enough light – build your own bracket and use one or two small flashguns to illuminate the subject from the side.

Landscapes
Landscapes are forever changing; good landscape photography is all about light and mood. Generally the first and last two hours of daylight are best, or when peculiar climatic conditions add drama or emphasise distinctive features.
* Never place the horizon in the centre – in your mind's eye divide the frame into thirds and exaggerate either the land or the sky.

Cameras
Keep things simple: light, reliable and simple cameras will reduce hassle. High humidity in tropical places can play havoc with electronics.
* For keen photographers, a single-lens reflex (SLR) camera should be at the heart of your outfit. Look for a model with the option of a range of different lenses and other accessories.
* Totally mechanical cameras which do not rely on batteries work even under extreme conditions. Combined with an exposure meter which doesn't require batteries, you have the perfect match. One of the best and most indestructible cameras available is the FM2 Nikon.

- Compact cameras are generally excellent, but because of restricted focal ranges they have severe limitations for wildlife.
- Automatic cameras are often noisy when winding on, and loading film.
- Flashy camera bags can draw unwelcome attention to your kit.

Lenses

The lens is the most important part of the camera, with the greatest influence on the final result. Choose the best you can afford – the type will be dictated by the subject and type of photograph you wish to take.

For people

- The lens should ideally should have a focal length of 90 or 105mm.
- If you are not intimidated by getting in close, buy one with a macro facility which will allow close focusing. For candid photographs, a 70–210 zoom lens is ideal.
- A fast lens (with a maximum aperture of around f2.8) will allow faster shutter speeds which will mean sharper photographs. Distracting backgrounds will be thrown out of focus, improving the images' aesthetic appeal.

For wildlife

- Choose a lens of at least 300mm for a reasonable image size.
- For birds, lenses of 400mm or 500mm may be needed. They should be held on a tripod, or a beanbag if shooting from a vehicle.
- Macro lenses of 55mm and 105mm cover most subjects, creating images up to half life size. To enlarge further, extension tubes are required.
- In low light, lenses with very fast apertures help.

For landscapes

- Wide-angle lenses (35mm or less) are ideal for tight habitat shots (eg: forests) and are an excellent alternative for close ups, as you can shoot the subject within the context of its environment.
- For other landscapes, use a medium telephoto lens (100–300mm) to pick out interesting aspects of a vista and compress the perspective.

Film

Two types of film are available: prints (negatives) and transparencies (colour reversal). Prints are instantly accessible, ideal for showing to friends and putting into albums. However, if you want to share your experiences with a wider audience, through lectures or in publication, then the extra quality offered by transparency film is necessary.

Film speed (ISO number) indicates the sensitivity of the film to light. The lower the number, the less sensitive the film, but the better quality the final image. For general print film and if you are using transparencies just for lectures, ISO 100 or 200 are ideal. However, if you want to get your work published, the superior quality of ISO 25 to 100 film is best.

- Film bought in developing countries may be outdated or badly stored.
- Try to keep your film cool. Never leave it in direct sunlight.
- Do not allow fast film (ISO 800 or more) to pass through X-ray machines.
- Under weak light conditions use a faster film (ISO 200 or 400).
- For accurate people shots use Kodachrome 64 for its warmth, mellowness and gentle gradation of contrast. Reliable skin tones can also be recorded with Fuji Astia 100.
- To jazz up your portraits, use Fuji Velvia (50 ISO) or Provia (100 ISO).
- If cost is your priority, use process-paid Fuji films such as Sensia 11.
- For black-and-white people shots take Kodax T Max or Fuji Neopan.
- For natural subjects, where greens are a feature, use Fujicolour Reala (prints) and Fujichrome Velvia and Provia (transparencies).

Nick Garbutt is a professional photographer, writer, artist and expedition leader, specialising in natural history. He is co-author of 'Madagascar Wildlife' (Bradt Travel Guides), and a winner in the 'BBC Wildlife' Photographer of the Year Competition. John R Jones is a professional travel photographer specialising in minority people, and author of the Bradt guides to 'Vietnam' and 'Laos and Cambodia'.

BUSINESS

Business visas can be arranged on arrival at Phnom Penh or Siem Reap airports with the minimum fuss for a fee of US$25, unlike in Vietnam where businessmen need to obtain an official invitation from a Vietnamese organisation.

Office hours are usually 08.00–12.00 and 14.00–17.30 Monday to Saturday (although some offices only work in the mornings on Saturdays) with government offices open 08.00–17.00 Monday to Friday with a break for lunch.

A very useful publication for businesspersons looking to establish business links, invest or open an office in Cambodia is the *Cambodia Business and Investment Handbook*, published by the Ministry of Commerce. The website www.cambodia-web.net has an online yellow pages section for businesses in Cambodia.

PUBLIC HOLIDAYS

1 January	New Year's Day
7 January	Makara Day
	Celebration of the liberation from the Khmer Rouge regime in 1979
8 March	International Women's Day
April	Bon Chaul Chhnam (Cambodian New Year)
	A four-day festival at the end of the harvest period when families spring-clean their homes and make offerings for the following year
Apr/May	Visaka Bochea Day
	Birthday of the Buddha
1 May	International Labour Day
May	Bon Chroat Preah Nongkoal (Royal Ploughing Ceremony)
	An agrarian festival whose ritual will predict the harvest for the coming year
1 June	International Children's Day
18 June	The Queen's Birthday
24 September	Constitution Day
30 October	The King's Birthday
	Two-day festival celebrating the birthday of King Norodom Sihanouk
9 November	Independence Day
	Celebrating Cambodia's independence from France in 1953
November	Bon Om Touk (Water Festival)
	A three-day festival marking the reversing of the current of the Tonle Sap River

TIME ZONE

Cambodia is seven hours ahead of Greenwich Mean Time (GMT) like Vietnam, Thailand and Laos. When it is midday in Cambodia it is midnight in New York, 05.00 in London and 16.00 in Sydney.

THE WATER FESTIVAL
Bon Om Touk

One of the highlights of the Cambodian cultural calendar, the three-day Water Festival attracts over 300 boats from all round the country to this annual boat race to mark a remarkable natural phenomenon. The waters of the Tonle Sap River run into the Mekong, but during the monsoon there is so much water that there is a build-up and the excess is forced to change direction and flow back into the Tonle Sap Lake.

People pour in from the provinces in cars and on bikes, buses and lorries and the area by the river becomes a mass of humanity as they watch the races and meander round the makeshift food stalls. There is a real carnival atmosphere which continues late into the night when a flotilla of boats glides down the river covered in lights. People crowd in front of the brightly lit Royal Palace to enjoy the display of fireworks that illuminate the night sky.

The 1999 Water Festival was the biggest seen in recent years as people enjoyed the optimism pervading daily life throughout the country. For many it was probably their first-ever visit to Phnom Penh. They come not only to see their capital city but to support the boats sent from their province. Many provinces send more than one boat to the races and the water is a riot of colour with the oarsmen in each boat, around 30 in total, sporting colourful T-shirts. The races start from near the Japanese Bridge and end in front of the Royal Palace where crowds throng the banks of the river. Winners from each race on day one compete the following day and are eliminated until the final race on day three when the winning boat takes the prestigious championship.

The date of the festival coincides with the full moon of the Buddhist calendar month of Kadeuk and is generally at the beginning of November. Around the country people gather to give thanks to the moon, burn incense and make offerings. It is a period when government offices, banks and many museums are closed and this can sometimes last for up to a week depending on which days the festival falls.

ELECTRICITY

Electrical voltage throughout the country is generally 220 volts AC, 50Hz, with round two-pin sockets. Power cuts are still a problem throughout the country but many larger hotels will have back-up generators which kick in should there be a power failure. In the smaller towns guesthouses may rely on generators only for their electricity supply and power will be confined to a few hours in the evening.

Part Two

The Guide

Phnom Penh

Phnom Penh is a dynamic, growing place where the present era of peace and stability has encouraged confidence in the future and new businesses are mushrooming. An expression of this confidence is the increase in the number of motorbikes and cars on the roads, particularly in the rush hour. However, the city still retains its charm with its colonial buildings, wide boulevards and riverside walks.

It is a city of contrasts. The riverside walk along Sisowath Quay is exceptional as so much of Cambodian daily life can be observed here. Many boulevards are lined with exquisite examples of colonial architecture but around the corner will be a street crammed with decrepit buildings and more potholes than road. Many visitors grant Phnom Penh only a cursory visit en route to its more glamorous sister, the temples of Angkor, but those who take the time find a city which blends some of its former character with a new dynamism as it emerges from troubled times.

Phnom Penh was founded in the 14th century by a woman named Penh who found four Buddha statues and then established Wat Phnom to house them. A small settlement grew up around the temple but Phnom Penh was not to become the capital for a few hundred years. The much underestimated capital of Cambodia is located at the confluence of three rivers – the Mekong, the Bassac and Tonle Sap – which are a focal point of life in the city. Phnom Penh became the capital of Cambodia in 1866, when it was moved from Udong, after the country had become a French protectorate. The city saw some troubled times during the 20th century when it was occupied by the Japanese during World War II and then when many thousand refugees flooded into it to escape the fighting in later years.

But life changed dramatically for the citizens of Phnom Penh on April 17 1975 when the Khmer Rouge entered the city and systematically began to evict the people. It is staggering to think that they went so easily but it is important to remember that they were told that they were being asked to leave for their own protection and would be able to return in a few days. In their absence the city was looted and there are some moving black-and-white pictures of the abandoned city streets with family possessions thrown down from apartment windows.

When the citizens began to move back into the city after the Vietnamese invasion, it appeared that they were just camping in the houses and apartments. So much had been destroyed. Now the lot of the citizens has improved but there are still problems with the water supply and the sewage system. In addition there are frequent power cuts and the state of the roads varies enormously: many are a patchwork of potholes. Visitors to Phnom Penh will be largely unaffected by these problems and, compared with the state of the city a number of years ago, the residents of Phnom Penh see them as mere inconveniences.

GETTING THERE AND AWAY
By air

As well as international flights (see *Chapter 3* for details) there are domestic flights between Phnom Penh and a few cities around the country. Three airlines link Phnom Penh with the provinces and an outline of their service is given below. The published timetables change regularly so do check days of operation and **do not fail** to reconfirm your booking two to three days before departure. It is also advisable to contact the airline again the day before departure to check that the flight time has not changed.

Royal Air Cambodge 206a Norodom Bd, Phnom Penh; tel: 023 428055/6; fax: 023 427910; email: Royal-Air-Cambodge@camnet.com.kh; web: www.royal-air-cambodge.net. Royal Air Cambodge have the most comprehensive timetable throughout Cambodia with flights as follows between Phnom Penh and the provincial cities. Siem Reap – two or three flights daily; Battambang – one flight daily, mainly in the morning; Rattanakiri – one flight daily, mainly around lunchtime; Mondulkiri – morning flight on Wednesday (via Rattanakiri on the outward flight) and Sunday (via Rattanakiri on the return flight); Stung Treng – morning flight on Monday, Thursday and Sunday, usually combined with the Rattanakiri flight. Flights on domestic routes are generally on ATR72 planes with a Boeing 737 on some flights to Siem Reap.

President Airlines 50 Norodom Bd, Phnom Penh; tel: 023 212887, 210338/9; fax: 023 212992. This is a private airline which has been operating since 1997. Their fleet consists of Antonov 24s and Fokker 28s. The latter are used on the Siem Reap route. Siem Reap – two flights daily, one in the morning and one in the afternoon; Battambang – one flight daily in the morning; Rattanakiri – late morning flights on Tuesday, Thursday and Sunday; Stung Treng – morning flight on Sunday only; Koh Kong – Monday and Friday from Phnom Penh (en route to Siem Reap) and Wednesday and Sunday to Phnom Penh (en route from Siem Reap).

Phnom Penh Airways 209 St 19, Sangkat Chay Chum Neah, Khan Daun Penh, Phnom Penh; tel: 023 217419/20; fax: 023 217420. This is the newest airline on the scene having been in operation only since October 1999 and with a small fleet of Antonov 24s. Siem Reap – two flights daily, one in the morning and one in the afternoon, but the morning flight stops in Battambang on the way back to Phnom Penh; Battambang – one flight daily in the morning but the flight stops in Siem Reap en route from Phnom Penh; Rattanakiri – one flight on Monday, Wednesday and Friday but the flight stops in Stung Treng en route from Phnom Penh; Stung Treng – one flight on Monday, Wednesday and Friday but the flight stops in Rattanakiri en route to Phnom Penh; Koh Kong – morning flight in both directions on Tuesday and Saturday with a stop at Sihanoukville en route from Phnom Penh on Tuesday and from Koh Kong on Saturday.

Arrival

As described in the *Red tape* section on page 43, arrival at Phnom Penh is very straightforward as long as you are in possession of one photo and the relevant visa fee. Taxis into the city can be found at the airport taxi station opposite the terminal building and the price is fixed at US$7. Most visitors will find a number of car and motorbike owners also waiting outside the terminal eagerly touting their services, each vying with the others to offer a lower price. Car drivers have been known to ask for as little as US$2 and motorbike owners US$1. The journey into town takes between 15 and 30 minutes depending on the time of day.

By boat

Speedboats are a good way of travelling around Cambodia, particularly until the roads are seriously improved. The most popular route is between Phnom Penh and Siem Reap but there is also a good service from Phnom Penh to Kompong Cham, Kratie and Stung Treng.

Boats to Siem Reap and the northeast depart from just north of the Japanese Bridge (Chruy Chang Va) on Route 5. The ticket offices for the daily service are by the river, north of the bridge, and tickets have to be bought in person or through a travel agent (who will charge for this service). The ticket offices, such as Soon Lee Express and Chang Na Express, are open daily 07.30–11.00 and 14.00–17.00. The one-way fare to Siem Reap is US$25, the boats leave at around 07.00 and the journey takes five hours. The boats to Kompong Cham and onwards leave at 07.00 and the one-way fare is 15,000 riels for the two-hour journey. The best time to travel by ferry is in the wet season: during the dry season smaller boats are used and these take longer.

By bus

There is a good, modern bus service to the towns around Phnom Penh operated by Ho Wah Genting Transport Company. Two other bus companies, GST Export Bus and DH Cambodia, also operate a service on the Sihanoukville route.

Phnom Penh Ho Wah Genting Transport Company Ltd Corner of Sts 217 and 67, Sangkat Phsar Thmey II, Khan Daun Penh, Phnom Penh; tel: 023 210359; fax: 023 215887. This is the largest bus company, located at the southwest corner of the Central Market, and it has the monopoly on all bus routes (apart from Sihanoukville) for the foreseeable future so is the best option for travel by public transport to provinces around Phnom Penh. An outline of the timetable for the main routes is given below.

Sihanoukville Four buses each day leaving at 07.30, 08.30, 12.30 and 13.30 from Phnom Penh and 07.00, 08.00, 12.15 and 14.00 from Sihanoukville. Journey time four hours. One-way fare 10,000 riels.

Kompong Cham Six buses each day at 06.45, 07.45, 09.30, 11.30, 13.45 and 15.45 from Phnom Penh and 06.45, 07.45, 09.30, 12.30, 13.30 and 15.30 from Kompong Cham. Journey time two hours. One-way fare 6,000 riels.

Udong Buses depart every 30 minutes. Journey time 1.5 hours. One way-fare 2,500 riels.

Takeo Nine buses each day at 07.00, 08.00, 09.00, 10.00, 11.30, 13.00, 14.00, 15.00 and 16.00 from Phnom Penh and 06.30, 07.30, 09.30, 10.30, 11.30, 12.45, 14.00, 15.30 and 16.30 from Takeo. One-way fare 4,500 riels.

Neak Leung This is the town on route 1 where it is necessary to cross the Mekong by boat. Buses stop here but it is possible to pick up shared taxis to the Vietnamese border after crossing the river. Buses leave Phnom Penh on the hour, every hour, from 07.00 to 16.00. This also applies to buses leaving Neak Leung for Phnom Penh. The one-way fare is 4,500 riels.

Kompong Chhnang Several buses daily leaving Phnom Penh at 06.40, 08.00, 09.00, 10.00, 11.30, 13.00, 14.00, 15.30 and 16.30. Buses from Kompong Chhnang leave at 06.30, 07.30, 09.30, 10.30, 11.00, 12.00, 13.00, 14.00, 15.30 and 16.30.

GST Export Bus Co St 13, Phnom Penh; tel: 023 725054. GST has four buses daily between Phnom Penh and Sihanoukville departing at 07.15, 08.15, 12.30 and 13.30. The one-way fare is 10,000 riels and 18,000 riels return. Buses also leave from the small bus station at the southwest corner of the Central Market.

DH Cambodia Group 66 St 63, Sangkat Psathmei II, Khan Daun Penh, Phnom Penh; tel: 012 840716 (mobile). DH has two buses per day to Sihanoukville departing at 07.30 and 12.30. The one-way fare is 10,000 riels. Buses also leave from the small bus station at the southwest corner of the Central Market.

By train

Train travel in Cambodia is agonisingly slow and rather uncomfortable, but the authorities do allow foreigners to use the service after a hiatus in the 1990s. Two routes depart from Phnom Penh – to Battambang in the west and Sihanoukville in the south. There is a daily service to Battambang departing at 06.00 and the journey takes around 12 to 14 hours. The Sihanoukville train leaves Phnom Penh on Monday, Wednesday, Friday and Sunday and returns on Tuesday, Thursday and Saturday and takes around 11 hours to reach its destination. The fare is a very modest 4,500 riels.

By taxi

Shared long-distance taxis depart from different locations around the city, depending on their destination.

Taxis for Kampot depart from Psah Dumkor Market near the Intercontinental Hotel. The fare is 8,000 riels per person in a car and 6,000 riels in a minibus; the journey time is 2–3 hours. The latest time to start the journey is around midday as many taxi drivers will not leave after this time.

The taxis for the Vietnamese border leave from Chhbar Ampov Market, across the Monivong Bridge; the journey time along Route 1 is 4 hours. One-way to the border is around US$20–30 per car with an onward taxi from the Vietnamese side to Ho Chi Minh City costing around US$40 per car.

Route 5 to Battambang is good as far as Kompong Chhnang and then it deteriorates badly for the rest of the way. The journey takes around 8 hours and taxis leave from the northwest corner of Central Market in Phnom Penh. The one-way fare to Battambang is 20,000 riels inside a pickup truck and 15,000 riels outside.

Kompong Cham can be reached in less than 2 hours along fast Routes 6 and 7. Taxis from the southwest corner of the Central Market in Phnom Penh cost 7,000 riels in a car and 5,000 riels in a minibus.

Route 6 to Kompong Thom is very good and can be reached from the southwest corner of the Central Market in around 2–3 hours for 7,000 riels in a car and 5,000 riels in a minibus.

The 8-hour journey to Siem Reap costs US$6 (about 23,000 riels) and taxis leave from the southwest corner of the Central Market. The road is good to Kompong Thom but deteriorates thereafter.

Taxis for Sihanoukville leave from the southwest corner of the Central Market for the easy drive along excellent Route 4. The journey in a car costs around 10,000 riels and takes around 3 hours.

GETTING AROUND THE CITY

Maps of Phnom Penh are plentiful in the markets and bookshops. Periplus publish a map of Phnom Penh together with a country map.

By taxi

There are no metered taxis in Phnom Penh but car owners wait around outside hotels and restaurants offering their services for short journeys or all-day hire. A price has to be negotiated before setting out and a short journey within the city should be around US$2–3 (a little more at night) and full-day hire around US$15. Vehicles also wait on Sisowath Quay opposite the Sofitel Cambodiana Hotel and can be hired for longer durations.

One taxi company advertises its services in the newspapers: Bailey's Taxis can be prebooked, their drivers speak English and the taxis are metered. They can be contacted on 023 310808 or 012 890000 and they work 24 hours.

By moto

Also known as *motodops* these are motorbike taxis whose owners wait around outside hotels and restaurants and even stop on the street to see if you need their services. They appear amazed that any foreigner can possibly wish to walk anywhere. Fares have to be negotiated and should be around 1,000–2,000 riels during the day and a little more at night. Make sure the driver actually knows where you want to go as many come into the city every day from the countryside looking for clients. Many do actually speak passable English and are willing to be your guide for a day around the city for about US$5–7.

By cyclo

There are still a few cyclos cruising the streets in Phnom Penh despite the proliferation of motos and the busy traffic. These are a more relaxing way of travelling, particularly if you are nervous about getting on the back of motorbikes. Cyclo drivers should charge around the same rate as motos but will obviously take longer to reach your destination.

Tipping

Tipping is not customary in Cambodia but greatly appreciated as incomes are very low and many of the drivers are trying to supplement meagre incomes in order to support their families. A few hundred riels will go a long way.

By bus

There is no city bus service as such so residents use motos to move around. Ho Wah Genting buses do stop on request in the city en route to the towns they serve around Phnom Penh.

Motorbike and bicycle hire

This should only be attempted if you are an experienced motorbike rider or cyclist and can cope with traffic coming at you from all directions. Motorbikes can be hired from Lucky! Lucky! Motorcycles at 413 Monivong Boulevard (tel: 023 212788) and Asia Trade and Travel – Auto Rental at 166 Norodom Boulevard (tel: 012 809192). Prices range from US$4–9 per day. Many guesthouses can arrange bicycle hire for a nominal sum. A driving licence is not required but there is also no local insurance available should you be in collision with a third party. Check the small print in your insurance policy to make sure this kind of transport isn't excluded.

Vehicle hire

Most of the travel agencies mentioned in this section can arrange for a car and driver to be hired for a day or longer and the price depends on the distance travelled. Alternatively car drivers hang around outside hotels offering their services for the day and you can expect to pay around US$15–20 per day. If you wish to hire a van or 4WD vehicle these congregate on Sisowath Quay opposite the Cambodiana Hotel and again the price will depend on the distance to be covered.

ACCOMMODATION

As to be expected in a capital city the selection of guesthouses and hotels is enormous, ranging from the simplest right through to sheer luxury. Location is not as important as in some other cities since it is pretty easy to move around.

Deluxe

Le Royal Hotel 92 Rukhak Vithei, Daun Penh (off Monivong Bd), Sangkat Wat Phnom, Phnom Penh; tel: 023 981888; fax 023 981168; email: raffles.hlr.ghda@bigppond.com.kh; web: www.raffles.com/ril. Once home to many NGO workers and journalists, the old Samaki Hotel reopened in 1997 following extensive refurbishment by its new owners Raffles International. The hotel has now

Previous page Painted bas-reliefs depicting scenes from the Ramayana and the life of Buddha decorate the shrines surrounding Wat Phnom, Phnom Penh. (JM)

Above Floating village on the Tonle Sap near Siem Reap. The villages are laid out in rows of houses with schools, shops and petrol stations. (AS)

Right The 11th-century hilltop temple, Phnom Chisor near Phnom Penh, much damaged by fighting between the Khmer Rouge and Lon Nol troops (AS)

Below House belonging to the Kreung people near Banlung in Rattanakiri province (AS)

Above Mining for rubies and sapphires near Pailin, a town now controlled by members of the former Khmer Rouge (AS)

Left Mining for gems in Rattanakiri province where makeshift villages have been thrown up to cater for the men drawn to the area by the lure of possible riches (AS)

Below Boiled spiders for sale at Skuon. The vendors will show you the live spiders to prove they are really fresh. (AS)

Above A saffron-robed novice monk performing duties in the monastery's paddy fields, Lolei village, south of Siem Reap (JM)

Below The moat surrounding Angkor Wat, some 5km in length, teems with youngsters from local villages collecting water weeds in woven baskets. (JM)

Below right At most temples in Cambodia there are numerous children who will act as informal guides to the ruins. (JM)

LE ROYAL HOTEL, PHNOM PENH

As it was part of the French colony of Indochina, much of the development of many towns in Cambodia was instigated by French officials. In the 1920s plans were drawn up to extend the city, and to build a market (now known as Psah Thmei or Central Market) and a hotel close to Wat Phnom. This area was particularly lovely with trees and wide boulevards and many European residences, government buildings, the Cercle Sportif and the hospital were to be found here. The plans for the hotel were particularly fine, although European in style rather than Khmer, which many had hoped for. The elegant design included shutters, dormer windows and cool corridors all designed to cope with the tropical climate.

The hotel opened in 1929 and immediately attracted an international clientele of royalty, celebrities, writers and adventurers who passed through, generally en route to visit the temples of Angkor. Tourism was in its heyday in the 1930s and again in the 1960s and Le Royal saw a steady stream of visitors who arrived in Cambodia by ship or overland by car from Bangkok or Saigon. During the early 1970s most of the rooms were occupied by journalists reporting on the civil war. The hotel was an oasis from the fighting all around until the Red Cross declared it a neutral zone and brought in refugees and treated injured people in a makeshift operating theatre. The hotel was abandoned with the arrival of the Khmer Rouge in April 1975 and all the foreigners resident there moved to the French Embassy before being escorted out of the country.

The hotel reopened in 1979 and was renamed the Samaki. Fortunately the hotel building had suffered little in the intervening years but was rather run down. It became home to many of the people working for the international aid agencies which flooded into the country and then to members of the UNTAC force in the early 1990s. A dramatic change took place when Raffles International began renovation work and reopened the hotel in 1997 when it returned to its original name, Le Royal. The main building remains but the bungalows in the hotel grounds were demolished to make way for three low-rise wings. The number of rooms and suites increased from 54 to 210 and all were refurbished in the original style of the hotel. The modernisation work which took place over the years was removed to restore the main building, and in particular the entrance lobby, to its original splendour.

been restored to its former glory and is pure timeless elegance. Previous guests include Jacqueline Kennedy and Charles de Gaulle. There are 210 rooms and suites decorated in art deco style, most of which are located in the new low-rise wings of the hotel, although some of the very luxurious suites are in the original, main building. The hotel

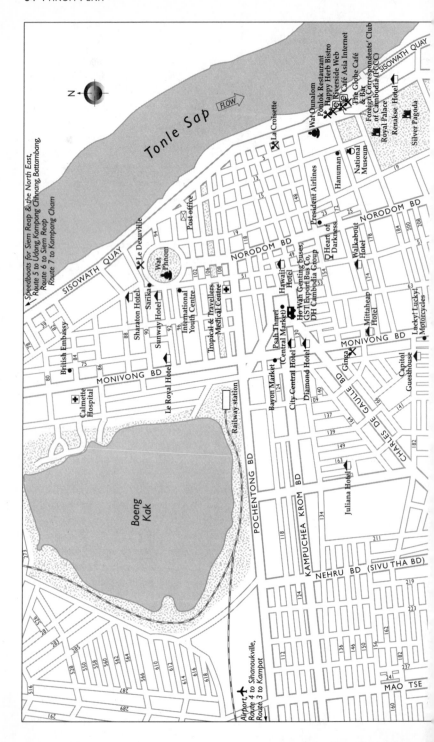

N

Tonle Sap

FLOW

Speedboats for Siem Reap & the North East,
Route 5 to Udong, Kompong Chhnang, Battambang,
Route 6 to Siem Reap
Route 7 to Kompong Cham

Wat Ounalom
Ponlok Restaurant
Happy Herb Bistro
Riverside Web
Café Asia Internet
The Globe Café & Bar
Foreign Correspondents' Club of Cambodia (FCCC)
SISOWATH QUAY
Royal Palace
Remake Hotel
Silver Pagoda

La Croisette

Hanuman

National Museum

President Airlines

NORODOM BD

Heart of Darkness

Walkabout Hotel

Le Deauville

Post office

SISOWATH QUAY

Wat Phnom

Sharaton Hotel
Sarika
Sunway Hotel

International Youth Centre

Tropical & Travellers Medical Centre

NORODOM BD

Hawaii Hotel

Hor Wah Genting buses
GST Export Bus Co.
DH Cambodia Group

Mittaheap Hotel

Lucky Lucky Motorcycles

British Embassy

Calmette Hospital

MONIVONG BD

Le Royal Hotel

Railway station

Psah Thmei
Central Market

Bayon Market

City Central Hotel

Diamond Hotel

Ginga

MONIVONG BD

Capital Guesthouse

BD GAULLE

Juliana Hotel

CHARLES DE GAULLE

Boeng Kak

POCHENTONG BD

KAMPUCHEA KROM BD

NEHRU BD (SIVU THA BD)

Airport,
Route 4 to Sihanoukville,
Route 3 to Kampot

MAO TSE

PHNOM PENH

building surrounds a cool, garden courtyard and two swimming pools and there is a selection of bars and restaurants throughout the hotel ranging from snack bars to smart establishments serving Chinese, Western and Khmer food. The hotel has a desk at Phnom Penh airport so can make reservations and arrange transfers on arrival or with advance notice. Room rates range from US$260 for a single and US$290 in a double per night for one of the 137 staterooms and US$350–2,000 for the suites.

Hotel Intercontinental Regency Square, 296 Mao Tse Tung Bd, Phnom Penh; tel: 023 424888; fax: 023 424885; email: phnompenh@interconti.com; web: www.interconti.com. The hotel has a desk at Phnom Penh airport so can make reservations and arrange transfers on arrival or with advance notice. Located in a new development area in the south of the city, it has all the facilities associated with this chain including pool, gym, casino, shops, restaurant, café and bars. The hotel is easy to spot as it is the only high-rise building in the city. Room rates start at US$120 for deluxe singles, US$140 for deluxe twins and US$300–1,500 for suites, all exclusive of breakfast. In addition there is 10% service charge and 10% tax.

Superior class

Sunway Hotel 1 St 92, Sangkat Wat Phnom, PO Box 633, Phnom Penh; tel: 023 430333; fax: 023 430339; email: asunway@bigpond.com.kh; web: www.Cambodia-web.net. Located in a peaceful area, close to Wat Phnom, the Sunway is a smart, stylish hotel with 140 rooms and suites. Do not be put off by its salmon pink exterior. It has extensive facilities including Mediterranean restaurant, lobby bar, health club, beauty salon, art and craft shop, ballroom, business centre and meeting rooms. Room rates are US$194–218 for singles and US$218–220 for twins. However, there are often special promotions where savings of over 50% can be made, so it is worth contacting the hotel in advance.

Sofitel Cambodiana 313 Sisowath Quay, Phnom Penh; tel: 023 426288; fax: 023 426290; emailsofitel.cambodiana@worldmail.com.kh. The Cambodiana was the first deluxe hotel in Phnom Penh in recent times, following its completion in the early 1990s. It was originally started in 1967 but the civil war and political situation meant that it stood half-finished for many years. The hotel now has serious competition but its location on the banks of the Mekong River still make it a popular choice as does its proximity to the Royal Palace and National Museum. All its 267 rooms overlook the river, although the view along the river is spoilt by the huge Naga casino boat moored behind the hotel. Facilities include several restaurants and bars, swimming pool, tennis courts, shops, business centre and meeting rooms. The hotel has a desk at Phnom Penh airport so can make reservations and arrange transfers on arrival or with advance notice. Room rates start at US$170 for a single and US$200 for a twin.

Royal Phnom Penh Samdech Sothearos Bd, Sankat Tonle Bassac, Phnom Penh; tel: 023 360026, 360697-8, 360899; fax: 023 360036. The Royal was the first hotel to offer an alternative to the Cambodiana in 1994. Its 75 tasteful rooms are set in delightful gardens with a restaurant serving Thai, Chinese and international food, a bar and a lounge. Other facilities include a swimming pool, health club, golf driving range and tennis courts. The size of the hotel means that its service is friendlier and more personal than some of the larger hotels in the city. Room rates range from US$162 for deluxe rooms to US$240 for junior suites, including breakfast.

First class

Princess Hotel 302 Monivong Bd, Khan Daun Penh, Phnom Penh; tel: 023 801089, 801066, 721960; fax: 023 801217. A modern, friendly hotel, located close to many of the embassies. Facilities include a Chinese restaurant with a few Western dishes, and small bar. The rooms all have air conditioning, satellite TV, IDD and mini bar as well as room service and laundry. Room rates are US$97 single and US$121 twin.

City Central Hotel Monivong Bd at 128 St, PO Box 533, Phnom Penh; tel: 023 722022; fax: 023 722 021; email: citycentralhotel@camnet.com.kh. Located at the heart of the commercial district close to shops and offices, the City Central Hotel is popular with both tourists and business travellers. The restaurant offers an excellent selection of Khmer, Asian and Continental cuisine and there is a well-equipped business centre with email and internet. The 67 rooms have air conditioning, satellite TV, IDD and safe as well as room service and laundry. Room rates are US$106–152 for singles and US$121–168 for twins.

Juliana Hotel 16 St 152, Phnom Penh; tel: 023 366070; fax: 023 880530. One of the original upmarket hotels which has now been renovated and is a constant favourite. Set in lovely gardens with swimming pool, fitness centre and business centre. Restaurants serve Chinese, Western and Asian food. The 100 rooms have all the usual facilities associated with international hotels. Competitive prices starting at US$60 for singles and US$70 for twins.

Standard class

Hotel Sampan 46 St 240, Phnom Penh; tel : 023 217143/147; fax: 023 217146; email: Sampanhotel@bigpond.com.kh. This small and friendly hotel, opened in October 1999 (only 15 rooms, all air-conditioned), offers a truly Cambodian style and atmosphere. Each bedroom is unique in its size and decoration with traditional furniture, antiques and wood panelling. The Bar des Explorateurs is informal but chic and the Bassac Restaurant serves good Khmer, Chinese and Thai cuisine. A real find in the heart of Phnom Penh and one to be recommended. Good value at US$30 for a standard room, US$45 for a superior room and US$65 for a suite. Room rates include breakfast.

Diamond Hotel 172–184 Monivong Bd, Phnom Penh; tel: 023 217326-7-8; fax: 023 426635, 216637; email: diamondhotel@bigpond.com.kh. The hotel is well located in the commercial district close to the Central Market, shops and restaurants. Its prime location on a busy interchange means that it can be quite noisy but it is a lively area to stay in. The 87 rooms have air conditioning, satellite TV, IDD, mini bar and safe. A simple restaurant is located on the ground floor. Room rates are US$50 twin and US$40 single including breakfast. From time to time the hotel offers special promotional prices.

Regent Park Hotel 58 Samdeach Sothearos Bd, Sangkat Chak Tomuk, Khan Daun Penh, Phnom Penh; tel: 023 427131; fax: 023 361999; email: regentpark@bigpond.com.kh. Friendly establishment located close to the Royal Palace, but rather spoilt by the huge pizza advertisement outside. Good rooms with air conditioning, satellite TV, IDD and mini bar. The restaurant serves Thai and European cuisine and there is a rooftop garden. Room rates are US$55 including breakfast.

Renakse Hotel 40 Samdeach Sothearos Bd, Phnom Penh; tel: 023 722457; fax: 023 428785. Lovely old colonial building set in large garden with superb location opposite the Royal Palace. Recently renovated, the rooms are competitively priced at US$30–45.

Hawaii Hotel 18 St 130, Phnom Penh; tel: 023 362679; fax: 023 426652. This hotel has long been popular with regular visitors to Phnom Penh and for those who have to stay for longer periods. Rooms have air conditioning, satellite TV and IDD. Good central location. Rooms cost US$20–40.

Sharaton Cambodia Hotel St 47, near Wat Phnom, Phnom Penh; tel: 023 360395; fax: 023 361199; email: lity@bigpond.com.kh. Well-located hotel with 100 rooms and good facilities including café/restaurant, swimming pool, disco, business centre and airport pickup (prebooking necessary). Rooms cost US$80 plus tax and service including breakfast.

L'Imprevu Hotel Prek Eng, Route 1; tel: 023 360405; fax: 023 310335. Not strictly in Phnom Penh but it is such a special place that it is worth a mention. Located around 7km from Phnom Penh on Route 1, on the way to Vietnam, this hotel is a real oasis from the hustle and bustle of the city. Simple bungalows are set in tropical gardens with fan or air conditioning and satellite TV. To pass the time there is a swimming pool, tennis courts, petanque, table tennis… Restaurant serves French and Thai cuisine. Bungalow prices range from US$20 with fan to US$30 with air conditioning on a room-only basis.

Budget

The Boddhi Tree Guesthouse 50 St 133 (in front of Tuol Sleng); tel: 012 893138 (mobile). I stumbled across this delightful guesthouse by accident as I visited Tuol Sleng Museum. Right across the street from the museum entrance, the Boddhi Tree started life as a café/restaurant and then converted the upstairs into five guestrooms in October 1999. The rooms are simple but bright and fresh and only local materials have been used. There is one shared bathroom. The excellent menu offers Asian, European and Japanese food and is very reasonably priced at around US$2.50 per dish. The small veranda overlooking the front garden is candlelit at night. The owner, Manuel Garcia, donates profits to projects in the countryside and also sells handicrafts made by widows with disabilities, who also receive any profits. Room rates US$7–10.

Mittapheap Hotel 262 Monivong Bd, Khan Daun Penh, Phnom Penh; tel: 023 213999; fax: 023 213331. Hotel located above a snooker club with simple but adequate rooms with air conditioning, satellite TV and private bathroom. Rooms cost US$15 on room-only basis.

Capitol Guesthouse 15 St 182, Phnom Penh; tel: 023 724104. Located just off Monivong Boulevard this is a great meeting place for travellers to swap information and stories. Can also arrange tours and transport from here and the friendly staff are happy to help with many practicalities. Prices are US$4–6 for room with fan and the more expensive have private facilities.

Walkabout Hotel Corner Sts 51 & 174, Phnom Penh; tel: 012 851787 (mobile); email: walkabout@bigpond.com.kh. Popular, friendly place with good restaurant serving hearty breakfasts. Regular pool competitions. Room prices with fan start at US$4 rising to US$10 with air conditioning. Even accepts credit cards.

Scandic Hotel 4 St 282, Phnom Penh; tel: 023 302388; fax: 023 312388; email: nisse@bigpond.com.kh. Friendly, small hotel with restaurant/ bar and rooms with air conditioning, TV and bathroom. Free airport pickup available. Singles cost US$15 and twins US$20.

RESTAURANTS/BARS

As in any big city, restaurants and bars come and go so I have tried to include venues that have been around for a while and are more permanent. However, do still check in the local press as they often move to new locations around the city. Most bars in Phnom Penh serve food as well so I have put restaurants/cafés/bars in the same section to avoid duplication.

The Globe Café & Bar 389 Sisowath Quay (first floor), Phnom Penh; tel: 023 215923; email: globepp@camnet.com.kh. I first went to this colonial-style bar when I was looking for a good vantage point to watch the racing on the river during the Water Festival. The Globe has a perfect site on the riverfront and the relaxed atmosphere and delicious food make it a popular choice. The menu has southeast Asian food as well as some Western dishes. The owners, Duncan, Nhan Dao and Mark, originally owned a bar in Hong Kong and moved to Phnom Penh in 1997. Jazz rock lovers will enjoy the Globe on Saturday nights as Duncan plays saxophone with anybody who will join him and it is a good foot-tapping session. He was the saxophonist with the Psychedelic Furs in the 1980s – remember them? The bar is open from 10.00 to late Monday to Friday and from 07.00 at weekends.

Ponlok Restaurant 319–323 Sisowath Quay, Sangkat Chey Chumneas, Khan Daun Penh, Phnom Penh; tel: 023 212025. Huge selection of Khmer dishes and seafood in a large and busy restaurant. Fortunately the menu has photos of the dishes to help with your selection. The first floor terrace has great views over the river. Good value.

Foreign Correspondents' Club of Cambodia (FCCC) 363 Sisowath Quay, Phnom Penh; tel: 023 724014. Lovely old colonial building open to the riverfront with welcome cooling breezes. Pleasant dining area and comfy bar with big armchairs. Well-known meeting place for journalists.

Le Deauville Wat Phnom, Phnom Penh; tel: 012 843204 (mobile). Friendly bar/restaurant with French ex-pat owner, André, serving excellent French and Continental food. Easy to find on the road surrounding Wat Phnom. Pool table. Open 07.00–24.00 but closed on Sundays.

Tamarind Bar 31 St 240, Phnom Penh; tel: 012 885164 (mobile); email: soklaw@camnet.com.kh. Small and relaxed, this bar serves a selection of Khmer and French dishes and also has a choice of two three-course set menus at a bargain price of US$4. Also has a roof terrace but this is only open during the dry season. Open 07.00–02.00.

Our Place 36 St 214, Phnom Penh; tel: 011 816120 (mobile). Formerly known as Papparazzi, the name change hasn't changed the lashings of excellent Italian food served in a relaxed atmosphere.

La Croisette Corner of Sisowath Quay and St 144, Phnom Penh; tel: 012 876032 (mobile). French restaurant serving a selection of good-value set menus from 07.00–23.00 every day. Emphasis on barbecued food.

Chiang Mai Restaurant 112A-B Samdeach Sothearos Bd, Phnom Penh; tel: 023 360502. Thai restaurant serving excellent range of dishes with all-you-can-eat buffets on Friday and Saturday evenings.

Athena 20 St 51, Phnom Penh; tel: 023 366836. New location but still offers some great Greek food and has even added some Italian dishes. Happy hour 17.00–19.00.

Ginga 297 Monivong Bd, Phnom Penh; tel/fax: 023 217323. I am always mystified why Japanese food is so expensive when there doesn't seem to be any cooking involved but Ginga is no different, so if you have money to spare this is the place to spend it.

Happy Herb Bistro 345 Sisowath Quay, Phnom Penh; tel: 016 881335 (mobile). Selection of pasta and pizzas with a little something extra sprinkled on the top, if desired! However, a recent clampdown by the government may mean that this optional extra will be permanently off the menu. But the pizzas are still good. Can also deliver meals.

Café Mogambo 139 Monireth Bd, Phnom Penh, tel: 023 881462. Located next to the Intercontinental Hotel. Lots of atmosphere. Serves hearty meals.

Kim's Kiwi Bar 180 St 130, Phnom Penh. Cold beer and good food and a regular spot for many expats.

Heart of Darkness 26 St 51, Phnom Penh. One of those bars in this part of the world that everybody knows about and just has to visit. Don't go until at least 23.00 as it is dead before then and after that the party continues until the last customer staggers out.

DMZ Bar 83 St 240, Phnom Penh. A particular favourite with expats living in the city with regular screening of major sporting events, Wednesday-night quizzes and ladies' nights. Open from 17.00 until the last person leaves from Monday to Friday and from 11.00 at the weekend.

To enjoy a Cambodian eating experience cross over the Japanese Bridge to the area known as Prek Leap where small and large restaurants line the road, all serving Khmer food. Very busy at night and during holidays.

TRAVEL AGENCIES
The list of travel agencies in Cambodia is long and it is important to check prices and the reliability of the services offered. A few to be recommended are as follows:

Apsara Tours 8 St R V Vinnavaut Oum, Sangkat Chaktomuk, Khan Daun Penh, Phnom Penh; tel: 023 216562; fax: 023 426705; email: apsaratours@camnet.com.kh.

Diethelm Travel 65 St 240, Phnom Penh; tel: 023 219151; fax: 023 219150; email: dtc@bigpond.com.kh.

Diethelm Travel 363 Sisowath Quay, Phnom Penh; tel: 023 214059; email: dtc.fccc@bigpond.com.kh.

Intra Co 2–3 St 118, Phnom Penh; tel: 023 428596; fax: 023 218578; email: intra@bigpond.com.kh.

Lolei Travel (Cambodia) 91 St 141, Sangkat Beoung Prolit Kh 7 Makara, 12252 Phnom Penh; tel/fax: 023 210089; email: info@loleitravel.com.

Mittapheap Travel & Tours 262 Monivong Bd, Khan Daun Penh, Phnom Penh: tel: 023 216666; 012 877888 (mobile); fax: 023 213331; email: mtours@camnet.com.kh; web: www.tourismcambodia.com.

Pichtourist 46 Norodom Bd, Phnom Penh; tel: 023 218948; fax: 023 426586; email: pcihtourist@camnet.com.kh. One of the leading travel agencies in Cambodia. Very switched on to your needs with excellent guides and drivers.
PTM Travel 200 Eo Monivong Bd, Phnom Penh; tel: 023 219268; fax: 023 428990; email: ptm-travel@camnet.com.kh; web: www.cambodia-web.net/t-agents/ptm.
Transpeed Travel 19 St 106, Phnom Penh; tel: 012 815855 (mobile); fax: 023 725594; email: sobhayou@hotmail.com
Vidotour 188 St 13, Phnom Penh; tel: 023 724022; fax: 023 427865.

ENTERTAINMENT
Cinemas
The **International Youth Centre** (Daun Penh Street, Phnom Penh; tel: 023 722722) shows English-language films every evening at 20.00 and is open to non-members. Films on show are advertised in the Friday edition of the *Cambodia Daily*.

Theatre
The **Chatomuk Theatre** occasionally holds Khmer dance and music shows so check the local press for information.
The **Sofitel Cambodiana Hotel** has classical dance shows every Friday evening.

Sports
Bowling
Superbowl 113 Mao Tse Tung Bd, Phnom Penh

Go karts
Kambol F1 circuit is located 8km past Pochentong airport on Route 4 and is clearly signposted. The track is 900m long. Reservations can be made on 012 804620.

Swimming
Olympic Stadium has a pool (entrance US$2) and some of the larger hotels, such as the Sofitel Cambodiana, allow non-residents to use their swimming pools for a fee.

Golf
Cambodia Golf and Country Club Route 4, south of Phnom Penh; tel: 023 363666; fax: 023 212036. This is currently the only golf club in Cambodia, although there is a driving range in the city. Located just off the main road to Sihanoukville around 35km south of Phnom Penh. Around 15km from Phnom Penh along Route 2 another golf club was being constructed but the investors pulled out after the coup of 1997. It is hoped that new interested parties will now come forward to complete the project.
Parkway Square Driving Range 113 Mao Tse Tung Bd, Phnom Penh. Rooftop driving range for golf enthusiasts.

PRACTICAL INFORMATION
Currency exchange
To change US dollars cash into riels in Phnom Penh it is best to go to the exchange shops, which are quite often located in jewellery shops around town

or in the markets. There are many on Monivong Boulevard, around the central market and in the market itself. Hotel exchange rates are not quite so good and the rate in the banks is usually worse.

Travellers' cheques can only be exchanged in the banks, although some of the large international hotels may change them for you. In a bank there is a commission charge of 1–2% on travellers' cheques. Banks in Phnom Penh can advance cash on a Visa card and the commission rate is 4%.

Banks are open from Monday to Friday generally between 07.00 and 15.30, although times vary from bank to bank. Most banks are closed at the weekend, although a few may open on Saturday mornings.

Communications
Post office
The main office is close to Wat Phnom on the corner of Streets 102 and 13. It is open every day from 07.00 to 18.00 for purchasing stamps and sending mail but is closed Saturday and Sunday for email and fax services. It is possible to make international calls from here and the rates are cheaper at weekends. Poste restante is available; it costs 300 riels per item and a passport is needed as identification. Mobitel phone cards are on sale as well as collectable stamps.

Phones
Street phones are all over the city and the relevant phonecards, either Mobitel or Camintel, can be bought at nearby shops.

Internet cafés
There are now a number of internet cafés dotted around the city.

Café Asia Sisowath Quay, Khan Daun Penh, Phnom Penh; tel: 023 217041; fax: 023 427758; email: cafeasia@FCC.forum.org.kh. Located underneath the FCCC and open daily 08.00–22.00 (although closed when I went there one Saturday evening). Serves bottomless coffee for US$1 plus a wide selection of soft drinks, cocktails, ice-cream, yogurt and cakes. Internet/email charge US$6 per hour.
Riverside Web 351 Sisowath Quay, Khan Daun Penh, Phnom Penh; tel/fax: 023 218028; email: riversideweb@hotmail.com; web: www.riversideweb.com. Small, friendly place serving free soft drinks during happy hours. Internet/email access US$5 per hour.
Khmer Web 150Eo Sihanouk Bd, Phnom Penh; tel: 012 846467 (mobile); fax: 023 217102; email: khmerweb@bigpond.com.kh. Not necessarily a café but internet access is charged at US$5 per hour.

SHOPPING
Phnom Penh is a great place to shop as there is a plethora of good quality handicrafts to buy as well as exquisite silks, silverware and carvings. There are also a number of upmarket fine arts shops selling antiques and traditional arts and details of these can be found in the newspapers.

Supermarkets

Bayon Market 133–135 Monivong Bd, Phnom Penh. Has a good stock of
international foodstuffs including imported meat, fruit, dairy products, cheeses and
wine. More expensive than local produce but still quite reasonable. Open every day
07.00–20.00.

Lucky Supermarket 160 Sihanouk Bd, Phnom Penh. Another shop selling a
selection of international goods. Open every day 08.00–18.30.

Bookshops

International Book Centre 37 Sihanouk Bd, Phnom Penh. As well as books
(mainly educational) also sells office supplies.

Monument Books 46 Norodom Bd, Phnom Penh. Excellent collection of books on
Cambodia covering a range of topics as well as a wide choice of fiction and non-
fiction in English and French.

The London Book Centre 65 St 240, Phnom Penh. Large collection of secondhand
books including a range of books on Cambodia.

Handicrafts

Wat Than Training Centre Wat Than Pagoda, Norodom Bd, Phnom Penh.
Workshops attached to the temple are a training centre for landmine and polio victims
who then return to their villages to earn a living from their new skills. While they are
being trained they sell the handicrafts that they make in a shop on site, particularly
silk items. There is a wide, quality selection and they make excellent gifts. Closed on
Sundays.

Apsara Handicrafts 116d Norodom Bd, Phnom Penh. Sells quality handicrafts
made by Cambodians with disabilities.

National Centre of Disabled Persons 3 Norodom Bd, Phnom Penh. Quality
handicrafts made by disabled people throughout Cambodia.

Fine arts/souvenirs

Hanuman 188 St 13, Phnom Penh. Good selection of handicrafts, art and antique
silks and silver.

Sarika Wat Phnom, Phnom Penh. Sells original creations of traditional and
contemporary silk, jewellery, sculptures and watercolours.

Rajana 170 St 450, Phnom Penh. Located by the Russian Market this classy shop
sells original Khmer art and crafts, silk paintings, jewellery and cards.

Markets

There are a number of markets around Phnom Penh but the ones of most
interest to visitors are the Central Market and Russian Market. They have a
good selection of items such as silk articles, silver ornaments, basketware, gold
and silver jewellery, gemstones, good-quality postcards and clothes.

Central Market (Psah Thmei)

The main market in Phnom Penh looks like a desert palace from a distance
and is overflowing with goods both inside and out. There is a fruit, vegetable,

meat and fish section, fresh flowers, shoes, clothes, books, cassettes, gems and jewellery. The inside of the market positively glitters with scores of gold stalls. There are also many gold shops in the street around the market. Open daily 07.00–17.00.

Russian Market (Psah Toul Tom Poung)

Situated in the south of the city at the corner of Streets 155 and 444 this market is a great favourite with visitors as it sells a vast selection of souvenirs including ceramics, silverware, gems, jewellery, curios, silk, CDs and bags. It is fun exploring the narrow, dark alleyways crammed with stalls and bargaining hard for desired items. Open daily between 07.00 and 17.00.

WHAT TO SEE IN PHNOM PENH
A walking tour of Phnom Penh

Start your walking tour at the colonial **railway station** which has certainly seen better days. The trains to Battambang (daily) and Sihanoukville (every other day) leave very early in the morning so you are unlikely to see one unless you are a train enthusiast and are prepared to be there at around 05.30. There is a lot of activity before the trains depart but during the rest of the day the station is virtually deserted. You are allowed to walk through the station and on to the platform and tracks. Turn left out of the station along Pochentong Street and turn north along Monivong Boulevard into the old **French Quarter** where you will find typical colonial buildings, some rather run down. As you pass the end of Street 92 you will see the beautiful colonial facade of **Le Royal Hotel** just down the road. Make a mental note to return there for a drink in the Elephant Bar to soak up the wonderful ambience. Continue north past the French Embassy to the roundabout and turn immediately right back down Vithei France (Street 47). At the end of the road is the small hill topped by **Wat Phnom**.

Wat Phnom

The temple is positioned on top of a small hill in the north of the city and marks the spot of the foundation of Phnom Penh. According to legend, a young woman named Penh discovered four Buddha statues deposited by river water. The temple was built on a hill to house the statues by Penh in 1372 and named Phnom Penh (the hill of Penh). It is reached by a flight of steps with *nagas* on either side. The temple has been rebuilt and renovated several times. The interior walls are decorated with frescoes depicting the life of Buddha and the Ramayana. A statue of Lady Penh can be seen in a small building next to the stupa said to contain the ashes of King Ponhea Yat (1405–67). Wat Phnom is an important spiritual site in the city and a magnet for residents who come to pray for good luck. The area around the hill is also popular for picnics at the weekends and there is even an elephant offering rides around the base of the hill.

Wat Phnom is open every day and foreign visitors must pay an entrance of US$1.

Leaving the wat, walk east along one of the roads heading towards the **Tonle Sap River**. Walk south along the riverfront along Sisowath Quay until the road divides. To the right, at the beginning of Samdeach Sothearos Boulevard, you will see impressive **Wat Ounalom**.

Wat Ounalom

Wat Ounalom, facing the Tonle Sap, is the most important temple in Phnom Penh as it is the headquarters of the Khmer Buddhist faith, but it suffered greatly from the excesses of the Khmer Rouge. They murdered the Buddhist leader, threw the statue of him (since rescued and on display) into the river, destroyed its precious library of religious books and severely damaged a marble statue of Buddha. Much has been done since 1979 to restore the wat. The marble Buddha has been reassembled but sadly nothing remains of the library.

Continue along Samdeach Sothearos Boulevard and just before you reach the Royal Palace you will see the distinctive red building housing the National Museum to the right, across an open area. You may find, following a visit to Wat Ounalom, that it is time for a lunch break so go back to the riverside (Sisowath Quay), which is visible from here, and walk northwards along the quay where there are numerous cafés and restaurants.

The National Museum

The **National Museum** was built by the French in 1917 in pseudo-Khmer style with red bricks. It houses an extensive collection of Khmer sculptures dating from the pre-Angkorian period (7th century) through to the post-Angkorian period (14th century). It has four galleries around a central courtyard. The differing styles of Khmer art are displayed in chronological order starting to the left of the entrance, with sculptures from various sites around the country. With the help of one of the English-speaking guides who will accompany you on request, it is possible to identify the subtle changes in styles by the variations in costume, hairstyle and jewellery. Pre-Angkorian is represented with examples of Phnom Da, Sambor Prei Kuk and Prasat Andet styles which all have a relaxed, natural feel and the influence of Hinduism is clear. The Angkorian period began with the reign of King Jayavarman II in 802AD and the sculptures become more formal and stylised as represented in examples of Kulen, Preah Ko, Bakheng, Koh Ker, Banteay Srei, Baphuon, Angkor Wat and Bayon styles. Hinduism and Buddhism coexisted in Cambodia until the end of the 13th century when Theravada Buddhism became prominent. It was the beliefs of the current king that dictated which religion was dominant at any one time. The post-Angkorian period is represented by the post-Bayon style which clearly shows the influence of the expanding Thai kingdom and of Buddhism.

The museum is open daily except Mondays and some holidays from 08.00 to 11.30 and 14.00 to 17.30. The entrance fee is US$2.

Go back to Samdeach Sothearos Boulevard and continue to the **Royal Palace** and **Silver Pagoda**.

Royal Palace and Silver Pagoda (Wat Preah Keo Morokat)

The **Royal Palace** is once again the residence of King Sihanouk. It has been extensively renovated and the roofs, covered in gold-coloured tiles, now positively gleam in the sunlight. The old main entrance used to be through the Chan Chaya Pavilion, but now it is through a side gate. The pavilion is occasionally used as a viewing platform by the royal family. The main residence is never open to visitors but the Throne Hall, built in 1917, is open and truly impressive. The roof is topped by a tiered tower with four faces in the Bayon style. The two huge thrones inside are only ever used for coronations, but the hall itself is used to receive important guests. The walls are decorated with colourful paintings depicting the Ramayana.

Close by is **Napoleon's Pavilion**, which looks totally out of place amongst the typically Khmer buildings surrounding it. It is, however, a delightful building which originally belonged to Empress Eugenie, before she presented it to King Norodom. This two-storey building is very French with shuttered windows and balconies. Inside are an assortment of royal family mementos including portraits, photographs, dinnerware and medals.

The **Silver Pagoda** is so named because the floor is covered with thousands of silver tiles weighing a formidable six tonnes. It was originally a wooden building but was rebuilt in 1962. The pagoda houses numerous priceless Buddhas including Wat Preah Keo or the Emerald Buddha (made from baccarat crystal) and a beautiful 90kg life-size golden Buddha encrusted with thousands of diamonds, one of which weighs 25 carats. Several smaller silver and bronze Buddhas surround it. The walls of the pagoda are lined with cabinets housing gifts from visiting dignitaries. The compound containing the Silver Pagoda and the stupas of previous kings is surrounded by a 642m wall covered with murals depicting scenes from the Ramayana, although very damaged in places. Remarkably the Silver Pagoda was left virtually unscathed by the Khmer Rouge, although some looting did take place.

Open daily 07.30–11.00 and 14.30–17.00 but closed during special events. The entrance fee is US$3 and there is a camera fee of US$2. No video cameras are allowed.

There are two other sights of interest around the city but you may find, depending on where you are staying, that they are too far to reach on foot. They may be better done by moto and combined with a souvenir shopping visit to the Russian Market.

Victory Monument

Built to celebrate independence from the French on November 9 1953. The monument took three years (1955 to 1958) to complete and is in the shape of a lotus. Located at the intersection of Norodom and Sihanouk Boulevards.

Tuol Sleng Museum

Personally I find this museum particularly moving and although I have visited it on several occasions it still has the same impact. The building was originally Tuol Svay Prey High School but during the Khmer Rouge years it was turned into the biggest prison in Cambodia. Classrooms which had rung with the sound of young voices were turned into cells and torture rooms through which passed peasants, doctors, engineers, teachers, students, monks, soldiers, government ministers, diplomats and even a few foreigners. It is believed that around 20,000 people were brought to Tuol Sleng and suffered at the hands of the murderous regime, either dying pitifully in the prison or else transported to the killing fields at Cheong Ek once they had confessed.

The Khmer Rouge were meticulous in documenting all their victims, many captured because they had completed the forms handed out when the city was emptied following the arrival of the Khmer Rouge. The people were told that they would return in a few days when they would be given similar jobs so the new regime had to know their current occupation. Once they were imprisoned they were tortured for information about friends, relatives and neighbours. All prisoners were photographed and thousands of these photos now line the walls of the former classrooms alongside photos of the youthful Khmer Rouge cadres. The hate in their eyes is chilling.

The first rooms are starkly simple in documenting the brutality which went on there. Each room has an iron bed with maybe a few items of ragged clothing and a metal box used as a toilet on the bloodstained floor. The large photo on the wall shows the body of the victim found there when the prison was liberated by the Vietnamese in January 1979. In total the Vietnamese found just 14 bodies and, miraculously, seven survivors. Most of the classrooms on the ground floor were crudely converted into tiny cells divided by rough brickwork, each with a manacle bolted to the floor. The upper floors were used for mass detention with prisoners crammed in and manacled together by their feet.

Statistics quoted in the museum claim that around three million people were killed, more than 140,000 were invalided, 200,000 children were orphaned and 650,000 houses, schools, hospitals and pagodas were destroyed. In addition the industrial infrastructure was dismantled and urban centres were abandoned.

The museum, located on St 113, is open daily except Mondays, from 07.30 to 11.00 and 14.00 to 17.00. Entrance fee US$2.

BOAT TRIPS

An organisation called Mekong Island sells tickets for boat trips for **sunset tours** at 13 Street 240 (open daily 07.30–10.30 and 14.00–16.30; tel: 023 427225). A boat departs every evening at 16.45 from in front of Wat Ounalom for a one-hour sunset cruise along the Tonle Sap, provided there is a minimum of two people. The charge is US$12 per person.

There are also daily departures for a full-day boat trip to **Mekong Island** itself. The boat departs from in front of Wat Ounalom at 09.30 and returns there at 15.00. The price is US$32 per person including lunch. On the island you will see handicraft production including silk weaving and a small zoo. There is a daily cultural show of music and dance.

THE CHIEF EXECUTIONER CONFESSES

It might seem unlikely that such a man could profess to be a born-again Christian trying to help the poor, dispossessed people of the regime he so wholeheartedly supported. Duch, as he was called then, was in charge of the Khmer Rouge interrogation centre in Phnom Penh, which became known as Tuol Sleng. Now under the guise of Ta Pin, he works with international aid groups and is a committed Christian. Once he was a servant of communism, but now he serves only God.

In his former life he ran Tuol Sleng where thousands of innocent Cambodians were tortured and murdered and taken outside the city to be buried in mass graves. The Khmer Rouge were meticulous in documenting everybody who passed through the prison and Duch's signature appears on many of these documents, some authorising torture and execution.

Duch was interviewed by a journalist from the *Far Eastern Economic Review* in April 1999 and his openness about his gruesome past suggests that he could be a pivotal witness if, as is hoped, many of the former Khmer Rouge leaders are brought to trial. So many of them defected to the government from the mid-1990s onwards and were given a royal pardon. But now calls for their prosecution are gaining impetus from the international community. Duch alone can position the key players in the genocidal regime and the extent of their responsibility for the events which took place.

EXCURSIONS FROM PHNOM PENH

All the following sites can be reached from Phnom Penh comfortably in one day either by car for anything between US$20 and US$30 per day depending on distance or by Ho Wah Genting Bus.

Cheong Ek

The site of one of the many killing fields around Cambodia is 15km away from the city. The memorial stupa near the entrance is the first thing you see and as it is stacked with hundreds of skulls it is quite shocking. Less shocking but equally disturbing are the 129 excavated mass graves that were found in the vicinity. Each one held hundreds of bodies and it is believed that over 17,000 people met their deaths here. Open daily 07.00–17.00 with an entrance fee of US$2.

Udong

The ancient capital of Cambodia can be reached easily from Phnom Penh along Route 5. There is a Ho Wah Genting bus every 30 minutes from near the Central Market. It takes around 90 minutes to cover the 35km and the fare is 2,500 riels each way.

The road to Udong follows the line of the waters of the Tonle Sap River. During the monsoon the water stretches into the distance on both sides of the road but in the dry season the waters recede and the area is used for growing rice. The road passes through several Cham villages whose main living is from fishing. It is worthwhile stopping at one of the mosques en route. There are also many temples to the new god of the 21st century, the car, in the form of huge petrol stations with gleaming shops selling nothing except bottles of oil. These seem very incongruous amongst the surrounding shacks. The first sighting of Udong in the distance is of a line of stupas on a hill, looking like a mystical fairytale castle.

Udong was once the capital of Cambodia and at its height of influence between 1618 and 1866 when the capital was transferred to Phnom Penh. Little remains of the original hundreds of buildings including temple sanctuaries and stupas, covering two ridges, as the area was used as a battleground between the Lon Nol and Khmer Rouge troops in the 1970s. Many of the stupas which contained the ashes of previous kings, including those of King Monivong (1927–41), were seriously damaged so new ones were built for them around the Silver Pagoda in Phnom Penh. Some of the stupas were covered with intricate patterns in ceramics and a few of these have survived. There is a new stupa under construction, although work has stopped because of a lack of funds. It is rumoured that this is for King Sihanouk but he is most likely to have a stupa erected in the grounds of the Silver Pagoda in Phnom Penh.

Enormous damage was inflicted on the area in the 1970s and there is evidence of fighting everywhere. One of the large temple buildings was used as a munitions dump by the Lon Nol army and this was totally blown apart including the statue of Buddha which it contained. A large reclining Buddha on the other ridge can only be identified by its feet. Mass graves were found close to Udong, containing the victims of the Khmer Rouge, and there is now a memorial to those that suffered as well as a gruesome mural depicting Khmer Rouge atrocities.

Open every day with an entrance fee of US$1. It's best to avoid Sundays as the site is popular with residents from Phnom Penh who go to picnic there.

Phnom Chisor, Ta Mau and Tonle Bati

A rewarding day away from Phnom Penh can be spent visiting the temples along Route 2. The bus to Takeo can stop at the various points along the main road leading off to each site. The remaining few kilometres can be covered by negotiating a ride with a moto. Buses leave virtually every hour on the hour from Phnom Penh starting at 07.00 and the last bus back leaves Takeo at 16.30.

Around 52km from the capital **Phnom Chisor** is an 11th-century hilltop temple which was constructed using bricks and laterite. The method of construction is interesting as the bricks were partially baked, then the walls were erected and finally wood was piled around the walls and a fire lit to finish the baking process. This accounts for the burnt appearance of some of the walls. Sadly much of the temple was destroyed by fighting between the Khmer

Rouge and Lon Nol troops as well as aerial bombing. There are stupendous views of the surrounding countryside and Tonle Om, the lake expanded by the Khmer Rouge. Also look for the straight irrigation canals built by the Khmer Rouge using slave labour.

Turning back towards Phnom Penh along Route 2, take the turn-off at the 39km stone towards **Phnom Ta Mau**. The temple area is a further 3km along the road and there is an entrance fee of 1,000 riels. Large areas have been fenced off and inside are water birds, otters, deer and bears. This is a privately run zoo but the animals are very difficult to see because of the vegetation. The 7th-century temple is on a small hill which is a little difficult to find. The way up is by the many food stalls at the bottom of the hill. The temple is rather small and built around a huge boulder which is now exposed as most of the building has suffered from age and weather. There is a lovely view over the forest but it is noticeable that the trees are very young as heavy logging took place here during the Vietnam War. The timber was then sold to Vietnam.

Tonle Bati

Tonle Bati is a very popular place to visit, particularly at weekends when Cambodians travel the 33km from the capital to picnic on the banks of the Tonle Bati River and hire swan-shaped boats to while away the time. Numerous food stalls crowd the banks of the river. The 12th-century temple, **Ta Prohm**, built by King Jayavarman VII, close to the water, is a very attractive laterite building surrounded by a small garden. A large statue of Buddha stands at the heart of the temple. Look for the interesting bas-relief which shows a young woman carrying a box on her head and a man bowing to a larger woman. This tells of the young mother who gave birth with the assistance of the midwife, but failed to show proper respect and was condemned to carry the afterbirth of the baby in a box on her head for the rest

CAMBODIA'S FIRST ZOO
Phnom Ta Mau

Cambodia's first zoo was officially opened in January 2000 by Hun Sen. The site is already popular with tourists from Phnom Penh, especially at weekends, as it has long been a picnic site. The zoo has been an animal collection centre since 1995 and now houses over 500 animals, most confiscated from smugglers. Species in the zoo include lions, tigers, bears, birds and reptiles. Many animals native to Cambodia fled during the recent wars. The situation was aggravated with the increase in illegal logging which destroyed much of the animals' natural habitat.

The new tiger enclosure has been paid for by British-based Care for the Wild International. In total the zoo needs to raise US$105,000 annually to pay for food and medicines for all the animals.

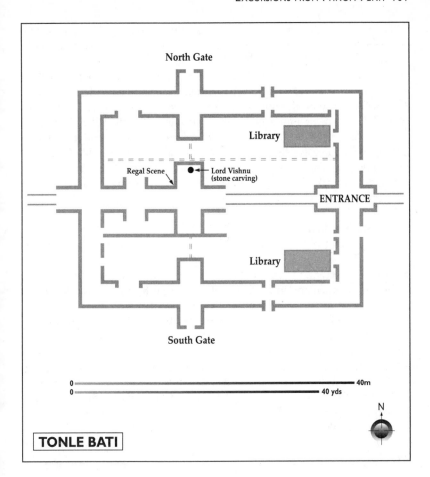

North Gate

Library

Regal Scene ← Lord Vishnu (stone carving)

ENTRANCE

Library

South Gate

0 ▬▬▬▬▬▬▬▬▬▬▬ 40m
0 ▬▬▬▬▬▬▬▬ 40 yds

N

TONLE BATI

of her life. The man is asking for forgiveness for his thoughtless wife. From time to time a group of young people play traditional instruments at the entrance to the temple. The five chambers and the linga inside were badly damaged by the Khmer Rouge.

Close by is another smaller temple, **Yeay Peau**, as well as a modern wat. Yeay Peau has an interesting legend attached to it. Peau was an attractive young woman who was loved by King Preah Ket Mealea. They had a baby son, Prohm, who was sent to live with his father at the court of Angkor. As an adult he returned to his mother but did not recognise her and asked for her hand in marriage as she was still very beautiful. He would not believe that she was his mother so Peau suggested that they each build a temple and if Prohm completed his first then he could marry her. The building took place at night and Peau, to ensure the outcome, created an early-morning star to fool the men helping Prohm. They went to sleep confident that Peau and her women helpers were nowhere near completion. Peau won the contest and Prohm acknowledged her as his mother.

The site is open every day and there is an entrance fee of US$2 per person.

If time allows it is perfectly possible to visit the temple of **Phnom Da** in one day from Phnom Penh, although you would need your own transport to take you on from Phnom Chisor. Alternatively, you could overnight in **Takeo** at the Phnom Sonlong Guesthouse and then arrange transport to the town of Angkor Borei and on to Phnom Da by boat. During the rainy season the area around Takeo turns into a huge lake and then it is only possible to reach Angkor Borei by boat. Phnom Da is a 9th-century laterite tower at the top of a hill which affords excellent views of the surrounding countryside. The town of Angkor Borei appears of little interest but was a centre of the state of Funan and there is a small museum in town which is worth visiting to understand the significance of the area.

Kirirom National Park

This is one of the few national parks in Cambodia and one that is easily accessible from Phnom Penh along Route 4. The area used to be popular with French colonists and there were a number of villas including a royal residence, all now abandoned and in ruins, mainly destroyed by the Khmer Rouge. Its accessibility from the capital makes it very popular at the weekend when tourists enjoy the cool forests, waterfalls and lakes. Turn right approximately 80km from Phnom Penh at the sign 'Preah Suramarit Kossomak National Park'. The entrance to the park is around 20km from Route 4 and there is an entrance fee of 3,000 riels for a car and its occupants. The road gradually climbs until a few pine trees appear and the main road ends up at the remains of an old house overlooking a large lake and the surrounding forest. Another road trails down to a river and a small waterfall on several levels with numerous wooden platforms used for picnics. There are believed to be a number of animals in the park such as tigers and leopards but these are rarely seen.

Southern Cambodia

SIHANOUKVILLE

Kampong Som was the original name for the town which has only been in existence since 1955 when the area was selected to be the main port for Cambodia following independence from France. During French colonial times most goods had been transported up the 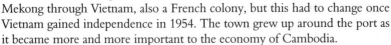 Mekong through Vietnam, also a French colony, but this had to change once Vietnam gained independence in 1954. The town grew up around the port as it became more and more important to the economy of Cambodia.

Sihanoukville is currently the only beach resort in Cambodia. Its lovely beaches are becoming very popular as a place to relax at the end of a tour of the country or as an escape from Phnom Penh for expats living there. Its attractions are many with four beaches, a choice of islands and watersports. For many years there have been rumours of a massive development planned by a Malaysian consortium, but this never materialised although new hotels and casinos have quietly opened. The unrest throughout Cambodia prior to the elections in 1997 was a blow to tourism here but once again Sihanoukville is attracting tourists, especially at the weekends.

Getting there and away

The town is reached along the busiest and best road in Cambodia, Route 4, taking approximately 3.5 hours from Phnom Penh. The downside is that many large lorries thunder along this route from the port to the capital, although most do travel at night. Trucks used to have to travel in convoy because of the security situation but the improvement in security during the early part of 1999 means that this is no longer a problem. Note the roadside spirit houses clustered together at Phnom Pichnil on Route 4 where travellers make offerings of bananas to the deities for a safe journey.

By air

There used to be regular flights between Phnom Penh and Sihanoukville as the land journey was very difficult. Since Route 4 was reconstructed using US funds in 1992/3 there has been no need for flights and until spring 2000 the airport was closed. Phnom Penh Airways have just introduced a stop at Sihanoukville on their flights between Phnom Penh and Koh Kong so the airport may fully reopen if there is demand.

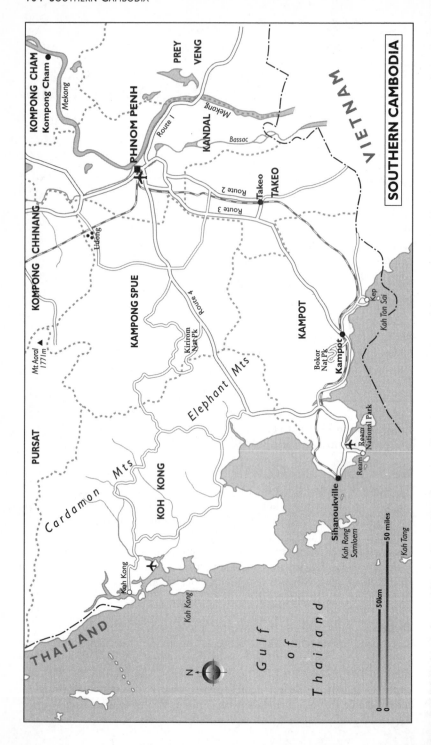

By boat

Sihanoukville can be reached by boat from Thailand (see the *Practical Information* chapter for details of border crossings). There is a daily speedboat from west of the town's port to Koh Kong, stopping at Koh Sdach. The journey time is 90 minutes to Koh Sdach and 3.5 hours to Koh Kong. The speedboat leaves Koh Kong at 07.30 and the return trip departs Sihanoukville at 12.00.

The entrance to the dock is through a gate marked 'Port of Passenger Ship'. The one-way fare is US$15 and tickets can only be bought the day of departure at the ticket office in the wooden building by the speedboats. The ticket office does not currently have a telephone. There is a small café and toilets for the use of passengers.

By bus

Three bus companies offer frequent services between Phnom Penh and Sihanoukville with a journey time of 3.5 hours along excellent Route 4. Each company has its own small bus station in Sihanoukville.

Phnom Penh Ho Wah Genting Transport Company Ltd 1D Ekareach St, Sihanoukville; tel/fax: 034 933888. This is the largest bus company. It has four services daily from Phnom Penh departing at 07.30, 08.30, 12.30 and 13.30. The return buses from Sihanoukville to Phnom Penh leave at 07.00, 08.00, 12.15 and 14.00. In Phnom Penh buses depart from near the Central Market. The one-way fare is 10,000 riels.

GST Export Bus Co Ekareach St, Sihanoukville. GST also have four buses daily between Phnom Penh and Sihanoukville departing at 07.15, 08.15, 12.30 and 13.30 in both directions. In Phnom Penh buses depart from near the Central Market. The one-way fare is 10,000 riels and 18,000 riels return.

DH Cambodia Group Ekareach St, Sihanoukville. DH have two buses per day in both directions departing at 07.30 and 12.30. The one-way fare is 10,000 riels. Buses depart from near the Central Market in Phnom Penh.

By train

There is one train on alternate days between Phnom Penh and Sihanoukville departing at 06.30 and arriving at 17.00. Trains leave Phnom Penh on Monday, Wednesday, Friday and Sunday and return on Tuesday, Thursday and Saturday. The journey is agonisingly slow and uncomfortable and it is far better to take the bus or a taxi. The railway station is close to the port and is very run down with no facilities.

By taxi

Shared long-distance taxis depart from the market area for Phnom Penh. A seat inside a pickup truck costs 6,000 riels and 5,000 riels on the back. The journey in a car costs 10,000 riels per person and takes around three hours. Taxis to Kampot also leave from here; the fare in a pickup is around 8,000 riels and the journey time is 3–4 hours. Taxis to Sihanoukville leave from near the Central Market in Phnom Penh and from near the Total station in Kampot.

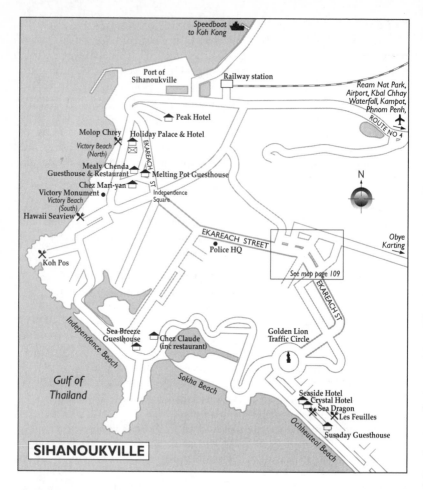

Getting around

The layout of the town is difficult to understand as much of it is nestled in the hills overlooking the sea and is rather spread out on a peninsula.

Motos are the main way to travel around Sihanoukville and a fare of 1,000–1,500 riels can be negotiated. Ensure you settle on a price before leaving as there have been reports of some drivers overcharging. Prices are likely to be higher at night. Alternatively motorbikes can be hired from an office at the GST bus station on Ekareach Street (tel: 034 933826) at a cost of US$5 per day. Passports have to be left at the office as security and any damage has to be paid for. Do check first that your travel insurance policy covers you for motorbike transport, as some don't. The Melting Pot Guesthouse (see *Accommodation* for details) also hires out motorbikes and mountain bikes. Cars can generally be arranged through your guesthouse or by negotiating with one of the taxis in the market. Expect to pay around US$15–20 for one day.

Accommodation

Currently there are far more places to stay in Sihanoukville than there are visitors so prices are competitive and hotel owners are sometimes open to negotiations, apart from at weekends and during public holidays. The layout of the town means that the centre is a long way from the beaches and as most people prefer to be near a beach I have mainly included hotels near or with easy access to this area.

First class
Peak Hotel Krom1, Mondol 1, Khan Mittapheap, Sihanoukville; tel: 034 320301; fax: 034 320300. Opened in July 1999, this Thai-owned hotel's main raison d'être seems to be the casino, although it is currently the best hotel in town. Located on a hill overlooking the port it is surrounded by pleasant gardens including a small zoo. The hotel offers a free transfer service to the town and beaches for guests. Other facilities include bar, restaurant, swimming pool, tennis courts, nightclub and karaoke. The casino is a favourite with Thais who come by boat from the Koh Kong border crossing for a few days' gambling (which is illegal in Thailand). Security is strict at the casino and all visitors must pass through an X-ray machine. Guns, grenades and knives are banned as are uniforms, helmets, shorts and vests. Rooms cost US$40–60 including breakfast.

Holiday Palace & Hotel Victory Beach; tel: 034 933807; fax: 034 933809. Another hotel with casino which is proving popular. It was being extended at the time of my visit. Good location just off Victory Beach. Rooms all have air conditioning and satellite TV. US$40–65.

Standard class
Seaside Hotel Ochheuteal Beach, Sihanoukville; tel: 034 933641/662; fax: 034 933640. This hotel has a great location on Ochheuteal beach and has been extensively renovated, making it very popular with weekenders from Phnom Penh. The rooms are bright and large with air conditioning, satellite TV and IDD. There is also a small restaurant. Rooms cost US$25–50 including breakfast.

Crystal Hotel Ochheuteal Beach, Sihanoukville; tel: 034 933523. Located next to the Seaside Hotel, this was being seriously renovated at the time of my visit and possibly extended in order to compete with its neighbour. Rooms likely to be of a similar standard to the Seaside Hotel so worth telephoning to check rates.

Chez Claude Sihanoukville; tel: 012 824870 (mobile); fax: 034 320032. Not the easiest place to find but everybody seems to know it and it has panoramic views over Independence Beach and Sokha Beach, although it is located on a hill inland. The owner, Claude, has lived in Cambodia for over seven years and the restaurant and guestroom reflect his fondness for the country. Much work is ongoing as it only opened at the end of 1998 but it is far from a building site. Quite the opposite, in fact, as it is so tranquil. The main business is currently the restaurant and bar (see page 109) but there is one bungalow with bathroom and private terrace which sleeps up to four people in two rooms. Claude will build up to 12 more bungalows in the future. The existing bungalow costs US$30 and the new ones will cost US$20. He can also arrange boat trips to the islands; the price depends on the destination. Trips to the nearest islands cost US$55 including use of diving equipment.

Sea Breeze Guesthouse Independence Beach, Sihanoukville; tel: 034 320217; 012 870423 (mobile). Set back from Independence Beach this smart-looking hotel has a lovely lobby and friendly staff. The 17 rooms all have simple bathrooms, air conditioning and satellite TV but smell rather damp. Single rooms cost US$15 and twin rooms US$25–30. No restaurant but there are plenty of food stalls on the beach.
Hawaii Hotel Ekareach St, Sihanoukville; tel: 034 933447. This Hong-Kong-owned, newly renovated hotel on the main street in town is of a good standard although many of the rooms have no window. The 34 rooms have private bathroom, air conditioning and satellite TV, and there is also a laundry service. Singles cost US$20 and twins US$25. Breakfast can be bought at the restaurant next door.

Budget

Chez Mari-yan Sankat 3, Khanmettapheap, Sihanoukville; tel: 034 933709. I hesitated to include this in the budget section as it is a wonderful place but the room prices put it at the cheaper end of the market. Set on a hill overlooking Victory Beach, Chez Mari-yan has ten rooms in traditional bungalows and six guestrooms. All have private bathrooms. The bungalow rooms are simple but adequate with fan and mosquito net and have lovely views. The guestrooms are very small, more basic and lower down so they do not enjoy the sea views. All rooms have private bathroom. The terrace restaurant serves mainly Khmer food but there are some Western dishes. The bungalow rooms cost US$10 and US$15 and the guestrooms US$5 each.
Semsak Hotel Ekareach St, Sihanoukville; tel: 034 320169; 015 831373 (mobile); email: marlin@camintel.com.kh. Located on Sihanoukville's main street this hotel, above the Marlin Bar and Grill (see Restaurant/Bar section), has 18 good rooms with private bathroom, air conditioning and satellite TV. Single rooms cost US$10 and twins US$10–15. Breakfast is extra.
Mealy Chenda Guesthouse & Restaurant Victory Beach, Sihanoukville; tel: 034 933472. Set back from the beach but with a great terrace restaurant (see page 110), this family-run establishment has 18 rooms with bathroom and fan. Another 20 rooms are being built and will be ready by the time this book is published. Singles cost US$6 and twins US$7. Breakfast is extra.
Angkor Inn Sophakmangkol St, Sangkat 2 Khan Mittapheap, Sihanoukville; tel: 034 933615. Very friendly owner attracts long-stay residents to this small, modern guesthouse just off the main street in the town centre. The 14 simple rooms all have their own bathroom and fan. Singles cost US$4 and twins US$6.
Melting Pot Guesthouse, hill overlooking Victory Beach, Sihanoukville; tel: 034 320285. Popular British-owned guesthouse opened in 1999 with small bar/restaurant serving Western and Indian food. Hires out bicycles, motorbikes and boats. Great meeting place for travellers to swap stories and information. Four small rooms with simple bathroom (cold water) and fan. Singles US$3 and twins US$4.
Susaday Guesthouse Ochheuteal Beach, Sihanoukville; tel: 034 320156. French-owned guesthouse also opened in 1999 with six simple rooms with private bathroom (cold water) and fan. Six more rooms with air conditioning will be built in 2000 but these will be more expensive. Lovely terrace restaurant facing the beach serving Khmer food adapted for Western tastes. Rooms with fan cost US$10 each.

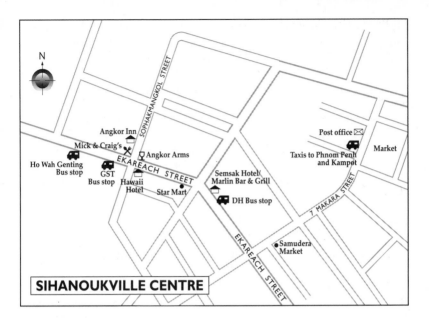

SIHANOUKVILLE CENTRE

Restaurants/bars

Angkor Arms Ekareach St, Sihanoukville; tel: 034 933847; 012 831608 (mobile). Part of the nightlife since 1996 this English-style pub was taken over by Bert in November 1999 and his bonhomie has brought a new lease of life to the place. Serves English pub grub at reasonable prices. Open 17.00–24.00; cold beer and warm welcome guaranteed.

Chez Claude Sihanoukville; tel: 012 824870 (mobile); fax: 034 320032. Stunning views across to the sea and Sokha Beach from the terrace restaurant/bar. Food served is mainly international with an excellent wine list. Interesting bar shaped as a boat. A little difficult to find but everybody in town knows its location.

Sea Dragon Restaurant Ochheuteal Beach, Sihanoukville; tel: 034 933671. Good Khmer, seafood and international food at reasonable prices. Great location by the beach and close to the hotels. Large terrace and friendly service. Open for Western breakfast.

Les Feuilles Restaurant Ochheuteal Beach, Sihanoukville; tel: 034 320156. Set one block back from the beach in a lovely garden setting. The excellent choice of food and good service make this a popular place. Billiards also available. Open for breakfast.

Molop Chrey Restaurant Mittapheap District, Victory Beach, Sihanoukville; tel: 034 933708. Open-air restaurant set in the trees by Victory Beach serving extensive Khmer menu including some interesting dishes such as lizard and boar. Plenty of seafood included. Not the cheapest place but always busy.

Hawaii Seaview Restaurant Mittapheap District, Victory Beach, Sihanoukville; tel: 034 933659. Large, open-air restaurant by the beach frequented by both locals and visitors. Extensive menu including excellent seafood. Similar prices to Molop Chrey Restaurant so again not particularly cheap.

Koh Pos Restaurant Sihanoukville; tel: 012 872825 (mobile). Open-air restaurant in a great setting right on the sandy beach on the point between Independence and Victory beaches. Excellent selection of Asian and Western food. A great favourite with visitors.
Mealy Chenda Restaurant Victory Beach, Sihanoukville; tel: 034 933472. Rooftop restaurant with views over the sea attached to the guesthouse. Serves good Khmer and international food at budget prices.
Mick & Craig's Sophakmangkol St, Sangkat 2 Khan Mittapheap, Sihanoukville; tel: 034 933615. Opposite the Angkor Arms, this small café serves Western food at good prices and is open 08.00–02.00.
Marlin Bar & Grill Ekareach St, Sihanoukville; tel: 034 320169; 015 831373 (mobile); emailmarlin@camintel.com.kh. Western food served from 07.00 until late. Relaxed, friendly atmosphere.

Practical information
Currency exchange
To change US dollars cash into riels in Sihanoukville it is best to go to the gold stalls in the market.

Travellers' cheques can only be exchanged in the banks such as the Canadia Bank (open Mon–Fri 07.30–15.30 and Sat 07.30–11.30) and the First Overseas Bank (open Mon–Fri 08.30–15.30 and Sat 08.30–11.30), both on Ekareach Street, where there is a commission charge of 2%. The Cambodia Commercial Bank (open Mon–Fri 08.00–15.00) can advance cash on credit cards and the commission rate is 4%.

Banks are open from Monday to Friday generally between 07.00 and 15.30, although times vary from bank to bank. They are closed at the weekend, although a few may open on Saturday mornings.

Post office
Located opposite the market and next to the long-distance taxi station, the office sells stamps and phonecards for the Camintel street phones which can be used to make international calls. It is open every day from 06.00 to 20.00.

There are several Camintel street phones around town and phonecards can be bought from shops close to each phone.

Email and the internet
The internet only arrived in Sihanoukville during 1999 and therefore prices are still high and connection somewhat erratic.

The Marlin Bar & Grill on Ekareach Street offers an email and internet service, although it is rather expensive. The rates are 40 cents per minute online and 20 cents per minute offline. There is a minimum charge of US$2.

It is also possible to use the internet at ABC Computer where the charges are US$2 for every 15 minutes. It costs 3,000 riels to send one email message.

Shopping
Psah Leu is the main market in town selling fruit, vegetables and toiletries. Star Mart on Ekareach Street (attached to the Caltex petrol station) sells a range of

imported food, drink and toiletries. Samudera Market on 7 Makara Street also sells imported food including meat, cheese, wine and chocolates so is ideal if you are having withdrawal symptoms during your stay in Sihanoukville.

What to see and do
Most people make their way to Sihanoukville for the beautiful sandy beaches. There are four in total, the main one being **Ochheuteal Beach** which is a long, wide stretch of sand with some protection from trees and a few palm-leaved shelters. **Independence** and **Victory** beaches are mainly very narrow and tend to be relatively busy because of the number of excellent restaurants nearby and their proximity to guesthouses. There are food stalls or restaurants by these three beaches. **Sokha Beach** is long with plenty of shade, a small restaurant and a few vendors and is really quite delightful.

The port area is a fascinating place to explore as it is a hive of activity with boats jostling to unload their goods and hundreds of sinewy men plying to and fro carrying the most impossible loads. Close by is a fishing village which is very photogenic, although rather smelly because of the fish being dried in the sun. A good time to visit the village is at the end of the day when all the boats leave for the night fishing.

Sports
Unlike other towns in Cambodia where there are more cultural pursuits to be followed, Sihanoukville is ideal for those who enjoy activities, particularly watersports.

Go-Kart fans will enjoy a spin on the track at Obye Karting, 2km from the market on Omui street. Owned by a Frenchman, Pierre, the track is open every day from 10.00 to 22.00 and the price for 30 minutes is US$14. Tel: 015 347001 (mobile).

Diving trips can be arranged through the Marlin Bar on Ekareach Street, Chez Claude on 012 824870 (mobile) and at Nagadive which is located on Ochheuteal Beach opposite the military base.

Excursions from Sihanoukville
The islands
There are a few interesting excursions to be taken from the town. A boat trip to some of the islands such as **Koh Pos**, **Koh Tas** and **Koh Rong Samloem** is a must. The beaches are totally unspoilt and there are snorkelling and even scuba diving opportunities on some of the islands. The best scuba diving is around **Koh Tang** and **Koh Prins** but both these islands would require an overnight stay camping on the beach or sleeping on the boat deck. Small boats can be hired for around US$25 from the fishermen along the beaches or contact Claude at Chez Claude (see page 109 for details). Steve at the Marlin Bar may be able to arrange boat hire as well. At the time of writing he no longer had a boat as it had sunk a few months earlier, but it is highly probable that he will acquire another at some stage.

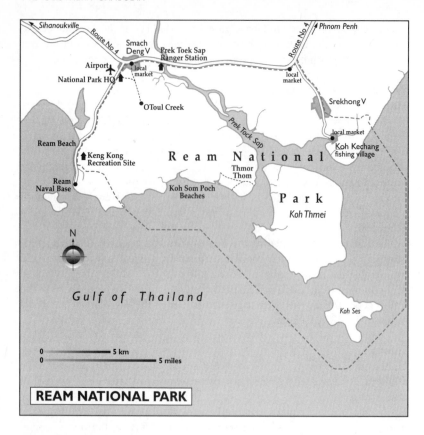

REAM NATIONAL PARK

Ream National Park

The park is 20km from town (along Route 4) close to the little-used airport and also home to the Cambodian navy. It was established in 1993 and the UN have introduced rangers and developed a park management programme including access for visitors. The park has lowland evergreen forest and mangroves along the river and coastal zone; coral reef and seagrass beds; 155 species of birds including fishing eagles and some threatened ones such as the lesser adjutant, milky and woolly-necked storks; and several other wildlife species such as monkeys, wild pigs, cats and reptiles.

Park rangers take boat trips along the Prek Toek Sap river through mangroves to some of the beaches on the mainland or on the island of Koh Thmei. They also guide half-day walks to OToul Creek and Meditation Mountain which has panoramic views of the park. A half-day boat trip costs US$20 for up to four people and US$5 for each additional person up to a maximum of twelve. Guided walks cost US$3 per person.

Ream also has its own secluded beach which is rarely visited except on public holidays. There is very basic accommodation near the beach for US$5 per room and visitors are welcome to eat with the rangers at the park headquarters.

To arrange a boat trip or guided walk or to reserve accommodation it is necessary to contact the park headquarters which is opposite Keng Kong Airport (the airport for Sihanoukville) or telephone 015 914174. The park can be reached by taxi or moto from the market in Sihanoukville.

Kbal Chhay waterfalls

North from town along Route 4, these are a wonderful location for a picnic lunch. The falls are easily reached by a new laterite road and are a series of pools and waterfalls in a delightful setting. Picnic platforms are placed around the waterfall area taking advantage of the little shade available here. Make sure you use a strong sunscreen and wear a hat as there are hardly any trees under which to shelter. However, it is a great place to cool off by swimming in the pools and is very popular at weekends.

KOH KONG

The only reason any traveller would go to Koh Kong is to use it as an overnight stop when travelling between Cambodia and Thailand. The town is very quiet, although quite pleasant, and there is a wat on a small hill and a Cham village nearby. The **Koh Pich Hotel** close to the pier has clean rooms with air conditioning and private bathroom for 300 baht in a single and 400 baht in a twin. Bungalow-style accommodation is available at the **Morokat Motel** with the same facilities for 300 baht. Many of the other guesthouses which proliferate throughout the town only rent rooms by the hour!

Details of the boat service are given in *Chapter 3* on page 40. Both President Airlines and Phnom Penh Airways have a flight between Phnom Penh and Koh Kong and President Airlines also have a link to Siem Reap. The fares with President Airlines are US$65 single and US$115 return on both the Phnom Penh and Siem Reap routes. Phnom Penh Airways is slightly cheaper at US$55 single and US$95 return from Phnom Penh. Details of the timetable are also given in *Chapter 3*.

KAMPOT

Kampot is a sleepy town with a very charming riverside area which has a few old French colonial buildings. There is little of interest in the town but it does make a good base for excursions to the crumbling hill station of Bokor and the abandoned beach resort of Kep. Kampot is reached along Route 3 which varies from good to bad and the journey from Phnom Penh takes around three hours. A fun place to stop is at Sruk Kandal Steng which has a weir where small fish can be seen jumping up against the flow of the water.

A poor road from Kampot follows the coast much of the way until it meets up with Route 4 to Sihanoukville. It is a very attractive route passing between the hills on which Bokor is situated on one side and the coast and numerous Cham fishing villages on the other. The road from Kampot to Route 4 is lined with very simple villages without electricity where life has changed little in decades. On reaching Route 4 the transition is dramatic as the fast road is lined with smart houses, shops, petrol stations and neon lights.

Getting there and away
By train
The run-down railway station is on the outskirts of town. The service between Phnom Penh and Sihanoukville stops at Kampot and the one-way fare is 2,800 riels. The train leaves Phnom Penh on Monday, Wednesday, Friday and Sunday and returns from Sihanoukville on Tuesday, Thursday and Saturday.

In February 2000 a unique event took place when a renovated steam train (Pacific 231) travelled the route between Phnom Penh and Kampot for the first time in over 30 years. There are plans for this luxury train to make further trips in the future so keep an eye on the local press for dates.

By taxi
Shared long-distance taxis depart from Psah Dumkor Market near the Intercontinental Hotel in Phnom Penh and drop off at the station in Kampot near the Total station. The fare in a car is 8,000 riels per person and 6,000 riels in a minibus and the journey takes 2–3 hours. The latest time to start the trip is around midday as many taxi drivers will not leave after this time. Taxis also depart for Sihanoukville from Kampot and the fare is 7,000 riels. The road is mainly laterite so can be pretty churned up at the end of the rainy season. The journey takes between two and three hours depending on road conditions at the time.

Getting around
Cars with drivers can be hired from the Phnom Kamchay Hotel (see below for contact details) for excursions in the vicinity for US$15–20 per day. A 4WD vehicle, again with driver, can be hired from the Marco Polo Restaurant (see below) for trips to Bokor hill station. A motorbike with driver can be rented from the Phnom Kamchay Hotel for US$10 per day for trips to Kep.

Accommodatiom
Blue Mountain (Phnom Khieu) Hotel Kampot; tel: 015 831851 (mobile); 012 820923 (mobile). Located in the town centre the hotel is rather functional but is bright and clean with 30 rooms with bathroom, air conditioning and satellite TV. Rooms cost US$15 each. There is no restaurant.

Phnom Kamchay Hotel & Restaurant Kampot; tel: 033 932916. Opposite the Blue Mountain Hotel this busy place has its own restaurant popular with the locals. The 41 rooms have bathroom, air conditioning and satellite TV and cost US$12 for singles, US$15 for twin and US$20 for triples. Breakfast is extra.

Hotel Bory Borkor Kampot; tel: 033 932826. Located behind Phnom Kamchay Hotel on Route 3, this good hotel, opened in 1998, has 52 rooms all with air conditioning and private bathrooms, also its own restaurant. Rooms cost US$15 single, US$20 twin and US$25 triple, excluding breakfast.

Marco Polo Guesthouse Kampot; tel: 015 330166 (mobile). This is mainly a restaurant (see *Restaurant/Bar* section) but it also has two simple rooms upstairs with shared basic bathroom. Each room costs US$5.

Ta Eng Guesthouse Kampot. Just down the road from the Marco Polo Restaurant this popular guesthouse has seven simple rooms with fan and mosquito net. Three of

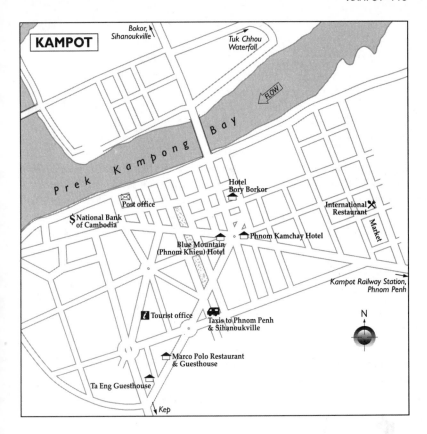

the rooms have their own basic bathroom and cost US$6 each; the four rooms with shared basic bathroom are US$5 each.

Restaurants/bars

Restaurant Marco Polo Kampot; tel: 015 330166 (mobile). Small, pleasant restaurant serving European food. It's mainly Italian as the owner is from Italy, but has a surprisingly unimaginative menu. Breakfast is more British – you can get cornflakes! – and the menu includes meals such as egg and chips. The food is rather indifferent and a little pricey but the staff are wonderfully friendly. There is talk that the restaurant may move to one of the properties by the river so check before making your way there.

International Restaurant 66 St 177, Kampot; tel: 033 932868. At the time of writing this restaurant was closed waiting for an upturn in visitors to Kampot. Located opposite the market, in the past it had a very good reputation so it's worth checking to see whether it has reopened.

Practical information

Currency exchange

The National Bank of Cambodia (the only bank) has a branch office on the road facing the river. At the moment they cannot exchange travellers'

KAMPOT TRADITIONAL MUSIC SCHOOL FOR HANDICAPPED AND ORPHANED CHILDREN

My travels around Cambodia have often brought me into contact with people who inspire and humble me when I learn how they have risen above terrible trauma and rebuilt their lives. My last visit there was no different, except this time it wasn't a Cambodian but a young British woman who, for me, was truly inspirational.

Catherine Geach studied and worked at the University of Fine Arts in Phnom Penh and felt that there was a role for her in reviving Cambodia's traditional Pin Peat and Mahouri music. Catherine herself is a solo violinist having graduated from the Royal Academy of Music in London. She established the school in 1994 and 25 orphaned, abandoned or disabled children now live there together with eight day students from very poor homes, all aged between seven and 19 years. Here Catherine and her Cambodian staff care for them, educate them and teach them about the rich culture of Khmer music and dance.

What is so striking about the school is the feeling of happiness and love everywhere. The dormitories, classrooms, dining room and bathrooms are very neat and simple but the children have everything they need, including each other, an education up to the age of 16 years (and therefore a bright future) and constant support from Catherine and her dedicated staff.

Catherine first came to Cambodia in 1991 and it has now been her home for the past nine years to the extent that she rarely speaks English, being

cheques and do not accept credit cards for cash advances, although this may change during 2000/1 when a private bank is rumoured to be opening a branch. The exchange rate is better in the market so very few people find their way to the bank which is not signposted and is not obviously a bank, more a run-down colonial residence. It is located next to Virean Hong Kong restaurant/hotel and National Bank guesthouse. I had to go through a door at the back and there is no public area to conduct business. English is not spoken although some of the older staff may speak a little French. The opening hours are 07.00–11.00 and 14.00–17.00 Monday to Friday.

Post office

Service in the post office is restricted to sending mail and parcels and it has no facilities for international calls. The post is sent up to Phnom Penh for onward despatch on Monday and Thursday.

The office is located on the road facing the river, quite close to the bridge. Open Monday to Saturday 07.30–11.00 and 14.30–17.00.

There are no public telephones in Kampot but there are several phone shops around town from where you can make international calls and send faxes.

fluent in Khmer. She now speaks her mother tongue with an accent and has a little difficulty in remembering some English words. Her demeanour has become Cambodian and, being a classical dancer, she moves with extraordinary grace. What is even more remarkable is that she can only be in her late twenties.

The children are accomplished musicians now and their skills include music theory and history so that their knowledge can be handed down to future generations. Catherine's success with the school has allowed the children to perform their music overseas and they have even produced two CDs of traditional music. From time to time Catherine appears in concert in Europe playing classical, Irish and Cambodian music.

The school is sponsored by Caritas Netherlands and Terre des Hommes (Netherlands) but there is always a need to find sponsors for the future should the situation change. Catherine's approach to the school is very low key and she prefers to work quietly with the children. Visits are not encouraged unless there is a genuine interest in music and education and then appointments should be made in advance.

Any organisation or individuals interested in helping Catherine and her staff with their work should contact them via the Khmer Cultural Development Institute, c/o PACT, PO Box 149, Central Post Office, Phnom Penh; tel: 033 932992; fax: 023 426746; or write direct to the school in Kampot town (there is no street name so just put the school name and the town). Catherine also runs a music and dance therapy project in Sarajevo, Bosnia Hercegovina.

Excursions from Kampot
Bokor Hill Station and National Park

One of the most interesting excursions is to the abandoned hill station of Bokor, which is now a national park. The French established Bokor in the 1920s because of the relative coolness here. At its zenith it had a hotel, casino, church and a few villas. The royal family even had a residence here. The civil war brought an end to the high life and it became far too dangerous to visit.

Bokor is reached by travelling along the road from Kampot to Sihanoukville and then turning right after approximately 10km to the entrance of the park. (The road was closed until 1998 because it was controlled by the Khmer Rouge and/or bandits and mined extensively; the UN has cleared the mines.) There is an entrance fee of US$2 and the park ranger hands over a black plastic sack for any rubbish. Journeys up to the hill station must be started before noon as the road is very narrow and two cars could not pass en route. It takes around two hours to reach the abandoned town from Kampot, but only one hour to return. There are plans to improve the road to Bokor but investment is needed to do this and no potential investors have come forward as yet.

The first 10km of road to the park entrance are in good condition, but thereafter it deteriorates dramatically into little more than a track and the next 32km climb is very bumpy and slow. After about 10km there is a wooden building where snacks, fruit and water can be bought as there is nothing at the very top.

The first ruins can be seen about 10km from the top of the hill. Here are the ruins of King Monivong's residence dating from the 1920s. At the very top, on a windswept plateau there are derelict houses dotted around, a church and a very large casino/hotel. Exploring the ruins of the casino gives an idea of the elegant lifestyle enjoyed by the French. It is almost possible to imagine you can hear the roll of dice and laughter of the people at the gaming tables. The view from the ramshackle terrace is stupendous and overlooks the coast and the road from Kampot to Sihanoukville.

There is a small, isolated guesthouse at the top with very simple rooms costing US$5 per person. Food has to be ordered in advance so that the staff can go into Kampot to buy it.

Three kilometres before the top the road divides and 4km to the right are the **Popovil Falls**. The road fizzles out and then there is a 2km walk along a track to the top of the falls. In the dry season it is possible to cross the rocky riverbed and clamber down to the bottom of the falls which are on two levels. This can be a little tricky, so good footwear is definitely needed, but it is worthwhile. You are quite likely to see elephant dung as you walk along, but there have been very few sightings of the elephants themselves.

Elsewhere in the park, despite the logging that has taken place there, over 300 species of birds have been recorded such as the great hornbill, which is thriving, and endangered species such as the grey-headed fish eagle, rufous-winged buzzard, blue-eared kingfisher, crow-billed drongo, chestnut-headed partridge and green peafowl.

Waterfalls and caves

If time allows there are some pleasant waterfalls and interesting caves in the area around Kampot. **Tuk Chhou** is a rather unspectacular waterfall reached by crossing the bridge out of town en route to Sihanoukville, and then turning right and driving for about 8km. The spot is popular with the locals at weekends and a lovely spot for a picnic.

Fairly close to the road between Kampot and Kep are a series of large caves which are holy sites. **Phnom Sia** is a must-see, as much for the riot of colour provided by the flame trees when they are in flower as for the caves. A series of paths and steps take you to various large caverns with stalactites inside. Although not the most spectacular of caves they are little visited apart from the few locals who come to pray at the shrines and altars which are dotted around.

Boat trips

Boats can be hired from the Marco Polo Restaurant (see page 114 for contact details) for trips to one of the islands or upriver. Boat hire ranges from US$30 to US$50 depending on the destination. The boats depart from near the bridge crossing the river.

KEP

A visit to Kep, 26km from Kampot, is as eerie as going to Bokor. This was a thriving, fashionable beach resort, established by the French, with many lovely villas along the waterfront until it was destroyed in the 1970s. Now it is very difficult to see the layout of the town as the forest has claimed many of the ravaged buildings and completely covered the derelict ones. Often the only evidence that a villa existed is the wall surrounding a property or an archway entrance, devoid of the metal gates. Other buildings have fared better but most are uninhabitable. People certainly live in the area but there are no schools, shops, banks or post offices – absolutely nothing.

The resort is still an attraction and can be busy at weekends. The beach is attractive but small and the sand is not the lovely white of the Sihanoukville beaches. Numerous tables are spread along the wall running along the beach and these serve the most delicious, fresh seafood. Once the order is taken the waitress disappears on a motorbike and comes back 15 minutes later clutching bowls of piping hot food.

Many people visit Kep from Kampot but it is possible to stay overnight here although the range of accommodation is limited.

Accommodation

Krong Kep Hotel & Restaurant Pliauv Kep, Kep; no telephone. No longer a restaurant, although the sign outside still claims this, the hotel is rather run down now. This must have been the best hotel in town in its heyday but now it just feels neglected, although there is a caretaker on site should any guests arrive. The 15 large rooms (US$7 each) all overlook the sea and each has its own bathroom and a fan. The generator is turned on for a few hours in the evening. Breakfast can be bought at the food stalls down the road.

Krong Kep Guesthouse Pliauv Kep, Kep. Just along the road from the hotel is a small guesthouse, also facing the sea, which appears livelier. It is family run and has six large rooms with simple bathroom and fan. Again there is only electricity for a few hours in the evening and breakfast can be bought at the nearby food stalls. Rooms cost US$5 each. The family can arrange boat trips to Koh Ton Sai for US$10 and the families on the island can provide picnic lunches.

Seaside Guesthouse Kep; tel: 012 820831 (mobile). Located on the road from Kampot before you reach the main beach area, this attractive house has three rooms with basic bathrooms and fan. Food can be provided by the family. The rooms cost US$8 each.

Le Bout Du Monde Guesthouse Kep; no telephone. Very simple accommodation close to the main beach and the waterfront restaurant tables. Rooms cost US$5 for a single and US$10 for a twin. Meals are extra.

Restaurants

There are no restaurants as such in Kep but there are food stalls by the beach or along the road which follows the coast. They all serve tasty and fresh seafood.

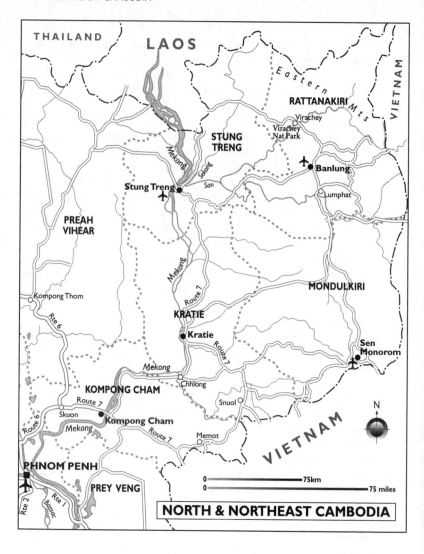

NORTH & NORTHEAST CAMBODIA

Northeast Cambodia
6

KOMPONG CHAM

Kompong Cham, on the banks of the Mekong River, is a pleasing town with some lovely colonial buildings and a busy waterfront area. Although a quiet, provincial town at the moment, the recent improvement of Route 7 to the town, the building of the bridge across the Mekong and eventually the upgrading of Route 7 onwards from Kompong Cham to the northeast will turn it into an important hub. There is already an air of prosperity because the speedboat from Phnom Penh to Kratie and Stung Treng stops here and the riverside bustles with activity in general, being on the all-important Mekong. Some say that the town has benefited from being the home town of the Prime Minister, Hun Sen.

Most people use Kompong Cham just as a starting point for their journey upriver to the northeast so don't explore it thoroughly. However, there are a few important temple sites within a few kilometres of town and a ferry ride across the river is a fun way of passing time.

Getting there and away

There is a very good road from Phnom Penh to Kompong Cham, Route 6 to Skuon and then Route 7. This journey takes 2.5 hours in total. The road is so good in places that there are even signs asking drivers to slow down when approaching towns en route. Kompong Cham is currently the end of the line for the good road and the only viable way to continue is by speedboat. However, this could change within the next two to three years as the Japanese are currently building a bridge across the Mekong at Kompong Cham and then there are plans to improve Route 7 to Kratie and eventually to Stung Treng and Rattanakiri.

By boat

Speedboats with 90–100 seats ply the Mekong from Kompong Cham to Phnom Penh in the south and Kratie and Stung Treng in the north. They leave from opposite the Mekong Hotel and tickets can be bought the day before. There is one boat a day between Phnom Penh and Kompong Cham which leaves Phnom Penh at 07.00 returning at 09.00 from Kompong Cham to Phnom Penh. The journey takes two hours and costs 15,000 riels. There are three boats to Kratie departing at 07.30, 08.30 and 09.30. The journey takes 3.5 hours with a few short stops at small towns and villages. Boats from Kratie to Kompong Cham depart at 06.00, 07.00 and 13.00. The one-way fare is 15,000 riels.

By bus

Phnom Penh Ho Wah Genting Transport (tel: 015 850784 mobile) operate a regular service between Phnom Penh (from close to the Central Market) and Kompong Cham (from the market, next to the long-distance taxi station). Buses leave Phnom Penh at 06.45, 07.45, 09.30, 11.30, 13.45 and 15.45 and Kompong Cham at 06.45, 07.45, 09.30, 12.30, 13.30 and 15.30. The one-way fare is 6,000 riels. The journey time is 2 hours 10 minutes in both directions.

By taxi

There are regular long-distance taxis between Phnom Penh and Kompong Cham. These depart from near the Central Market in Phnom Penh and by the market in Kompong Cham. A seat costs 7,000 riels in a car and 5,000 riels in a minibus. Cars take up to seven passengers and the minibuses 15 passengers.

Accommodation

Mekong Hotel Kompong Cham; tel: 042 941536; fax: 042 941465. The most popular hotel in Kompong Cham because of its riverside location. It has 60 bright clean rooms with air conditioning or fan, satellite TV and private bathroom. For some strange reason it has cavernous hallways on each floor. The rooms overlooking the river can be noisy in the early mornings but as most people are staying there to take the morning speedboat to Kratie this is an excellent alarm call. Rooms cost US$10 each and breakfast US$1.50.

Mittapheap Hotel Kompong Cham; tel: 042 941565; fax: 042 841465. Within walking distance of the river area, a simple hotel with 30 rooms, all air-conditioned with satellite TV and private bathroom. Not much character but the rooms are fine. No restaurant but the Apsara Restaurant is around the corner by the market and it serves breakfast. Rooms cost US$10 each.

Monorom Guest House Kompong Cham. Close to the river, this 17-room guesthouse is adequate. Each room has air conditioning or fan, satellite TV and simple bathroom. However, there is a noisy karaoke bar at the front of the building. Rooms cost US$12 with air conditioning and US$5 with fan. There is no restaurant.

Restaurants

There are numerous unnamed restaurants around the town and many food stalls in the market area. The **Apsara Restaurant** opposite the market is a good choice and not far to walk should your accommodation not provide breakfast.

Practical information

Currency exchange

The best rates for exchanging money are to be found at the jewellery stalls in the market. The Canadia Bank can exchange travellers' cheques with a commission rate of 2%. It cannot yet advance cash on credit cards. The bank is open Monday to Friday 08.00–15.30 and Saturday 08.00–11.00.

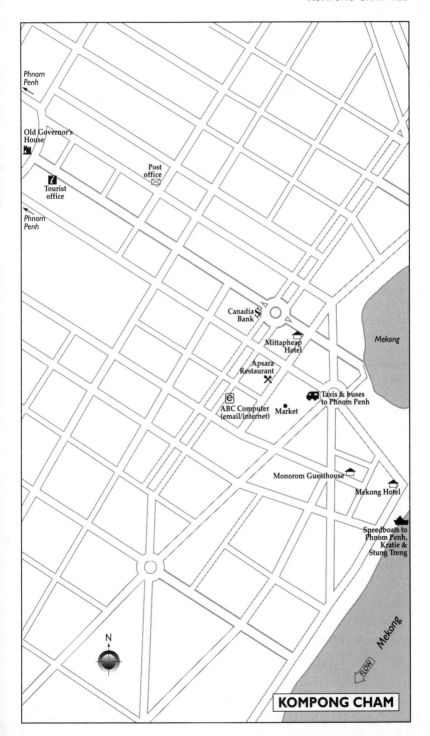

Post office
The post office sells stamps and Mobitel phonecards for the street phones. The post is sent to Phnom Penh on Tuesday, Wednesday and Friday for onward despatch. The office is open daily from 07.00 to 17.00.

Email and the internet
ABC Computer (tel: 042 941477) has an internet service for US$6 per hour with a charge of US$1 for each email sent. The office is open Monday to Saturday 07.00–19.00.

What to see
There is little of particular interest in the town itself other than it is an attractive, quiet town to walk around with a few colonial buildings. There is plenty of activity on the waterfront and this never fails to fascinate. En route to Kompong Cham, the village of **Skuon**, where Route 7 starts, has a most interesting roadside market. Women sell enormous fried spiders for 500 riels each. I am reliably informed that they taste like crab but they are rather crunchy as the skeleton is consumed at the same time. In order to prove that they are fresh the women hold bags full of live, writhing spiders and howl with laughter when one is placed on your chest for the obligatory photo. I declined this offer.

Further on towards Kompong Cham are two ancient temples, **Phnom Bros** and **Phnom Srei**. These temples represent man (Bros) and woman (Srei); Bros is a large temple on a small hill and Srei is a smaller temple on a higher hill. The legend attached to them tells that there was a competition held to see whether the men or the women could be the first to build their temple one night. The women lit an enormous fire to confuse the men by making them think it was morning; then the women went on to complete their temple first. Phnom Bros was originally wooden but has been rebuilt several times. It is currently under renovation again as much damage was caused by the Khmer Rouge. The area was used as a prison and a few mass graves were discovered at the foot of the hills. Many of the skulls have been stored in a derelict building close to several small stupas. Look for the small lion statue outside Phnom Bros where one side of the rear end has been flattened by the constant sharpening of the knives used to kill the prisoners. In order to bring villagers to the killing grounds without arousing their suspicions, the Khmer Rouge told them that they were being taken to inspect new housing. Loud music was played over loudspeakers to cover the sounds of the shots and the screams of the victims. At the back of the temple are a couple of food stalls selling fruit, but it is quickly obvious that the slightly nervous macaques in the trees above are the main customers. There are plans under way to landscape the area around the temples and make it easier to walk between the two hills.

Two kilometres from Kompong Cham is a fascinating 12th century temple called **Wat Nokor** which is remarkably well preserved. It is possible to see how the temple was constructed using individual blocks of stone without any evidence of cement holding them together. It can also be seen that the reliefs were carved after the building was erected as one face may be made up of two or more blocks of stone. Some of the temple appears to be on the point of collapse and it is a miracle that these parts stay upright. However, there are plans to preserve the temple actively rather than leave it to chance. There is also a legend attached to this temple. A young man returned after living in China for many years and unknowingly married his mother. When they found out the truth they had to build a temple to expunge their sins.

KRATIE

Sleepy Kratie (pronounced Kratchay) nestles on the banks of the Mekong River and very little disturbs its languid lifestyle. First sighting of the town is a pleasant one and you will not be disappointed. It is worthwhile strolling around the streets and along the riverbank, but the main places of any interest are out of town.

Getting there and away
By boat
Speedboats with 90–100 seats ply the Mekong to Kompong Cham in the south and Stung Treng in the north. They leave from opposite the Santepheap Hotel and tickets can be bought the day before at the small booth at the top of the steps leading down to the boat jetty. There are three boats to Kratie from Kompong Cham departing at 07.30, 08.30 and 09.30 and from Kratie to Kompong Cham departing at 06.00, 07.00 and 13.00. The one-way fare is 15,000 riels and the journey takes 3.5 hours with a few short stops at small towns and villages. The boat from Kompong Cham continues on to Stung Treng for another five hours and the fare is 25,000 riels.

By road
The road from Kompong Cham (Route 7) to Kratie is virtually impassable and, as there is an efficient boat service from there, very few people opt for the land route. However, long-distance taxis travel along the very bad 141km (also Route 7) from Kratie to Stung Treng every day. Only 4WD pickup trucks can attempt the journey and the vehicles have certainly seen better days. The route is peppered with enormous potholes and passengers inside and on the back are constantly thrown around. Unless you sit in the front passenger seat it only becomes bearable once you have passed through the pain barrier and can no longer feel your backside.

The whole route is guarded by very small groups of soldiers, although guarding mainly means dozing in hammocks. The driver's assistant, who sits on the back of the pickup to help push the vehicle out of holes or negotiate narrow bridges, throws a few hundred riels to the soldiers as the vehicle passes. Some soldiers don't even bother to show themselves and just set up bamboo tripods covered with a *krama* to indicate their presence and collect their dues. It is a strange system but one that works: the soldiers do not hassle the drivers as they need them to continue to use the route so that their meagre army income is supplemented. At the same time the drivers need the presence of the soldiers along the route to ensure their continued safety. One soldier actually stopped the car but then proceeded to hand bundles of money to the driver. On questioning it turned out that it was the wages for some of the soldiers further down the road and the driver was given handwritten instructions as to the exact location of the lucky recipients. What trust!

All along the route men were walking along carrying weapons and even hand-held rocket launchers. But at no stage did the soldiers try to extract more money because there was a foreigner in the taxi; in fact they almost seemed to lose interest on seeing me in there.

The journey takes six hours from Kratie to Stung Treng and the fare is 30,000 riels per person. Taxis leave from near the wat in Kratie.

Accommodation
Santepheap Hotel Kratie; tel: 072 971537. Good hotel overlooking the river, opposite the jetty where the speedboats dock. Has 20 rooms with air conditioning or fan, satellite TV and private bathroom with cold water only. No restaurant. Rooms cost US$15 with air conditioning and US$7 with fan.
Heng Heng Hotel Kratie; tel: 072 971405. Small hotel overlooking the river with 11 rooms but no restaurant. Adequate rooms with air conditioning or fan, satellite TV and simple private bathroom with cold water only. Rooms with air conditioning cost US$12 and US$6 with fan.

Restaurants
Phen Chhent Restaurant 22 St 9, Kratie. One of only two main restaurants in town serving excellent Khmer food, cooked to order.
Restaurant 30 December Kratie. Located opposite the river this place is popular with the resident NGOs. Not much to look at but very friendly service with excellent Khmer food. Also has a few rooms with shared bathroom for 10,000 riels.

Practical information
Currency exchange
The best place to change money is in the market. The National Bank of Cambodia, located in the centre of town between Streets 8 and 9, does not

exchange travellers' cheques but has plans to introduce this facility during 2000. There are no plans to bring in credit card transactions.

Post office
Located near the river end of Street 12 the office only deals with mail. The post is sent to Phnom Penh only six or seven times a month for onward delivery.

The only place to make international phone calls in Kratie is from the Camintel portakabins on Kosamak Street off Street 15. The portakabins were left behind by the UN in 1993.

What to see
Freshwater dolphins
The highlight of any visit to Kratie is to take a boat along the river to try to see some of the 60 freshwater dolphins that live there. The dolphins average 2 to 2.8m in length and weigh up to 180kg. Their numbers are dwindling but now a positive effort is being made to protect them. There is a viewing platform around 12km from Kratie and this can be reached by road or river. It is a peaceful location to watch for the dolphins and very rewarding when you do see them. Small speedboats can be hired from in front of the Santepheap Hotel for around US$20 and the owners take pride in making sure you see the dolphins. The local tourist office is planning to introduce its own boat trips at some stage so look out for information on arrival.

Sambok Pagoda
Ten kilometres north of Kratie, along the river road lined with typical wooden houses, many with original ornate roofs, is the Sambok Pagoda on a hilltop with stunning views of the Mekong. A small community of monks and nuns live there looking after the pagoda, meditating and studying Buddha's teachings. The pagoda is reached by a flight of steps and at the top is a small building with a series of gruesome paintings depicting different forms of torture and brutality in the Buddhist form of hell. The pagoda is not particularly large or attractive but its setting is so tranquil and the monks and nuns are particularly welcoming. The head monk had broken his leg in a motorbike accident and was very happy to receive me and to pray for continued success in my travels.

STUNG TRENG
On the banks of the Sekong River, where it meets the Mekong River, is one of those towns that doesn't have a lot going for it but for some strange reason is an enjoyable experience. Probably because there are no 'sights' as such, you have time to really explore Stung Treng. There is certainly a sense of lawlessness here because of its isolation, but at no time did I feel threatened. On the contrary I was quite charmed by this backwater. The town only ever sees a handful of tourists, but there are certainly NGOs in the area.

The rainy season could well see some serious disruption to any plans to travel here. The roads to Kratie and Rattanakiri could well be impassable and planes unable to land. All may not be lost though as the speedboat from Phnom Penh is in its element at this time when the river level is high. During the dry season the boat is not really an option.

Getting there and away
By air
Three airlines currently offer a few flights each between Phnom Penh, Rattanakiri and Stung Treng. However, flights are regularly half empty so by the time this book is published some may well have been cancelled. The flight time is approximately 45 minutes from Phnom Penh and 20 minutes from Rattanakiri to Stung Treng. The published timetables change regularly so do check days of operation and always reconfirm your booking two to three days before departure. It is also advisable to contact the airline again the day before departure to check that the flight time has not changed. There is a domestic departure tax of US$4 from Stung Treng.

Phnom Penh Airways Stung Treng; tel: none at the time of writing. The airline has three flights per week on Monday, Wednesday and Friday. The Monday and Friday flights from Phnom Penh stop at Rattanakiri on the way back to Phnom Penh and the Wednesday flight stops at Rattanakiri en route from Phnom Penh. Booking office open daily 07.00–17.00. Fare to Phnom Penh US$45 single and US$85 return; fare to Rattanakiri US$30 single and US$60 return.
President Airlines Stung Treng; tel: 074 973790. This airline also has three flights per week on Monday, Wednesday and Friday (although their timetable only lists a Sunday flight) but these are only between Phnom Penh and Stung Treng. Booking office open daily 07.00–17.00. Fare to Phnom Penh US$45 single and US$80 return.
Royal Air Cambodge Stung Treng; tel: 074 973788. RAC have flights on Monday, Thursday and Saturday between Phnom Penh and Stung Treng but the Saturday flight stops at Rattanakiri en route from Phnom Penh. Booking office open daily 07.00–12.00 and 13.00–17.00. Fare to Phnom Penh US$45 single and US$90 return; fare Rattanakiri to Stung Treng US$30 single.

By boat
There is a daily speedboat service between Kompong Cham, Kratie and Stung Treng. The larger 90–100-seater boats operate between August and October but during the dry season only very small boats can navigate the river, if at all. The boats depart at 07.00 to travel south and the journey takes five hours to Kratie and over eight hours to Kompong Cham. The boat from Kratie arrives in Stung Treng at around 17.30. The one-way fare from Kompong Cham is 40,000 riels and from Kratie 25,000 riels.

By road
The journey between Stung Treng and Kratie has been described in the Kratie section (see page 125). It is also possible to travel overland by long-distance taxi the 150km to Rattanakiri. It is difficult to believe that this section of Route 7 is even worse than the one to Kratie. The road passes through rubber

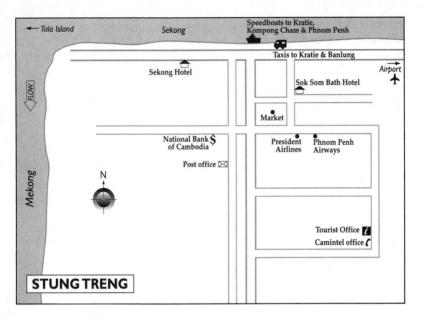

plantations and heavily logged forest where the road has been churned up by the huge logging lorries, working there illegally. The result is a road which is heavily cratered or so impassable that the 4WD pickup trucks, which act as taxis, have to leave the road and drive through the forest.

As on the road from Kratie to Stung Treng there are soldiers guarding the route to keep it open and not under threat from bandits. It appears that they turn a blind eye to the activities of the loggers as all along there are felled trees and signs that the loggers will be back. Many of the remaining large trees have had a 5cm band of bark hacked off so that they will die and be easier to fell at a later stage.

If the taxi driver is willing, an ideal place for a short stop is at Ou Pong Noan where there is a waterwheel in a picturesque setting by a local café selling cold drinks. It is likely that the waterwheel system, which supplies the village with electricity, was constructed by the UN as hundreds of their personnel were stationed in this area up until 1993.

Accommodation

Sekong Hotel Stung Treng; tel: 074 973762. Pleasant and friendly hotel on the riverfront with large but dingy rooms with simple bathrooms. There are 16 rooms with fan and five air-conditioned rooms. No restaurant but does serve drinks. Lovely to sit out on the swinging seat in the warm evening air. Rooms cost US$10 with fan and US$20 with air conditioning.

Sok Som Bath Hotel. This appeared to be another, newer hotel opposite the market. However, it was not clear whether it was being prepared for opening or had simply never opened for business as we were unable to find anybody in the building to ask.

Practical information
Currency exchange
As in any provincial town, the best place to change money is in the market at the jewellery stalls. There is a branch of the National Bank of Cambodia in the town but tourists never go there to change money. This may alter during 2000 as there are plans to start exchanging travellers' cheques.

Post office
The post office only deals with mail. Letters and parcels are sent to Phnom Penh on Wednesday and Friday for onward delivery. It is open daily 07.00–11.30 and 14.00–17.00.

What to see
Stung Treng is rather a backwater; the town is very quiet and not particularly attractive. It has a fascinating local market – many of the traders there are ethnic Lao and it is common to hear that language spoken around the town. Laos is only 45km away from Stung Treng and there is a lot of cross border activity between the two countries, although the crossing is not yet open to foreigners.

The waterfront has some activity but it is not as busy as Kompong Cham or even Kratie. The most exciting thing to happen, and one which draws the crowds, is the arrival of the daily speedboat from Kratie. I even found myself caught up in the excitement as the boat approached. By this stage of the journey I had become obsessed with spotting other foreigners, but I was to be disappointed as none ever disembarked.

A small, long-tailed boat can be hired for US$5 to cross the river to **Tala Island** where there is a very old but rather uninteresting temple, Preach Ko. There is a small community on the approach to the temple and the families here are mainly of Lao origin. If you take the boat across at the end of the day, the sun setting across the river and the island is rather lovely.

BANLUNG
Rattanakiri or Banlung or Labansiek seems to have an identity crisis. The province is definitely called Rattanakiri but the main town is also referred to as Rattanakiri in airline timetables whereas the locals call it Banlung. However, I am reliably informed that the name of the town is actually Labansiek and Banlung is the name of the district. I have decided to go with the flow and call the town Banlung and the province Rattanakiri. Whatever it is called it is in a remote area, bordered by Laos to the north and Vietnam to the east, and few visitors make their way there at the moment. This is partly because of its inaccessibility overland, although there are now regular flights from Phnom Penh over 600km away. Flying into Banlung does seem a little like cheating and I feel that I earned my spurs (as well as a huge bill from the chiropractor) by travelling overland from Phnom Penh! It is very satisfying to reach Banlung after several days, covered in dust and to the obvious admiration of the locals who aren't used to seeing foreigners arriving by that route.

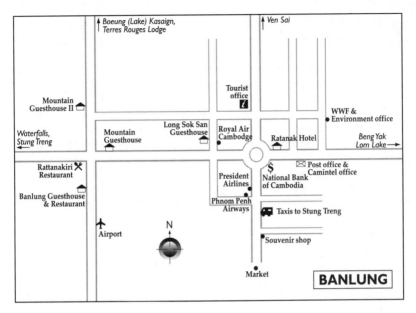

This remote area of Cambodia is home to rainforests, mountains, thundering waterfalls and hill tribes or *chunchiet* who worship the spirits and their ancestors. They practise slash-and-burn techniques, clearing vast areas of forest to make fields and then moving on after a few years. There are no magnificent temples emerging from the all-encroaching forest in this part of Cambodia but a natural beauty which is equally impressive.

Getting there and away
By air
Competition is fierce on the route between Phnom Penh and Banlung and the flights often operate with only a few passengers. Two of the airlines also stop at Stung Treng en route to Phnom Penh. Flight times are approximately one hour from Phnom Penh and 20 minutes from Rattanakiri to Stung Treng. The published timetables change regularly so do check days of operation and always reconfirm your booking two to three days before departure. It is also advisable to contact the airline again the day before departure to check that the flight time has not changed. There is a domestic departure tax of US$4 from Banlung.

Phnom Penh Airways Phoum 1 Khum Labaseak, Banlung; tel: 075 974147. The airline has three flights per week on Monday, Wednesday and Friday. The Monday and Friday flights from Phnom Penh stop at Stung Treng on the way and the Wednesday flight stops at Stung Treng en route to Phnom Penh. Booking office open daily 07.00–12.00 and 13.00–17.30. Fares from Phnom Penh US$55 single and US$110 return. Fares from Stung Treng US$30 single and US$60 return.

President Airlines Banlung; tel: 075 974059/974065. Fly three times per week on

THE FIGHT OF GLOBAL WITNESS AGAINST ILLEGAL LOGGING

Illegal logging in Cambodia is an old problem, once controlled by the Khmer Rouge and used to provide much needed funds for their campaigns. Despite the Khmer Rouge being a spent force, logging continues unabated but now those at the heart of the problem are the military and even government officials. Trees in the once extensive forests in Cambodia are being cut down at such a rate that the forest reserves are likely to be depleted within a few years. Satellite images of Cambodia's forest cover, taken in 1997, show that it has shrunk by around three million hectares since 1969 when the last series of satellite maps were taken. This number accounts for around 20% and it is believed that the majority of logging occurred in the 1990s. In total the forest cover has declined from over 70% of land area in the 1970s to around 30–35%.

An environmental pressure group, Global Witness, based in the United Kingdom, is monitoring the situation closely and has evidence that illegal log exports have not stopped despite a ban by the Cambodian government. Global Witness, acknowledged by the World Bank, the IMF and the US State Department as an authority on illegal logging and deforestation in Cambodia, has been gathering evidence of the connivance of the military and government officials who work together to export unprocessed logs to neighbouring countries. Although senior government officials sign export orders at the request of the military the profits from the transaction do not go into government coffers. Every year the Cambodian treasury loses millions of dollars to illegal operators. Global Witness has also seen documents signed by the Rattanakiri Provincial Governor, Kham Khieu, authorising the province's military commander, Nuon Channa, to collect logs to build a military base. This is in direct violation of Hun Sen's declaration against illegal logging in early 1999. Kham Khieu has long been known to be at the heart of the problem in Rattanakiri since he was the head of the provincial police there.

In 1998 Global Witness revealed that garden furniture sold throughout Britain was a major contributor to the destruction of the forests in Cambodia. Furniture advertised as being 'eco-friendly' and manufactured from 'genuine plantation timber' actually came from Cambodia, where it was illegally exported to Vietnam to be made into garden furniture for the international market.

For further information on the important work of Global Witness their contact details are: PO Box 6042, London N19 5WP; tel: 020 7272 6731; fax: 020 7272 9425; email: mail@globalwitness.demon.co.uk; web: www.oneworld.org/globalwitness. In Phnom Penh they can be contacted at PO Box 501, Phnom Penh; tel: 012 819115 (mobile).

Tuesday, Thursday and Saturday. Booking office claims to be open 24 hours. Fares from Phnom Penh are US$55 single and US$100 return.

Royal Air Cambodge Banlung; tel: 075 974067. There are daily flights between Phnom Penh and Banlung with the Saturday flight stopping at Stung Treng on its way back to Phnom Penh and the Sunday flight stopping at Mondulkiri en route to Banlung. Booking office open daily 08.00–12.00 and 13.00–17.30. Fares from Phnom Penh US$55 single and US$100 return.

By road

The route from Stung Treng is worse than that from Kratie to Stung Treng. The road is very churned up in places (mainly by the enormous logging trucks) with potholes so enormous that they are impassable, so vehicles have to drive into the forest and around the trees. It is a miracle if any vehicle travels the whole route without getting bogged down at some stage. Although the distance is only approximately 150km it takes around eight hours to reach Banlung. Long-distance taxis travel the route every day and the cost for a seat in a high-clearance 4WD pickup truck is 35,000 riels per person.

Getting around

If you have time to spare a few days in Banlung the Banlung Guesthouse can arrange a programme of visits to villages and waterfalls by car or motorbike together with a guide. Cars cost US$50 per day for up to four people and motorbikes can be hired for around US$7 per day. The Mountain Guesthouse also rents out motorbikes. Unless you know your way around it may be better to find a moto to make sure you get to where you are going.

Accommodation

Banlung Guesthouse & Restaurant Banlung; tel: 075 974066. Virtually opposite the entrance to the airport, this is the best place in town to stay. All rooms have air conditioning and private bathrooms with cold water. There is a small restaurant serving tasty Western and Khmer food.

Terres Rouges Lodge Boeung Kasaign, Banlung; tel: 075 974051; email: terresrouges1@aol.com. By the time this book is published a new guesthouse will have opened on the outskirts of Banlung which will set new standards for accommodation there and may encourage a flurry of such places. Terres Rouges is a typical, large wooden traditional house with 14 rooms, each with a fan and private bathroom with HOT water. The rooms are decorated in local, ethnic style and there is a huge terrace overlooking the garden and lake (Boeung Kasaign). Facilities also include a bar and restaurant and rooms cost US$35 including breakfast. The guesthouse can arrange excursions by jeep, boat, mountain bike and motorbike as well as treks and elephant rides, all with local and expat guides.

Long Sok San Guesthouse Banlung; no telephone. Small, traditional guesthouse in the centre of town. Seven rooms with fan, mosquito net and shared bathroom with cold water only. Food can be provided with prior notice. Rooms cost US$3.

Ratanak Hotel Banlung; tel: 075 974033. Large building near the monument in the centre of town which looks rather out of place. Charmless place which appears rather dirty and unfinished although they say they it opened in 1995. The attraction for visitors is that some rooms have hot water. There are 30 rooms in total all with private bathrooms. Rooms with fan cost US$5, with air conditioning US$10 and with air conditioning, satellite TV and hot water US$20.

Mountain Guest House Banlung; no telephone. Friendly, traditional wooden guesthouse with eight rooms with fan and shared bathroom (cold water only). Faces the airstrip. Meals can be arranged on request. Lovely veranda at the front which is wonderful until the karaoke starts next door. The owner meets every flight into Banlung. Rooms cost US$5.

Mountain Guest House II Banlung; no telephone. Owned by the same woman, this establishment is on the airport road and is also an old house with a lovely veranda which is very peaceful. Rooms also cost US$5 with fan and shared bathroom with cold water.

Restaurants
A number of food stalls are located around the market selling rice and noodle dishes.

Rattanakiri Restaurant Banlung. Small place which is popular with the NGOs working in the area because it has Western dishes on the menu which the chef has been taught to cook by various foreigners passing through.

Banlung Guesthouse & Restaurant Banlung; tel: 075 974066. Small restaurant attached to the guesthouse serving tasty Western and Khmer food.

Practical information
Currency exchange
The only place to change US dollars in Banlung is at the jewellery stalls in the market.

Post office
The post office only deals with mail and this is sent by every plane to Phnom Penh for onward delivery. It is possible to make international phone calls from here. The post office is generally open every day.

Shopping
Rattanakiri is not a shopping metropolis but those interested will be able to buy gems mined in the area, either in the market or uncut versions from the prospectors themselves who occasionally come into town. Handicrafts, in particular baskets and jewellery, can be bought in the tribal villages or from a shop in town, close to the market, with a sign saying 'There are souvenir things for sell'.

Tourist office
The Ministry of Tourism office in Banlung is pretty dynamic compared with most in Cambodia. They realise the potential for ecotourism in the region and have put together a simple leaflet outlining the possibilities in the area. This

alone won't bring in vast hordes of visitors but they do understand that they have something marketable here and I hope that they manage it without losing the charm of the place. The staff were even talking about finding investors to develop a safari park where tourists can drive through safely and see the animals in their natural habitat.

What to see

Banlung is a sprawling town with wide laterite roads and a small central area with a few shops and offices (government and airlines) and market. The market building has stalls selling a variety of household items, clothes, shoes, jewellery and gems. Outside the main market the people from the tribal villages sell their fruit and vegetables which they carry in baskets into town in the early morning.

Although Banlung itself is a little disappointing the surrounding area is delightful. There are many tribal villages around Banlung and the ethnic minorities make up around 65% of the population of Rattanakiri province. There are eight main ethnic groups here – Tumpuon, Kreung, Kavet, Kachak, Charai, Prouv, Phnong and Loung. They make their living from traditional ways of cultivation as well as being hunters. Many of the villages are within driving distance of the town itself, but it is important to have a local guide with you as the subtle differences in the housing, in particular the roofs, for each tribe will be lost on the casual observer. Often the villages are almost deserted apart from old people and young children as the men and women of working age will be out in their fields which can be many kilometres away.

Unlike the tribes in Thailand and Vietnam the hill tribes here wear very simple, dark clothing, not dissimilar to regular Cambodian dress worn in the countryside elsewhere. Occasionally you come across a small group of women walking along the road wearing only sarong-like skirts, smoking pipes and carrying traditional baskets full of vegetables. Some of the old people have facial tattoos and earlobes that have been pierced and stretched to accommodate large pieces of jewellery, or, in vogue during my visit, plastic bottle-tops.

The open deciduous woodland that predominates in the lowlands of the northeast, both here and in Mondulkiri, is ideal for spotting birds such as flocks of parakeets, eagles, storks and woodpeckers and is also the favoured terrain of wild cattle such as gaur and banteng. In the evergreen forests up in the hills you are likely to come across reptiles such as snakes, tortoises and monitors and large numbers of squirrels and may be lucky enough to spot gibbons and hornbills.

The area around the town is rich in waterfalls although the roads to reach them are appalling, which is probably why they are still so unspoilt. My particular favourite is **Cha Oung Waterfall**, as it is possible to walk behind the waterfall and the drop is so steep that the cascade of water dwarfs anybody standing under it. The bumpy road passes through rubber and coffee plantations and then there is a short walk along a track to the fall. **Kachang Waterfall** is not as spectacular as it is far more gentle, but there is a lovely pool at the bottom for swimming which is popular with the locals. We tried to reach **Katieng Waterfall** but had to abandon our attempt despite being in a 4WD vehicle. Large, brightly coloured butterflies are often seen fluttering through the trees, their wings caught in the beams of sunlight that stream through.

A beautiful spot for a picnic and swim is the volcanic lake **Beng Yak Lom** around 5km from town. It is 50m deep and has beautifully clean water. There is a path around the lake and very few visitors other than at weekends and during holidays. By the lake is a reconstruction of the Kreung man and woman stilt houses, now seen less and less in the villages themselves. These houses, the tall one for the men and the shorter one for the women, were used by young unmarried people... Sadly there was a small souvenir shop being constructed at one side of the lake. There is an entrance fee of 1,000 riels for foreigners.

For a taste of the 'gold rush' take a trip to the gem-mining area around 30km from town. The unnamed village is a temporary one where simple shacks have been thrown up to accommodate the hundreds of men who dig for gems in the vicinity. Small makeshift restaurants with rows of benches have also appeared. Deep circular holes are dug by hand in the red earth and then the contents are sieved to find yellowish gems. The whole area is pockmarked with holes under the burning sun and men intensely inspecting the crumbly soil. In one or two years' time the men will move on to another area to start again. The road to the mining area passes through large areas of rubber trees and villages belonging to the Tumpuon people. The main gem-mining town is Bokeo, but there is little of interest there and it is better to find the working mines.

The former provincial capital of **Lumphat** can be visited in a day from Banlung. Derelict government buildings show that it was once a bustling town but now it is a pretty lethargic place. The journey from Banlung can be done in around two hours in the dry season and this just allows enough time to look around town and take a leisurely boat trip on the Tonle Srepok.

Ven Sai, to the northwest of Banlung, on the San River, is a small, dull town but you can cross the river here to visit the old Chinese village on the other side. In addition there are Lao and tribal settlements belonging to the Tumpuon and Kavet peoples, but a local guide is needed to locate them and to smoothe your arrival. An old jalopy makes the journey from Banlung to Ven Sai every day in the early morning from the market and returns in the late morning.

VIRACHEY NATIONAL PARK

This is the largest national park in Cambodia and a management programme is being developed in conjunction with the Worldwide Fund for Nature (WWF). A park headquarters close to Ven Sai, funded by the WWF, has information on animals believed to be in the park although any other work is still in the planning stage. Many animals were killed during the civil war and there are plans to introduce some from Laos and Thailand if studies find that many native populations have been wiped out. The park headquarters has posters indicating various species of animals that may be in the park. These include wild water buffalo, tiger, panther, javan rhino, elephant, pig-tailed macaques, gibbons, kauprey (*Bos sauvel*), gaur (*Bos gaurus*), banteng (*Bos javanicus*), sarus crane (*Grusantigone*), black-necked stork (*Ephippiorhynenus asiaticus*), red-headed vulture (*Sarcogypsgalvus*), and rock python (*Pythos molurus*). If you wish to visit the park contact the Environment Office in Banlung where the WWF staff are based. The best time to visit is during the dry season when rangers can take you to observe animals coming to the waterhole.

SEN MONOROM

Mondulkiri, although one of the largest provinces in Cambodia, has the smallest population at around 25,000–30,000 thus making its northern neighbour, Rattanakiri, appear overpopulated. Only a few visitors make their way to Sen Monorom, the capital, as it is possibly an even tougher trip than reaching Banlung in Rattanakiri province. Once there you must chill out and enjoy the languid way of life as nothing happens very fast. In fact nothing really happens… Nature lovers will enjoy the unspoiled countryside and the chance to ride an elephant through some spectacular scenery. The predominant open deciduous woodland shares the province with evergreen forests in the hills. The woodland is home to parakeets, eagles, storks and woodpeckers, reptiles such as snakes, tortoises and monitors and wild cattle such as gaur and benteng. Gibbons, hornbills and vast numbers of squirrels are more likely to be seen in the forests.

The province is inhabited by several *chunchiet* tribes, the main one being the Phnong, with significant numbers of Stieng, Kraol and Tumpuon. Khmers account for only 20% of the population. Like the *chunchiet* of Rattanakiri province, the dress is indistinct from that of the general population, although some women may have tattooed faces and wear only sarongs. As most of the villagers work away in the fields during the day there are usually only a few old people and children around.

Getting there and away
By air
The only airline to operate flights to Sen Monorom is Royal Air Cambodge, which is strange considering the competition from the other two airlines for the few passengers on the Rattanakiri route. The flight time is around 50 minutes direct from Phnom Penh and one hour 50 minutes when routed via Rattanakiri. The airline operates two flights a week between Phnom Penh and Mondulkiri. The Wednesday flight is via Rattanakiri on the outward leg and the Sunday flight is via Rattanakiri on the return leg. The airline operates French ATR72s on this route and the return fare is US$110. The arrival of the twice-weekly flight causes great excitement and animals are cleared from the airstrip in preparation. The published timetables change regularly so do check days of operation and always reconfirm your booking two to three days before departure; also contact the airline again the day before departure to check that the flight time has not changed. There is a domestic departure tax of US$4 from Sen Monorom.

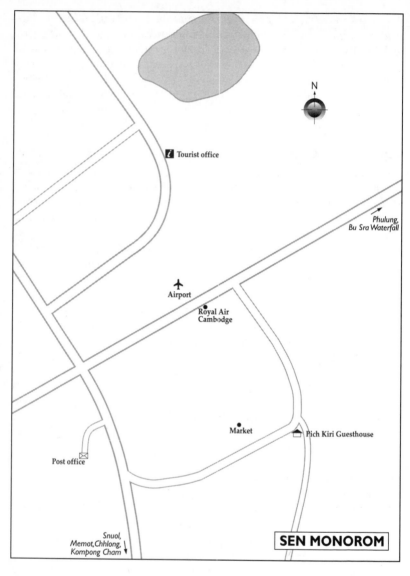

By road

There are two routes to Sen Monorom overland and both involve a degree of determination. The security situation should also be checked prior to setting out. The first route is to take a ferry across the river at Kompong Cham and find a shared 4WD taxi on the other side to take you along appalling Route 7 as far as Snuol via Memot. At Memot it may be necessary to change to another taxi as it could be the end of the road for the first one. The fare to Snuol is around 15–20,000 riels, depending on your negotiating skills. Sen Monorom is reached along a relatively good logging road and the three-hour journey costs 20,000–25,000 riels. Not so many vehicles travel along this route and you may find yourself having to overnight in Snuol where there are a few basic guesthouses. In a few years' time, once the bridge across the Mekong has been completed at Kompong Cham and Route 7 upgraded, it may be possible to cruise along to Snuol in a saloon car. But until then discomfort is the order of the day, although there has been some recent work on the section between Kompong Cham and Memot.

A better way is to take the 07.30 speedboat from Kompong Cham to Kratie and get off at Chhlong, a journey of around 2.5 hours. From here you can pick up the new logging road which goes all the way to Sen Monorom in around 5 hours, although it may be necessary to change taxis in Snuol. The fare all the way from Chhlong to Sen Monorom is around 25,000 riels.

Getting around
Motos and 4WD vehicles can be hired for the day but be prepared to pay a little more than in other places because of the difficulty of the terrain and the small number of tourists visiting. Motos cost in the region of US$8 and 4WDs US$50 (depending on the distance you want to travel).

Accommodation
The choice is extremely limited here and most people choose to stay at one guesthouse. There is only power in the evening from 18.00 to 22.00 and the altitude means that there is no need for air conditioning or even fans.

Pich Kiri Guesthouse Sen Monorom. The rooms are rather simple but quite adequate. There are cabins with private bathroom or rooms in the main building with shared facilities. Rooms cost US$10 in the cabins and US$5 in the main building including breakfast.

Restaurants
This heading is rather optimistic as there are in fact no restaurants but only food stalls in the market area although you can get hot noodles and rice dishes. Be warned that they close early so the choice is between eating early and stocking up on delicious baguettes or giving the owners advance warning that you will want to eat in the evening.

Practical information
Currency exchange
The only place to change US dollars in Sen Monorom is at the jewellery stalls in the market.

Post office
The post office deals only with mail and this is sent to Phnom Penh on the twice-weekly plane for onward delivery. The post office is generally open every day.

What to see and do

Sen Monorom, the capital of Mondulkiri province, is more of a large village than a town, surrounded by grassy hills, forests and coffee plantations. Most activity occurs in the market, especially in the early morning when the women from the hill tribes come to sell their fruit and vegetables. The most noise comes from the karaoke bars (powered by batteries) which seem to attract the tone deaf at any time of day. The town is almost charming because of its lack of attractions, and it is the only place to base yourself to explore further. The gentle countryside around town is ideal for strolling around, just relaxing and enjoying the views.

Tourism is totally undeveloped in the province whose main attraction is its natural beauty. There are several waterfalls around Sen Monorom, the main one being **Bu Sra Waterfall**, around 40km from town along an unbelievably bad road. However, it is possible to reach, and the waterfall, on two levels, is worth seeing. The journey itself is also enjoyable as it passes through some attractive Phnong villages en route. The town of Bu Sra is a few kilometres beyond the falls, but there is little of interest here other than a place to have a drink and something to eat. Watch out for hornbills and peafowl as you move around.

Mondulkiri is the best place to arrange **elephant rides** as most villages have their own working elephants. **Phulung**, north of town, is a good place to do this and you should either go in the early morning to sort this out or ask for help from the guesthouse to arrange a ride in advance. Do not plan to go anywhere in particular because the lumbering pace of the elephants only allows for short distances to be covered. Just enjoy this fun (although not particularly comfortable) way of getting into the forests, visiting waterfalls and passing through villages. You may even be lucky enough to see some of the animals that live in the region such as wild elephants, tigers, deer and gaur.

Because of the remoteness of the province, which has very few roads but many trails, it is always wise to have a local guide with you to make sure you reach your destination and get back again. However, as tourism has not yet arrived in Mondulkiri in any significant sense, they are very unlikely to speak English. The situation could change, though, as it is a prime area for the development of ecotourism and the Ministry of Tourism is looking into this.

Northwest Cambodia

SIEM REAP

Siem Reap (pronounced See-em Re-ep) is in the fortunate position of being the gateway to the great Angkor temples and now it is a bustling town with hotels, guesthouses, restaurants and travel companies  mushrooming. Despite its growth in recent years it is still far more relaxed than Phnom Penh and the river running through the centre of town gives it a very spacious feel. Although tourists have always found their way to Siem Reap and Angkor, for many years there was a rather 'wild west' feel to the town and at times it was not too safe for visitors. In 1993 I was asked by reception staff to come inside when I was sitting out by the main entrance enjoying the cool night air. They were worried that somebody would take a pot shot at me as they drove past. Development was slow during the ensuing years but in 1999, following the return of stability, the town has blossomed and I only hope that this is controlled so that Siem Reap does not lose its charm.

Getting there and away
By air
Siem Reap is the only town in Cambodia, other than the capital, which can accept international flights and the airport is expanding significantly to cope with the expected increase in visitors. Both Royal Air Cambodge and Bangkok Airways have flights between Bangkok and Siem Reap which take one hour. Following the announcement of an 'open sky' policy by Hun Sen, a number of regional airlines are now seriously planning to operate direct flights into Siem Reap. There are also three airlines flying between Phnom Penh and Siem Reap with a flight time of approximately 30 minutes. There is a domestic departure tax of US$4 from Siem Reap. The airport is 7km from town. Cars and motos meet all flights coming in and you can negotiate around US$5 and US$1–2 respectively for a trip into town.

Bangkok Airways 6 St 571, Phum Salakanseng, Khum Svay Damkum, Srok Khet, Siem Reap: tel: 063 380191/2; fax: 063 380191. There are five flights per day timetabled between Bangkok and Siem Reap although this can be reduced at different times of year. At the end of 1999 a flight was introduced from Siem Reap to Phuket (not the other way around) on Tuesday, Thursday and Saturday. In March 2000 another route was added from Sukhotai to Siem Reap, also on Tuesday, Thursday and Saturday. Booking office

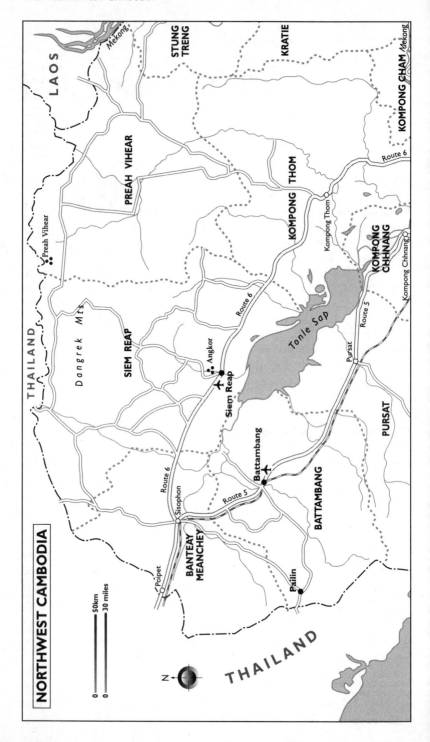

NORTHWEST CAMBODIA

LAOS

Mekong

STUNG TRENG

KRATIE

KOMPONG CHAM

Mekong

THAILAND

Dangrek Mts

PREAH VIHEAR

Preah Vihear

SIEM REAP

Angkor

Siem Reap

KOMPONG THOM

Kompong Thom

Route 6

Route 6

KOMPONG CHHNANG

Kompong Chhnang

Tonle Sap

Route 5

Pursat

PURSAT

Battambang

Route 6

Sisophon

Route 5

BATTAMBANG

BANTEAY MEANCHEY

Poipet

Pailin

THAILAND

50km
30 miles

0
0

N

open daily 08.00–17.00. Fares from Bangkok US$155 single and US$310 return. One-way fare Sukhotai to Siem Reap US$220 and Siem Reap to Phuket US$288.

Phnom Penh Airways 113 Svay Dang Kum, Siem Reap; no telephone at the time of writing. This new airline has twice-daily flights between Phnom Penh and Siem Reap, one morning and one afternoon. Booking office opens daily 07.30–11.30 and 14.00–19.30. Fares from Phnom Penh US$55 single and US$110 return.

President Airlines 56 Sivota Road, Siem Reap; tel: 063 964338. President have twice-daily flights between Phnom Penh and Siem Reap, one morning and one afternoon, with additional flights which fly Phnom Penh–Koh Kong–Siem Reap–Phnom Penh on Monday and Friday and Phnom Penh–Siem Reap–Koh Kong–Phnom Penh on Wednesday and Sunday. Booking office opens daily 07.00–20.00. Fares from Phnom Penh US$55 single and US$105 return.

Royal Air Cambodge Villa 362 St 6, Siem Reap; tel: 063 963422. RAC have two flights daily between Phnom Penh and Siem Reap, one morning and one afternoon, with additional morning flights on Tuesday, Friday and Saturday. Booking office opens daily 07.30–11.30 and 13.30–17.30. Fares from Phnom Penh US$60 single and US$120 return.

By boat

The daily speedboat service between Phnom Penh and Siem Reap is the best way to travel between the two towns if time is short, as the journey is only five hours and definitely more comfortable than road travel at the moment. The boats depart approximately 13km from town at Chong Khneas, although further away during the dry season when the water level of the Tonle Sap drops dramatically. Tickets can be bought in many places in Siem Reap, particularly along Sivota Road. The boats leave from Phnom Penh and Siem Reap at 07.00 and the one-way fare is US$25. The boats can be reached by private taxi from Siem Reap (a price can be negotiated of around US$3–5) or by moto for around US$1–2.

By road

The road from Phnom Penh to Siem Reap is very good up to Kompong Thom, deteriorates until approximately 1.5 hours outside Siem Reap, then becomes pretty good again. The journey takes roughly eight hours for around 300km. However, during 2000 work should start on improving this route and already there was evidence of trees being chopped down in order to widen the road.

Shared long-distance taxis depart from the southwest corner of the Central Market in Phnom Penh and by the market Psah Leu (on the road to Phnom Penh) in Siem Reap; the fare is US$6 per person. Taxis also travel to Battambang from Siem Reap; the fare is US$7 for a journey of six to eight hours. Sisophon towards the Thai border can be reached for around US$4 with an onward trip to the border costing around US$2.

Getting around

Motos can be hired for around US$7 per day. Many of the drivers speak some English and can provide basic explanations about the temples. For short

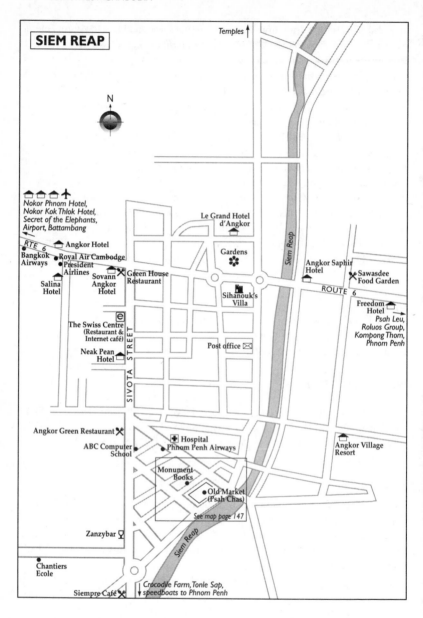

journeys around Siem Reap expect to pay in the region of 1,000–1,500 riels per trip. A car and driver can be arranged through one of the many travel agencies in town for a fee of US$20–30 per day. Some of the guesthouses and cafés hire out bicycles for US$2 per day.

The local authorities have just relaxed the rules and it is now possible to rent a motorbike for around US$7 per day. The renters of motorbikes and bikes usually ask that you leave your passport as a deposit. Make sure that your insurance policy covers you for this activity. Also it is worth remembering that the theft of motorbikes is a real problem in Cambodia and when you park your bike at one of the temples it will be unattended. You will then find yourself forking out to replace the bike if it is stolen. Also there are no signposts around the temple complex so it is easy to get lost unless you know your way. Personally I feel that a moto is the best option; often the drivers know quite a lot about the temples and are very helpful.

Travel agencies

Terre Cambodge PO Box 18, Siem Reap; tel: 012 843401 (mobile); email: tc@worldmail.com.kh; tercamb@hotmail.com. For those who have time to spare and want to see some of the less visited temples Terre Cambodge arrange day trips either by road or boat to temples such as Beng Mealea and to Prek Toal bird sanctuary. Longer trips can also be arranged travelling by traditional wooden boat and staying in villages.

Apsara Tours opposite the hospital, Siem Reap; tel: 063 963992; fax: 063 380198. Large travel agency offering tours for groups and individuals in a variety of languages.

Pichtourist 502 Khum Svay Dongkhum, Siem Reap; tel: 016 816677 (mobile). One of the leading travel agencies in Cambodia with enthusiastic and knowledgeable guides. Can make arrangements for groups and individuals and are very good at understanding and carrying out special requirements.

Accommodation

Most hotels in Siem Reap are located close to the river in the centre of town or along the airport road, Route 6.

Deluxe

Currently there is only one contender in this category but the Royal Phnom Penh Hotel is planning to open a sister hotel by the end of 2000 and a Sofitel will also open around the same time. This may result in some serious competition in this price bracket and prices may fall as a result.

Grand Hotel d'Angkor 1 Vithei Charles de Gaulle, Khum Svay Dang Kum, Siem Reap; tel: 063 963888; fax: 063 963168; email: ghda@worldmail.com.kh; web: www.raffles-intl.com. The Grand rivals its sister hotel, Le Royal in Phnom Penh, for style and sheer magnificence. Established in 1932 the hotel was untouched and very run down until it was restored and extended in 1997 by Raffles International. The result is exquisite and quite a transformation from my first visit to the hotel in 1990. Some of the original rooms in the main building have been converted into shops and meeting rooms although there are still some wonderful guestrooms there. The rooms in the new wings are very tasteful and some overlook the huge pool behind the hotel. There are even two small villas in the grounds by the pool. Guests are spoilt for choice when it comes to dining as there are eight restaurants and bars, some very chic and others more relaxed. The hotel has a desk at Phnom Penh and Siem Reap airports so can make reservations and arrange transfers on arrival or with advance notice. As expected the room rates reflect this luxury at US$310–460 for a single and

US$360–510 for a twin. However, these rates include both breakfast and dinner. The villas cost a staggering US$1,900 each – per night! They were both occupied when I visited the hotel.

First class

Angkor Hotel St 6, Phum Sala Kanseng, Sangkat Svay Dong Kom, Siem Reap; tel: 063 964301; fax: 063 964302; email: angkor_hotel@worldmail.com.kh. A new hotel, built in the Khmer style on the edge of town on the road to the airport. Despite its design it has more of an international feel than Cambodian. It has 110 rooms and four restaurants and bars with an excellent selection of Khmer and Western cuisine. Other facilities include a health club, swimming pool, business centre, library and shop. Rooms cost US$121–254 for singles and US$151–254 for twins including breakfast.

Angkor Village Resort Siem Reap; tel: 063 963563; fax: 063 380104; email: angkor.village@bigpond.com.kh. One of the loveliest and friendliest hotels in Siem Reap with wooden rooms surrounding a central restaurant and all set amongst lush, tropical gardens. Opened in 1995, it is owned and designed by Khmer and French architects and their influence is clear. Currently there are 18 rooms with 14 standard, 3 apartments and one deluxe suite. There are plans to add 12 deluxe rooms in 2001 and these will be bungalows on stilts. The rooms are quite delightful with a unique style not seen elsewhere in the country. All have balconies. Other facilities include a pool, business centre and across the road the Apsara Theatre, which has nightly traditional Khmer dance performances including dinner (three times weekly in the low season). Room rates are US$86–144 in the high season (November–April) and US$69–121 in the low season (May–October). All meals are extra and cost US$5 for breakfast, US$7 for lunch and US$9 for dinner. There is a set Khmer menu for both lunch and dinner which accounts for the reasonable price.

Nokor Phnom Hotel Airport Road, Phum Salakanseng, Siem Reap; tel: 063 380106; fax: 063 380033. Modern hotel with 114 rooms all with air conditioning, satellite TV, mini bar and IDD. Hotel facilities include swimming pool, business centre and restaurant serving Khmer, Chinese and Western food. Room rates US$70 single and US$90 twin. Breakfast extra.

Nokor Kok Thlok Hotel Rd 6, Siem Reap; tel: 063 380201; fax: 063 963550; email: Nokorkokthlok@worldmail.com.kh. Large hotel which used to be the best one in town. Now the competition has taken over and its location out on the airport road is a disadvantage. However, rooms have air conditioning, satellite TV and IDD although looking a little jaded now. Swimming pool. Room price of US$80 includes breakfast.

Standard class

Salina Hotel 125 Taphul Village, Rd 6, Siem Reap; tel: 063 380221; fax: 063 380035. Located in a quiet road, 15 minutes' walk from the Grand Hotel, this is a friendly hotel in a pleasant setting, popular with tour groups. The hotel has a large restaurant serving Khmer and international food, a business centre and a gift shop. The 50 large rooms have air conditioning, satellite TV, IDD and mini bar as well as room service and laundry. Single rooms cost US$45 and twin rooms US$55 including breakfast.

Previous page Contemporary carved sandstone bust in the Khmer style, Angkor Wat (JM)

Above Close up of one of the many hundreds of bas-reliefs to be found in the outer gallery of the Bayon (AS)

Below Bas-reliefs of great beauty decorate the walls of Angkor Wat. Here, Devatas, or female divinities, grace the walls of the upper level of Angkor Wat (JM)

Below right Enigmatic faces at the Bayon (AS)

Left Boddhisatva at 12th-century Wat Nokor near Kompong Cham (AS)

Left The Terrace of the Elephants (or Royal Terrace) was built by Suryavarman I in the 11th century and forms part of a series of terraces within the walls of Angkor Thom. (JM)

Above The 12th-century complex of
Ta Prohm has a 'lost world' charm. (JM)

Below A functioning Buddhist shrine
within the crumbling 12th-century
ruins of Banteay Kdei, Ta Prohm (JM)

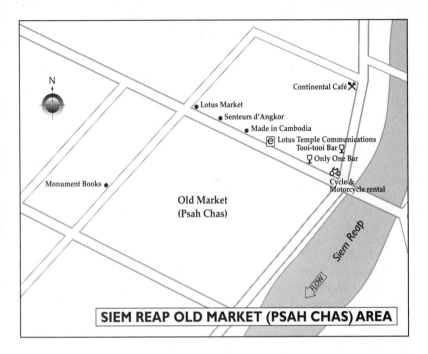

SIEM REAP OLD MARKET (PSAH CHAS) AREA

Angkor Saphir Hotel 82 Route 6, Siem Reap; tel/fax: 063 963566/380213. This Cambodian-owned hotel benefits from its location within walking distance of restaurants and shops. Opened in 1998 its 37 pleasant rooms all have air conditioning and satellite TV. There is also a small restaurant with an open-air terrace. What the hotel lacks in atmosphere is compensated for by its friendly service. Room rates range from US$30–60 on a room-only basis.

Secret of the Elephants Rd 6, Siem Reap; tel/fax: 063 964328; web: www.Angkor@travel.com. This delightful guesthouse is my favourite in Siem Reap. Although it's located slightly out of town on the airport road the ambience, stylish décor and congenial hosts are definitely worth the short journey. Each of the seven rooms is decorated uniquely, designed by the owners Jean Yves and Methia. The three downstairs rooms have private bathrooms and the four rooms upstairs share three small bathrooms. The whole traditional wooden house has been converted sympathetically in Khmer style and has a pleasant veranda as well as a small garden with a barbecue at the front. Evening meals can be prepared if requested in advance. The downstairs rooms cost US$30 single and US$35 twin; upstairs US$20 single and US$25 twin including breakfast.

Neak Pean 53 Sivota Rd, Siem Reap; tel/fax: 063 380073. This is a pleasing converted old house (formerly belonging to the Deputy Governor of Siem Reap) in a central location with 55 rooms with private bathroom and television. Rooms cost US$35–45 including breakfast.

Budget

Sovann Angkor Hotel 63 Mondol II, Sangkat II, Siem Reap; tel/fax : 063 964039. Centrally located on the airport road and within walking distance of restaurants and shops, this simple, clean hotel has 34 large rooms with either fan or air conditioning and satellite TV. The hotel does not have a restaurant but there are some excellent outlets nearby which are open for breakfast and other meals. Room rates US$15–20.

Freedom Hotel Airport Road, Siem Reap; tel: 063 963473. Modern hotel with 50 rooms located out towards the main market. Good rooms with fan or air conditioning and satellite TV. Restaurant. Rooms with fan cost US$10 and those with air conditioning and TV US$15–25.

European Guesthouse 0566 Group 21, Banteaychas, Slorkram Commune, Siem Reap; tel: 012 890917 (mobile); fax: 063 380262; email012890917@mobitel.com.kh. British-run homely guesthouse in quiet garden setting with twelve good-sized rooms with fans with four shared bathrooms (hot showers). Meals are extra but guests are tempted with muesli for breakfast and popular set Cambodian meals for lunch and dinner. An outrageously cheap US$4 for all you can eat. Owners are happy to meet you at the airport and help with travel plans. Twin rooms cost US$7 and singles US$5. Discounts for stays longer than one night.

Restaurants/bars

The Swiss Centre 66 Sivota Rd, Siem Reap; tel: 015 638808 (mobile). As the name suggests this place is run by a Swiss national who has lived in Siem Reap for several years. Pleasant setting in small garden. Has a restaurant serving Khmer and European food.

Continental Café 353 St, Stung Siem Reap, Siem Reap; tel: 015 850312 (mobile). Small, relaxed café facing the river, close to the market. Serves Western food including pizza. Owned by the Foreign Correspondents' Club in Phnom Penh. Open every day 06.00–24.00.

Angkor Green Restaurant Sivota Road, Siem Reap. Very pleasant place serving a wide selection of Khmer, French, Chinese, Thai and vegetarian food at reasonable prices. Do not go there if you're in a hurry as the choice is so great and it is all very tempting.

Green House Restaurant Airport Road, Siem Reap. Popular restaurant located in town, next to the Sovann Angkor Hotel and with exactly the same menu as the Angkor Green Restaurant above.

Tooi-tooi Bar Stung Siem Reap, Siem Reap. Small bar and café with menu of the day close to the Old Market.

Sawasdee Food Garden Siem Reap; tel: 063 380199. Agreeable restaurant serving delicious Thai food at really good prices. Take the road to the Psah Leu and turn first left past the Angkor Saphir Hotel. Not open for breakfast.

Only One Bar Siem Reap. Located next to the Psah Chas (Old Market) this trendy bar serves food but is on the expensive side. Popular with the resident expats.

Siempre Café Siem Reap; tel: 012 843956 (mobile). Lovely house with well decorated terrace and warm welcome. Open from 14.00 until late. Happy hour 19.00–20.00.

Zanzybar Sivota Road, Siem Reap. Busy bar popular with both expats and visitors. Open into the wee small hours.

Shopping

Psah Chas (Old Market) Despite being a newly built market in the centre of town it is referred to as the old market. Range of products available of interest to visitors including maps, books, handicrafts, clothes and jewellery. Good place to try out your bargaining skills.

Monument Books 502 Khum Svay Dongkhum, Siem Reap. Phnom Penh and Cambodia's leading bookstore opened a new shop in Siem Reap at the end of 1999 and stocks an extensive collection of books on Angkor.

Made in Cambodia is a small shop run by and for Cambodians with disabilities. It sells good-quality products made from hand-woven silk, leather, coconut and wood and any profits go towards training and employing vulnerable Cambodians. Products on sale include purses, wallets, bags, scarves and carvings. The shop is located opposite the market in the centre of town. A worthwhile cause to support.

Senteurs d'Angkor 275 Psah Chas, Siem Reap. Located in the old market and sells good choice of handicrafts, pottery, silk items and flowers.

Chantiers Ecoles sells Khmer crafts, woodworking and stonecarving.

Lotus Market This small supermarket is located opposite the old market and has a limited stock of imported items for visitors with hankerings.

Practical information
Currency exchange
Several banks have branches in Siem Reap and they will all exchange travellers' cheques with a commission charge of 2%. Some banks can even advance cash on credit cards (such as Visa, JCB and MasterCard); there is a charge of 5% for up to US$250 and 2% on higher amounts.

Post office/telephones
The most dynamic post office outside Phnom Penh, selling postcards and colourful stamp collections. International calls can be made from here at a cost of US$5 per minute to Europe, Australia and the USA. The post is flown every day to Phnom Penh for onward delivery. The office is open daily 07.00–17.00 and is located by the river just south of the Grand Hotel d'Angkor.

Street phones are all over the city and the relevant phonecards, either Mobitel or Camintel, can be bought at nearby shops. As in Phnom Penh it is possible to make overseas calls from these phones.

Internet/email/fax
Internet and email services in Siem Reap were rather intermittent at the time of my visit and could not be relied on. The situation will probably have improved significantly by the time this book is published. The charges are rather high as it involves a long-distance call to Phnom Penh, but these should drop if the connection improves. Faxes can be sent from many hotels and also from the Swiss Centre and Lotus Temple Communications.

The Swiss Centre 66 Sivota Rd, Siem Reap; tel: 015 638808 (mobile); email: angkorswiss@worldmail.com.kh. As well as being a restaurant the Swiss Centre offers business services and some translation work (German and French). The internet and email were not working at all when I was visiting so no rates were available. They did plan to reintroduce this service at a later date.

ABC Computer School Sivota Rd, Siem Reap. Mainly a venue for individuals to learn computer skills but also offers an internet and email service. Rather expensive at US$4 for five minutes, US$5 for ten minutes, US$7 for 20 minutes, US$9 for 40 minutes, US$11 for 50 minutes and US$13 for one hour. Each email sent costs US$1.
Lotus Temple Communications tel: 012 884107 (mobile); fax: 063 380065; email: lotus@lotus-temple.com. Located next to the market and has facilities for fax, email and internet. Can also assist with car rental, local guides and travel arrangements.

What to see

The only reason visitors make their way to Siem Reap is to see the temples of Angkor, but if you have time it is worth checking out some of the town's other sights.

Something any visitor to Siem Reap really should make time to see is the floating villages and the Prek Toal bird sanctuary. A visit can be made by boat through **Osmose Nature Tours** who arrange full-day tours to Prek Toal and the villages for US$60 per person (children under ten US$30) including breakfast and lunch. The goal of Osmose is to promote conservation and sustainable development through the proceeds of ecotourism, so it's worthwhile giving them your support. They involve the local communities so that the Cambodians can appreciate the value of their environment and gain some benefit from helping to preserve it. As well as helping to protect the bird life, they also support the economy of the villages on the lake.

Osmose can be contacted on 012 832812 (mobile) or email: osmose@lotus-temple.com.

THE LANDMINE MUSEUM

The Landmine Museum is one of Siem Reap's more curious visitor sights. Located just off the road to Angkor Wat, the 'museum' is just a shack but it is full of a wide variety of ordnance including landmines, bomb casings, grenade launchers and rifles. The museum is owned by Aki Ra, a former soldier, who appears to have changed sides several times. Once responsible for laying mines as a teenager he later joined in the quest to clear them.

Outside the museum a scrubby area has been set outside which conceals an array of mines and booby traps, showing how difficult it is to spot them. Aki Ra assures visitors to his museum that all devices are safe, but there are still signs saying 'Don't touch'.

Floating villages on the Tonle Sap

The Tonle Sap lake has a rich ecosystem and is a protected area. Most visitors take boat trips on the lake to see the picturesque floating villages scattered around. The villages are perfectly formed communities with rows of houses, schools, shops, petrol stations and even a police station in one village.

Prek Toal bird sanctuary

On the northwest bank of the lake lies Prek Toal, a conservation reserve which has been designated a Biosphere Reserve by UNESCO. It is an undisturbed flooded forest and a hatching place for migrating waterbirds. It is one of the most important places in the region for the conservation of endangered species such as painted, adjutant and milky storks, spot-billed pelicans, oriental darter and black-headed ibis. The best time to visit is during the dry season, from December to March, when the concentration of birds is greater because the area of water has shrunk.

Landmine Museum

A couple of kilometres out of town on the Angkor Wat road is an extraordinary museum housing an extensive collection of mines and bombs. There is even a chance to test your skills at locating (defused) mines. Entrance is free but donations are invited for the upkeep of the museum.

Crocodile farm

Around 1km along the road to Phnom Krom is the crocodile farm which is open every day from 07.00 to 18.00 with an entrance fee of US$1.

THE TEMPLES OF ANGKOR

The temples of Angkor literally rise out of the jungle and each one is truly magnificent. It is easy to see why they are the symbol of Cambodia and a source of such fascination for visitors. The Angkorian period of Cambodian history is acknowledged to have begun in the 9th century with the crowning

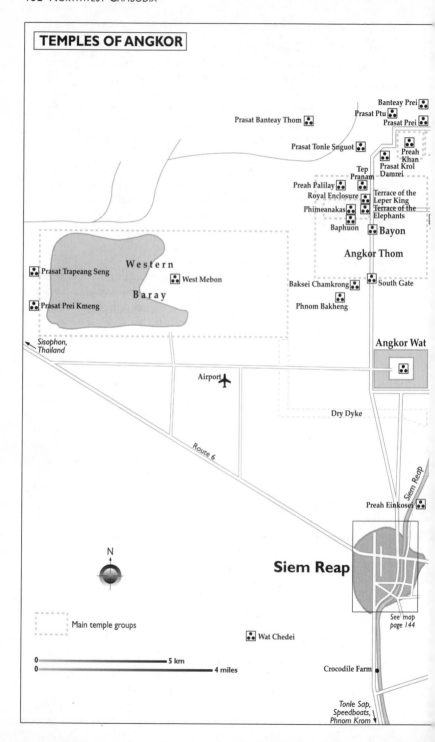

TEMPLES OF ANGKOR

Banteay Prei
Prasat Ptu
Prasat Prei
Prasat Banteay Thom
Prasat Tonle Snguot
Preah Khan
Prasat Krol Damrei
Tep Pranam
Preah Palilay
Royal Enclosure
Terrace of the Leper King
Phimeanakas
Terrace of the Elephants
Baphuon
Bayon
Angkor Thom
Western Baray
Prasat Trapeang Seng
West Mebon
Baksei Chamkrong
South Gate
Prasat Prei Kmeng
Phnom Bakheng
Sisophon, Thailand
Angkor Wat
Airport
Dry Dyke
Route 6
Siem Reap
Preah Einkosei
See map page 144
N
Main temple groups
Wat Chedei
0 — 5 km
0 — 4 miles
Crocodile Farm
Tonle Sap, Speedboats, Phnom Krom

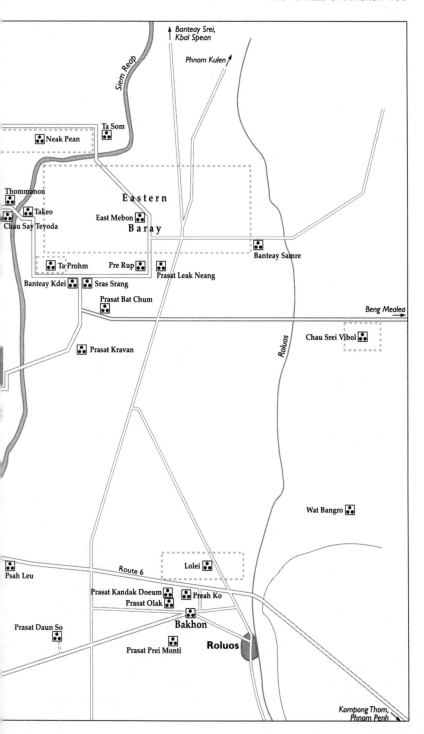

of Jayavarman II as the first god-king in 802 and ended when the kings relocated to the area around Phnom Penh in 1431.

After Angkor was abandoned to the jungle in 1431, although the locals always knew of its existence, it only came to the attention of Europe following the writings of Henri Mouhot on his expedition. The Ecole Française d'Extrême Orient was established in 1898 and by 1907 a group of archaeologists from this august institution had begun to study and restore Angkor. Work continued throughout the 20th century but this was interrupted during the civil war of the 1970s. At that time work on some of the monuments was at a delicate stage so before the conservators left they tried their best to make sure that the work they had carried out wouldn't deteriorate because it had to be abandoned in a hurry. Temple walls had to be shored up and some of the bas-reliefs were covered with special canopies to protect them.

The conservation of Angkor is now an international collaboration under the auspices of UNESCO. Angkor became a UNESCO World Heritage site in 1993 and archaeologists from many countries including Japan, America, Italy, Germany, Indonesia, France and China can still be seen working to restore some of the many temples. The Cambodian government is now actively involved in protecting the monuments and promoting the region.

THE LOOTING OF ANGKOR

A constant problem for the authorities has been looting and it is not a recent one. The first documented arrest for looting was that of the French journalist, André Malraux, who later became Minister of Culture under President de Gaulle. He was arrested just before he was due to leave Cambodia and found to be in possession of hundreds of kilos of stones from Banteay Srei temple. Photos dating from the 1920s show that even then many of the heads of statues had been looted. Much damage occurred during the civil war and when the country was under the control of the Khmer Rouge, who often used the temples as bases or hospitals. Looting continued when the country was liberated by the Vietnamese army and again once the country reopened when art collectors became interested and theft became more organised and professional. Collectors, particularly from Thailand, took advantage of the poverty of the people and paid them small amounts of money to steal artefacts which they then sold on for a fortune. Nowadays there is a special team who guard the temples and make regular checks. As a result, attempts to steal statues or cut out bas-reliefs are regularly foiled, although sadly not all the time. Bangkok is still the main conduit for looted items and some have been known to turn up in the most prestigious of institutions such as the Metropolitan Museum of New York. But attempts to stem the looting are too late for many exquisite statues or sections of bas-reliefs as is evident in the temples. It is all too obvious that many of the best artefacts have already been stolen and may never be returned.

The few visitors going to Cambodia when it reopened at the end of the 1980s found that nature was once again beginning to reclaim the temples of Angkor, with the jungle encroaching on the ruins and greenery growing through and over the walls. Sad though it was to see, the mysticism of the temples still shone through. Nowadays visitors are in for a treat as the area around the temples has once again been cleared and the work being carried out with international cooperation is ensuring that at least some of the vast number of temples will be with us for centuries to come.

Entry to the temples

The main temples are open from sunrise until sunset, and are easily accessible from Siem Reap by either moto, car or organised tour. The road system around the temples has been improved dramatically and the jungle cleared around the sites giving them a rather pristine appearance. Some of the temples further afield are reached along bad roads, but are definitely worth the effort. The authorities have become very organised and now there is a system of passes for access to the temples; these are checked regularly. A one-day pass costs US$20, 2–3 days US$40 and 4–7 days US$60. Passes can be bought at checkpoints en route to the temples or at the temples themselves if there is no checkpoint. Since mid-2000 the company which manages the pass system at Angkor has imposed a new ruling requiring all visitors to supply a passport-sized photograph on arrival. This will be attached to the permit to prevent any fraudulent use. Visitors arriving without photos can pay to have a polaroid photo taken.

Planning your trip

However interested you are in temples you may end up with temple burn-out because there are just so many wonderful examples here. The list of possible day visits below should help you to plan your time. I suggest that you allow a minimum of two days to see the major temples and preferably more to see some of those that are less visited, as well as some of the other sights (described above) that Siem Reap has to offer. A whole week around Angkor would be ideal. I've given details of the temples in the order in which they're shown in the list below.

Day one The two most famous temples are featured as well as two of the lesser ones. Angkor Wat, Angkor Thom, Chay Say Tevoda, Thommanon.

Day two Some lesser-known and smaller temples, giving an understanding of other periods in Angkor's history. Prasat Kravan, Banteay Kdei, Pre Rup, East Mebon, Ta Som, Neak Prean, Preah Khan, Takeo, Ta Prohm.

Day three These sites have been unsafe to visit until recently. You will definitely need a guide to take you to these as they are poorly signposted. Depending on the road conditions at the time these may take longer than one day to visit but try not to miss any. Banteay Srei, Kbal Spean, Phnom Kulen.

Day four The Roluos group of temples, Phnom Krom. (Try to get to Phnom Krom in time to watch sunset over Tonle Sap lake!)

Day five Banteay Samre, Western Baray

Day six Other sights in the Angkor area

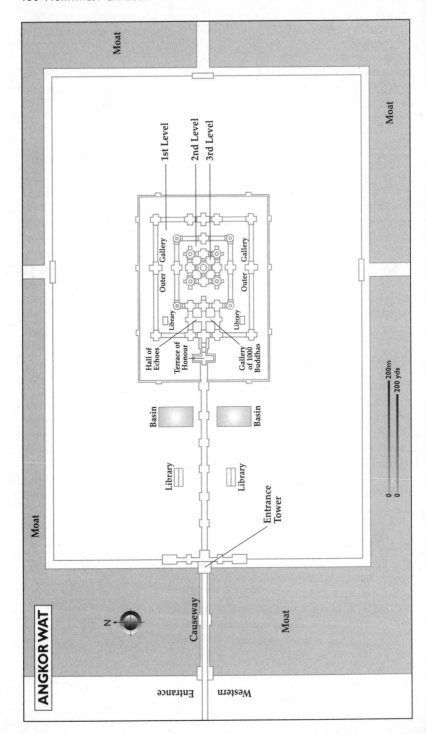

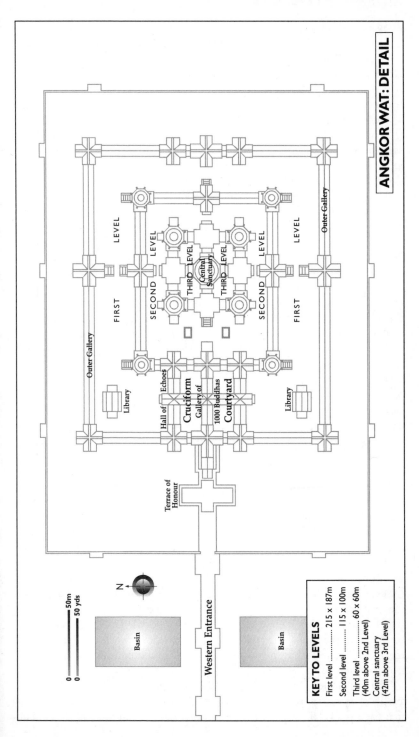

ANGKOR WAT: DETAIL

LEVEL

LEVEL

LEVEL

LEVEL

THIRD LEVEL

(Central Sanctuary)

THIRD LEVEL

FIRST

SECOND

SECOND

FIRST

Outer Gallery

Outer Gallery

Library

Library

Hall of Echoes

Cruciform Gallery of 1000 Buddhas

Courtyard

Terrace of Honour

N

Western Entrance

Basin

Basin

0 ____ 50m
0 ____ 50 yds

KEY TO LEVELS

First level .... 215 x 187m
Second level .... 115 x 100m
Third level .... 60 x 60m
(40m above 2nd Level)
Central sanctuary
(42m above 3rd Level)

Angkor Wat

This is the largest of the temples in the whole of the Angkor complex, the most visited and the most magnificent because of its size and location. Anybody seeing Angkor Wat for the first time will not be disappointed. It is still incredibly well preserved, probably because it was never totally abandoned but lived in by monks when it was converted to a Buddhist temple. Angkor Wat was built during the reign of Suryavarman II in the early 12th century and is believed to have taken up to 30 years to complete. The detail and the standard of construction are outstanding as it was the only temple built by the king and it took a long time to finish. It was constructed as a Hindu temple dedicated to Vishnu and is the only one of the temples to face west.

The temple is reached by crossing a 250m causeway over a vast moat. The authorities have renovated half the causeway and the walls bordering the moat to one side. The part of the causeway and walls left in their original state give an idea of what the temple endured through the ravages of time and climate. The main entrance, with galleries leading off either side, leads into an open area with a 350m walkway approaching the temple which is built on three levels and topped by five conical towers. It is only possible to see all five towers from certain angles. Only three towers are evident from the main entrance and this is the image depicted on the national flag of Cambodia. By leaving the walkway and crossing the grassed area you can get a good view of the temple including all of the towers. To either side of the walkway are two small buildings, believed to be libraries, which are beautifully preserved.

The first level of the temple itself has a gallery all the way round with some wonderful bas-reliefs. The sandstone carvings depict various stories and historical events and should be viewed from left to right. In a few places the carvings are very shiny, probably the result of visitors touching the walls. On entering the gallery from the main walkway it is best to go anti-clockwise around the walls. The first story is that of the Hindu epic, the Mahabharata, which tells of the battles between two families and has graphic detail of the two armies at different stages of the fighting. Turn the corner and the south-facing wall also has scenes from historical battles led by Suryavarman II. It clearly shows the methods used, ranks of fighting elephants, typical dress and helmets worn. Another section, renovated by the French in 1947, shows what can be expected in the afterlife in both heaven and hell. Note that a number of small square holes have been cut into the walls. It is not known when this was done but they may have contained valuable items or been an attempt to find such items. The panel in the east gallery depicts another Hindu myth of the Churning of the Ocean of Milk where the gods and demons work together to produce an elixir to make them immortal. The north gallery has scenes from the Ramayana and represents the war between the demons and the gods. Finally back at the west gallery the last section depicts a battle scene from the Ramayana.

The second level has covered galleries around small pools and the walls are decorated with figures of *apsaras*. On close inspection it becomes evident that each of the figures is different with varying hairstyles and dress. The third level of Angkor Wat was for the king and high priest only. Twelve sets of steps ascend to the upper level, eleven of which are at an angle of 70 degrees and one at 45 degrees. Do not attempt to climb them if you suffer from vertigo, but one of the steeper steps has a handrail to help descend. At the time of my visit it was not possible to use the less steep steps because one night a security guard heard a loud noise and in the morning it was discovered that an enormous crack had appeared. The top level has a tower at each corner with a taller one at the centre. The four towers are joined by galleries and from these you can enjoy some stupendous views of the surrounding jungle.

Good views of sunrise or sunset over Angkor Wat and Tonle Sap lake can be seen from nearby **Phnom Bakheng**. However, it is a far from mystical experience because you will be in the company of crowds of people who have

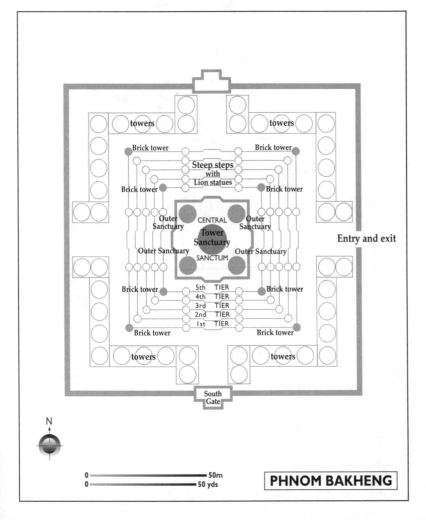

PHNOM BAKHENG

Central Tower, Angkor Wat

hauled themselves up the steep incline. A more leisurely, although rather expensive way to get there is to ride an elephant to the top. The temple at the summit of the hill was built during the reign of Yasovarman I and was the first temple to be built with five sandstone sanctuaries on the top level of seven tiers. In addition, the base had 44 towers and each of the five levels had 12 towers. Sadly, most of these have collapsed.

Angkor Thom

Angkor Thom was the capital city of Jayavarman VII, built during the end of the 12th century and early 13th century and was home to a huge population.

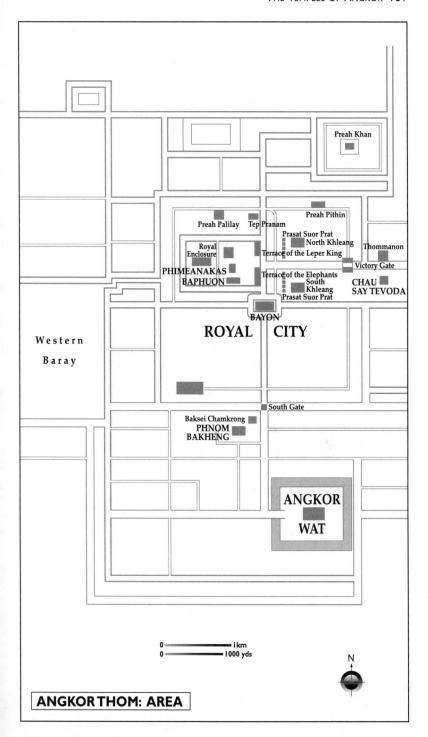

Preah Khan

Preah Pithin

Preah Palilay   Tep Pranam

Prasat Suor Prat
North Khleang

Thommanon

Royal
Enclosure

Terrace of the Leper King

PHIMEANAKAS

Victory Gate

BAPHUON

Terrace of the Elephants
South
Khleang

CHAU
SAY TEVODA

Prasat Suor Prat

BAYON

ROYAL   CITY

Western

Baray

South Gate

Baksei Chamkrong

PHNOM
BAKHENG

ANGKOR

WAT

0 ▬▬▬ 1km
0 ▬▬▬ 1000 yds

N

ANGKOR THOM: AREA

Many of the original buildings within the walls were made of wood and these have disappeared; but the surviving stone edifices within the walls of the city give a glimpse into life in this impressive capital. The city is surrounded by a vast laterite wall which had five entrances, four facing north, south, east and west, with an additional one along the east wall. Each entrance is reached across a causeway, flanked by 54 gods and 54 demons holding a *naga*, over a

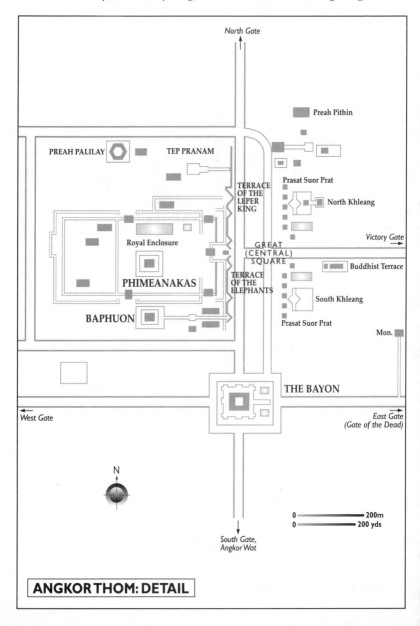

ANGKOR THOM: DETAIL

South Gate, Angkor Thom

wide moat. Many of the heads have been stolen or moved for safekeeping and the few examples there are generally copies. Each entrance has a 24m gate with four heads facing different directions and three-headed elephants at each corner of the base. Originally there would have been wooden doors and one or two of the entrances still have the remains of wooden beams. The best-preserved entrance is the *south* gate and it is particularly attractive in the morning light.

The Bayon

At the heart of the city of Angkor Thom is the Buddhist temple, the Bayon. Originally the temple was thought to be Hindu by archaeologists, but later discoveries revealed that it was in fact Buddhist. Fifty-four towers dominate the temple, each with four enigmatic faces. It is claimed that the faces are the image of the King, Jayavarman VII, and each one has a rather secretive smile.

The temple is built on three levels but its layout is maze-like and the levels are indistinct. Unlike Angkor Wat the temple has suffered: many columns have tumbled down and ceilings collapsed. However, this does not distract from the majesty of the building and it is a great favourite with visitors. The pillars on the first and second levels are decorated with some delightful dancing *apsaras*. Modern dancers come to the temple to study the carvings in order to recreate some of the ancient dances. Two small libraries are located on the east side of the first level and these have been carefully renovated by Japanese craftsmen.

The extensive bas-reliefs in the Bayon are quite exquisite and, unlike those at Angkor Wat, depict scenes from daily life. Those on the outer wall depict historical events and scenes include fishing, hunting, cooking, women looking after children, the playing of games, cockfighting and even some humour with a turtle biting the behind of a man. In addition there are many battle scenes and military processions including the fighting between the Khmers and the Chams which show that the hill tribes and possibly even the Chinese fought alongside the Khmers. The battle scenes on the west side appear to be unfinished. The bas-reliefs on the inner walls are mainly mythological subjects.

The temple was converted to a Hindu one in the 13th century by Brahmins after the death of Jayavarman. Scores of buddhas in niches on the second level

Details of bas-relief, The Bayon

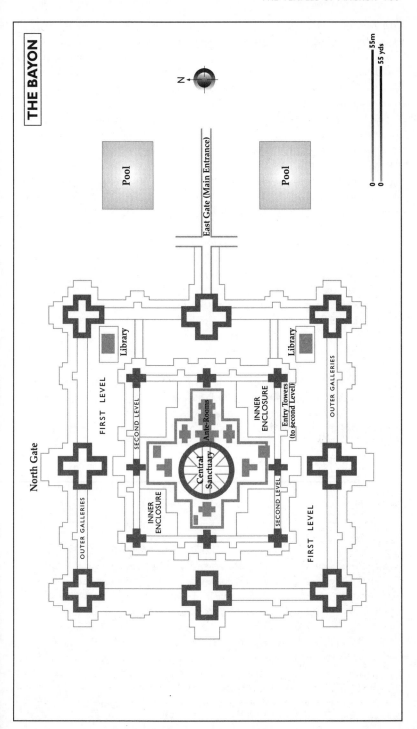

THE BAYON

N

Pool

Pool

East Gate (Main Entrance)

North Gate

Library

Library

FIRST LEVEL

SECOND LEVEL

INNER ENCLOSURE

Ante-Rooms

Entry Towers (to second Level)

Central Sanctuary

INNER ENCLOSURE

SECOND LEVEL

FIRST LEVEL

OUTER GALLERIES

OUTER GALLERIES

55m
55 yds
0
0

THE BAS-RELIEFS OF THE BAYON

Extensive bas-reliefs decorate the galleries running around the first and second levels of the Bayon Temple. The outer gallery is particularly fascinating for visitors as it depicts daily life in great detail as well as scenes from historical battles. Being deeply carved the bas-reliefs are generally in a good state of repair and Cambodian scholars have learned much about Khmer life from them. Although the reliefs are virtually complete there are a few areas where they have never been finished.

Starting on the eastern side and moving in a clockwise direction the outer gallery begins with military scenes divided into three panels. The procession shows the warriors of the two armies (Khmer and possibly Chinese), King Jayavarman VII and his commanders mounted on elephants, the carts used to carry supplies and the women following on to cook for the king's entourage. The bas-reliefs of the southern gallery, again on three tiers, show the battle between the Khmers and the Chams on the Tonle Sap and the fighting boats and galleys packed full with armed warriors. The bottom tier depicts life for the Khmers on the banks of the Tonle Sap and it is particularly honest and even humorous. Family scenes are shown with the women tending the children, playing games, preparing meals, while men are fishing, hunting and cockfighting.

The section of the bas-reliefs on the western side are incomplete and again depict scenes from battles with hand-to-hand fighting. The northern section has some combat scenes but there is a delightful section with entertainers such as jugglers and acrobats as well as a procession of animals. Part of the northern side has completely collapsed.

Unlike those in the outer gallery, the bas-reliefs of the inner gallery are not continuous as the galleries are divided into smaller rooms and contain many mythical scenes of Hindu origin. Again starting on the eastern side and walking in a clockwise direction the first rooms have countryside scenes including hunting followed by military processions. The southern gallery has a mix of military processions, combat scenes and daily life and then images of Siva and Vishnu appear. The first small room on the western side shows heavenly *apsaras* performing in the palace to the accompaniment of musicians; the following rooms have Vishnu superimposed over a scene of workers constructing a temple, Siva and Vishnu together and palace scenes. The next section contains images from the Hindu epic, the Churning of the Ocean Milk, where gods and demons churn the ocean milk for 1,000 years to make an elixir of immortality. (The most famous bas-relief of this Hindu epic is sculpted on the east gallery of Angkor Wat.) Finally, the northern gallery has a mix of scenes from the palace and then images of Siva, Vishnu, Brahma and Ganesh. Other scenes represent Siva in meditation.

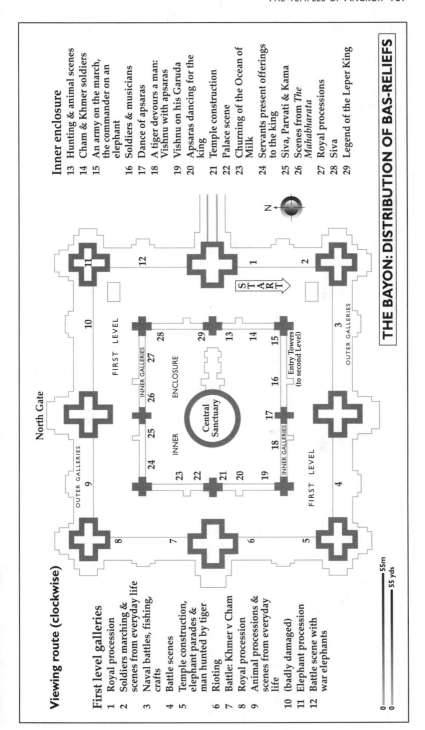

Viewing route (clockwise)

First level galleries

1 Royal procession
2 Soldiers marching & scenes from everyday life
3 Naval battles, fishing, crafts
4 Battle scenes
5 Temple construction, elephant parades & man hunted by tiger
6 Rioting
7 Battle: Khmer v Cham
8 Royal procession
9 Animal processions & scenes from everyday life
10 (badly damaged)
11 Elephant procession
12 Battle scene with war elephants

Inner enclosure

13 Hunting & animal scenes
14 Cham & Khmer soldiers
15 An army on the march, the commander on an elephant
16 Soldiers & musicians
17 Dance of apsaras
18 A tiger devours a man: Vishnu with apsaras
19 Vishnu on his Garuda
20 Apsaras dancing for the king
21 Temple construction
22 Palace scene
23 Churning of the Ocean of Milk
24 Servants present offerings to the king
25 Siva, Parvati & Kama
26 Scenes from *The Mahabharata*
27 Royal processions
28 Siva
29 Legend of the Leper King

North Gate

FIRST LEVEL

OUTER GALLERIES

INNER GALLERIES

INNER ENCLOSURE

Central Sanctuary

Entry Towers (to second Level)

START

N

THE BAYON: DISTRIBUTION OF BAS-RELIEFS

0 — 55m
0 — 55 yds

were taken out and it can be seen where attempts were made to transform a buddha carving into a flower. They also tried to chisel the eyes of the huge statues so that they appeared open rather than shut.

Baphuon

Despite being in a very bad state of repair this Hindu temple, built in 1060 by Udayadityavarman II, is being painstakingly repaired by a team from France. Because of the degree of destruction the work is like assembling a puzzle and the area is strewn with numbered pieces of stone which are slowly being put back in their original place. Work actually began at the beginning of the 20th century but it was interrupted several times, particularly by the civil war in the 1970s. Although work began again in earnest in 1995 it is believed that it will be 2003 before the reconstruction is complete.

Plans on display indicate that the temple was dedicated to Siva. Reports from the 13th century state that the temple was originally covered in bronze but none of that remains today and, as much of the temple is collapsed, it is difficult to imagine how magnificent it would have been. The temple, on five levels, is approached by a raised walkway but the central tower collapsed a long

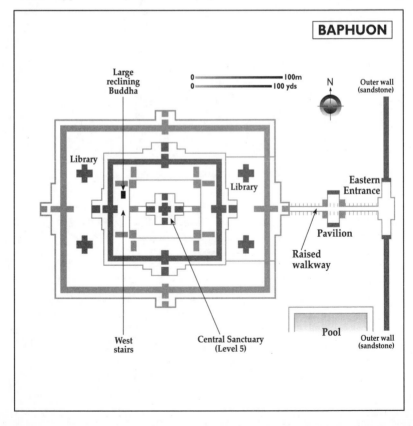

time ago. The walls of the Baphuon are famous for their bas-reliefs showing scenes from the Ramayana and depicting daily life. Regrettably, it is not currently possible to explore the structure itself because of the ongoing work, but once finished it will be a real treat to visit.

Royal Enclosure

This was the area of Angkor Thom where the royal family and servants lived but because many of the buildings would have been made from wood nothing survives and it is impossible to say how it would have looked. At the east side of the enclosure are two terraces, which still remain, and inside is the temple of Phimeanakas and two bathing pools. Most of the surrounding wall was destroyed by encroaching vegetation.

Phimeanakas

Built in 944, this Hindu temple was dedicated to Siva and was used personally by the king. Phimeanakas was built of sandstone and laterite on three tiers with a gallery on top and is believed to have been covered in gold. This was the first time such a gallery was seen. Each layer has an elephant in and lions decorated the set of steps on each side. Close by are two bathing pools, one for men and one for women.

Terrace of the Leper King

This terrace is actually a raised platform which is thought to have been used for ceremonial cremation. The walls of the laterite terrace are covered with

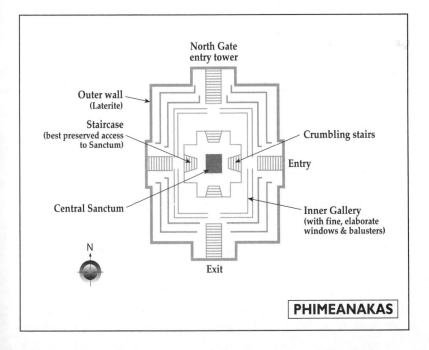

bands of sandstone bas-reliefs showing *garudas*, *nagas* and *apsaras*. On top of the platform is a statue which is said to represent the Leper King. However, it is not clear exactly who the Leper King was, but there are theories that it is either Jayararman II or Yasovarman I who may both have had leprosy. Alternatively the statue may have been so named because of the lichen growing on it which looks rather like the ravages of leprosy. The terrace has been extensively rebuilt and the Leper King statue is actually a copy.

Terrace of the Elephants
The larger Terrace of the Elephants is around 300m in length, running between the Baphuon and the Terrace of the Leper King, and has a few platforms which may have been used for viewing by the king and other dignitaries. Originally there would have been wooden shelters to protect the royal party while they were watching the entertainment but, at the same time, allowing the king to be seen by his people. The terrace is beautifully decorated with impressive bas-reliefs of elephants in profile, hunting and fighting. One set of steps going up to the platform is flanked by three-headed elephants and another is decorated with lions and *garudas*.

Facing the terraces of the Leper King and the Elephants are 12 crudely built laterite towers known as **Prasat Suor Prat**, whose purpose is disputed, and behind them are the **North** and **South Kleangs** which are thought to have been accommodation for foreign dignitaries.

Chau Say Tevoda
This is a 12th-century Hindu temple which is in bad repair. The main entrances have totally collapsed and the external wall has completely disappeared. The columns of the causeway have small stone pegs on top which would have held the walkway in place. The rectangular temple has a central sanctuary with some intricate carvings on the columns and false doors and lovely female statues in niches. Chay Say Tevoda is currently being renovated by a team from China.

Thommanon
Across the road is another 12th-century Hindu temple which has similar features and has been totally renovated by the French. The outer walls have disappeared although the east and west entrance gates still remain. The central tower has four doorways, three of which are false, all well decorated. To one side is a small building which was used as a library.

Prasat Kravan
On first sighting this temple almost looks modern because of the light, clean bricks. However, it is one of the oldest, built in 921, and has some remarkable brick bas-reliefs inside which are not found elsewhere. The five towers, unusually arranged in one straight row, have all been renovated by the French and many of the exterior bricks had to be replaced hence the new appearance of the buildings. The interior bricks were renovated and there

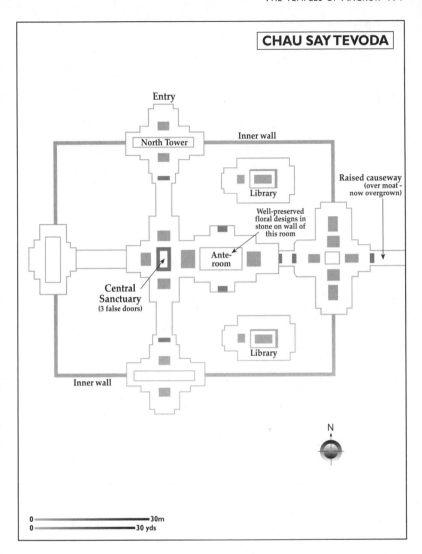

CHAU SAY TEVODA

Entry

North Tower

Inner wall

Library

Raised causeway
(over moat -
now overgrown)

Well-preserved
floral designs in
stone on wall of
this room

Ante-
room

Central
Sanctuary
(3 false doors)

Library

Inner wall

N

0 ▬▬▬▬▬ 30m
0 ▬▬▬▬▬ 30 yds

are superb sculptures of Vishnu in the central tower and of his wife Lakshmi in the end one.

Banteay Kdei

Banteay Kdei has never been restored so it is not easy to imagine how it would have looked at its height. Built by Jayavarman VII in the 12th century, around the same time as Ta Prohm, it is believed to be dedicated to his teacher. At each main entrance there is an elaborate gateway flanked by four *garudas* which were a particular favourite of the king. In front of the east entrance is a large artificial lake called Sras Srang, probably used for ritual bathing. In the dry season it is possible to see the foundations of an old temple in the middle of the lake.

East Mebon

Built by King Rajendravarman II in 952 and dedicated to Siva, this temple is built on a platform because at one stage it could only be reached by boat as it was surrounded by water, the **Eastern Baray**. Standing on the uppermost of the three tiers you can imagine how impressive it must have been when it stood in the middle of a huge lake, now a vast area of rice paddies. The temple itself was one of the last structures to be built using brick but it also incorporates laterite and sandstone. The five towers clustered at the top are of brick with sandstone doors. Holes in the bricks indicate where plaster was originally attached and it is possible to see the outline of an *apsara*.

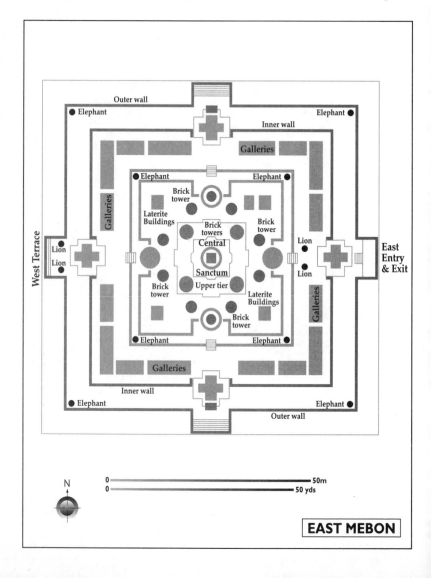

EAST MEBON

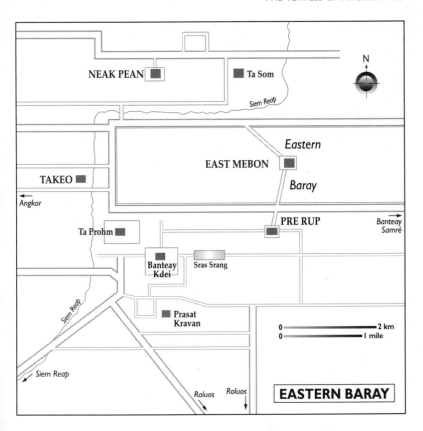

Magnificent sandstone elephants which stand at each corner of the first two tiers appear quite realistic from a distance.

Pre Rup

Like the East Mebon, this was also one of the last brick temples, built in 961 by the same king and dedicated to Siva. Similar in design to East Mebon, it also has five towers on the third and top level which were once covered in plaster. The temple was thought to have been used for funerary purposes as there is a pedestal at the foot of the stairs on the east side which archaeologists believe was the site for cremations. The name means to turn the body, being a ritual of cremation where the outline of the deceased is traced using the ashes at different aspects. The temple is currently being renovated by a team from Italy.

Ta Som

This temple is beautiful despite its advanced state of dereliction. Much of it has collapsed and there are termite hills blocking many of the doorways. Built in 1191 by Jayavarman VII, this temple, like Ta Prohm, has been left in its natural state and is very atmospheric in its dilapidation. It is built on a single

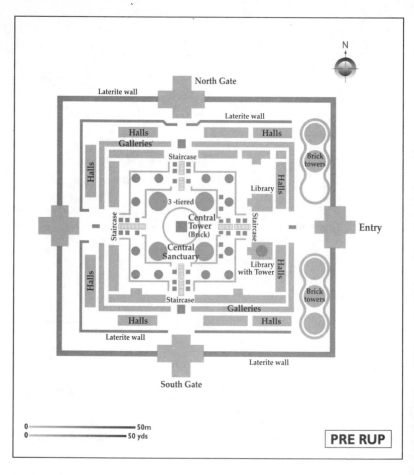

level with entrances on the east and west sides. You can enter the temple but it does involve a certain amount of scrambling over fallen blocks to be able to see the central tower.

Neak Pean

This unusual temple could be reached only by boat in its heyday and was used as a place to consult an astrologer and take the waters for a cure or to absolve sins. The small temple, built in the 12th century, is set on a small seven-tiered base which is encircled by two *nagas* at the very bottom in a large pool, surrounded by four smaller pools. The central tower stands on lotus flowers. The small pools each have a small building housing the head of an animal from whose mouth the holy water from the main pool flows. Pilgrims consulted an astrologer who decided which animal head, either human, elephant, lion or horse, they should go to and they then washed themselves in the water pouring from its mouth. Even now the weed growing in the pools is harvested for its curative properties.

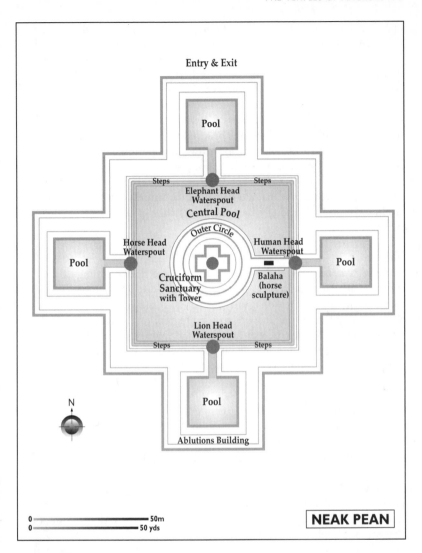

Entry & Exit

Pool

Steps   Steps

Elephant Head
Waterspout

Central Pool

Outer Circle

Horse Head
Waterspout

Human Head
Waterspout

Pool

Pool

Cruciform
Sanctuary
with Tower

Balaha
(horse
sculpture)

Lion Head
Waterspout

Steps   Steps

N

Pool

Ablutions Building

0 ———— 50m
0 ———— 50 yds

NEAK PEAN

Preah Khan

The World Monument Fund have a particular interest in this temple and regularly carry out conservation work on site. Just inside the gate is a small exhibition centre showing aspects of their work. There is an enchanting avenue with columns either side leading up to the temple which lies deep in the jungle. As the sun sets each evening, the area is alive with the calls of many birds.

Constructed in 1191 by Jayavarman VII it was originally a Buddhist temple, but was gradually changed to a Hindu temple during the 13th century after the death of the king. Evidence of this can be seen where small Buddhas in niches in the walls have either been transformed into Hindu statues or taken out completely. A short causeway over a man-made moat is lined by guardians on one side and demons on the other pulling a *naga*. This is a smaller version of the one found at the south gate of Angkor Thom, but here most of the heads have been taken. At the centre of the temple four passageways intersect and here you can see the structure of the galleries in all four directions. In the central tower is a stupa which replaced the statue of the king's father in the 16th century. A large hall is decorated with a series of *apsaras* on the lintels and is referred to as the Hall of Dancers. To the left is a two-storey building with rows of round columns which was believed to be a library although there are no stairs leading to the second floor. Round columns were the last of the Angkor style and subsequent columns were square.

Much of the temple is very tumbledown and archaeologists have left one side of the structure in its natural state with the tendrils of tree roots entwined around the walls, although in many cases these are actually holding the structure together.

Takeo

Built by Jayavarman V at the end of the 10th and the beginning of the 11th century, this is a Hindu temple dedicated to Siva. The temple was never finished and the exact reason is unknown other than that the king died in 1001 and this may have brought work to a premature end. It is a very imposing temple built on five levels with five towers, originally surrounded by a moat. Unlike many of the other temples around Angkor, it has no decoration as the type of sandstone used was very difficult to carve.

Ta Prohm

Apart from Angkor Wat and the Bayon, this temple must be one of the most recognisable because of the oft-shown photo of a tree and its gigantic roots spreading out over the walls. In fact there are numerous trees which are growing through the temple and archaeologists have left it virtually as it was found. There are two reasons for doing this. One is to show the state of many of the temples before they were reclaimed from the jungle and another is because the tree roots are often holding the structure together. One can imagine how the first explorers must have felt when discovering these mysterious temples, so long hidden by the jungle.

Ta Prohm was built in 1186 by King Jayavarman VII as a Buddhist temple and dedicated to his mother. It is a particularly attractive building as it is made up of small galleries and courtyards linked by passageways, although many are impassable because so much of the temple has tumbled down. In fact the appearance of the temple gives the impression that there has been a severe earthquake as the causeway over the dry moat is higgledy-piggledy and blocks of stone are strewn around inside the complex. The whole temple is surrounded by a laterite wall. It was clearly a very important temple because Sanskrit inscriptions indicate that over 79,000 people were needed to run the temple and that it owned over 3,000 villages. Listed among the items owned by the temple were diamonds, pearls and precious stones.

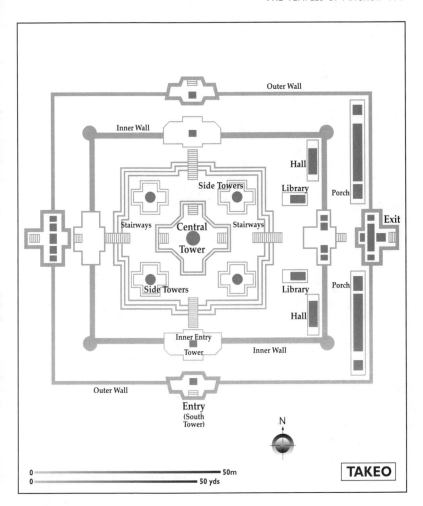

Outer Wall

Inner Wall

Hall

Library

Porch

Side Towers

Stairways Central Stairways
           Tower

Side Towers

Library Porch

Hall

Inner Entry

Tower Inner Wall

Exit

Outer Wall

Entry
(South
Tower)

N

0 ━━━━━━━━━━ 50m
0 ━━━━━━━━━ 50 yds

TAKEO

Banteay Srei

For so long out of bounds because of the security situation, this temple is now a great favourite with visitors and is a real gem. Although only 32km from Siem Reap it is reached along a bumpy road and the trip can take up to two hours, depending on the season. Banteay Srei, built in 968, is only a small temple but it is particularly attractive and beautifully preserved because of the type of sandstone used. Pink sandstone is soft when it is carved allowing for very deep sculptures. The sandstone becomes harder as it weathers and this results in an extraordinary state of preservation of the hundreds of ornate bas-reliefs. The temple was built by the Brahmin teacher to King Jayavarman V.

The temple is surrounded by walls which enclose a now dry moat over which there is a laterite causeway decorated by lotus-bud columns. Inside are a series of small galleries and enclosures. Photographers will be spoilt for choice as some of the finest examples of Khmer carvings are to be found

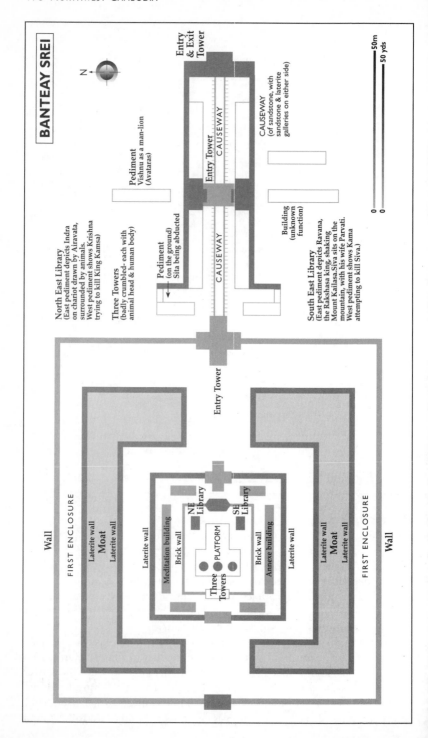

BANTEAY SREI

N

Entry & Exit Tower

Entry Tower

CAUSEWAY

CAUSEWAY

Pediment
Vishnu as a man-lion
(Avataras)

North East Library
(East pediment depicts Indra
on chariot drawn by Airavata,
surrounded by animals.
West pediment shows Krishna
trying to kill King Kamsa)

Three Towers
(badly crumbled- each with
animal head & human body)

Pediment
(on the ground)
Sita being abducted

South East Library
(East pediment depicts Ravana,
the Rakshasa king, shaking
Mount Kailasa.Siva sits on the
mountain, with his wife Parvati.
West pediment shows Kama
attempting to kill Siva.)

CAUSEWAY
(of sandstone, with
sandstone & laterite
galleries on either side)

Building
(unknown function)

0 ___ 50m
0 ___ 50 yds

Wall

FIRST ENCLOSURE

Laterite wall
Moat
Laterite wall

Laterite wall

Meditation building

Brick wall

NE Library

PLATFORM

Three Towers

SE Library

Brick wall

Annexe building

Laterite wall

Laterite wall
Moat
Laterite wall

Entry Tower

FIRST ENCLOSURE

Wall

everywhere on lintels, walls and doors. In addition there are intricate scenes from the Ramayana and some wonderfully detailed figures in niches.

The temple was renovated in the 1920s and 1930s by the French and there are some sections of wall which have been blackened where they burnt away the jungle.

Kbal Spean

Located around 10km past Banteay Srei, Kbal Spean, or River of a Thousand Linga, is a particularly pleasant, little-visited site of riverbed carvings believed to date from the 11th century. It is worth taking a guide with you as it is rather difficult to find. A barrier marks the entrance to the area and then there is a 30-minute walk to the top of the hill and on to the river. Soldiers are generally posted at the barrier and may act as your guide for a fee. The riverbed carvings have bas-reliefs with representations of Vishnu, Rama and Lakshmi as well as hundreds of linga, from where the name comes. The river is located upstream from Angkor and the linga were placed there to bless the water before it ran down to the royal city.

Phnom Kulen

Phnom Kulen is the most sacred site in Cambodia for the Khmers and is a sandstone plateau overlooking Banteay Srei temple. Here in 802AD Jayavarman II proclaimed himself to be the God King and independent from Indonesia, and so began the Angkor period. The area is now quite safe to visit apart from a strong warning not to stray from established paths as it has not yet been demined. The area is guarded by the military and they indulge in a little private enterprise, charging up to US$20 per person to enter the site. It takes around two hours to reach the top of the mountain where there is a small pagoda nestled between some rocks. Here there is a huge reclining Buddha carved into the rock. En route up the mountain you cross a river where you can see hundreds of linga sculpted into the riverbed. To the right from the pagoda is a path which leads to some waterfalls where you can enjoy a refreshing swim following your exertions.

Roluos group

The Roluos group is reached by taking Route 6 past the market for around 16km. Three temples make up this group, all dating from the late 9th century and all dedicated to Hindu gods. They are all built using brick and sandstone and are among the earliest examples of this form of construction.

Lolei

This temple is raised up on a platform and consists of four brick towers originally surrounded by water. It is believed the water was used to supply the city of Hariharalaya as well as for irrigation purposes. It was built by King Yasovarman I in 893. There is evidence that the king originally planned to erect six towers but it is not known why they were never completed. The towers have numerous decorations and inscriptions on their sandstone

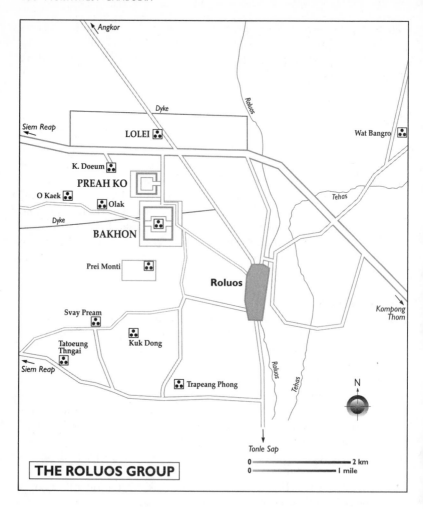

THE ROLUOS GROUP

entrances including the panels on false doors and particularly attractive lintels. Little niches on the sides of the towers still have exquisite figures inside them. One very attractive aspect of this temple is that there is still a community of monks living here.

Preah Ko

The simple beauty of Preah Ko or sacred ox is one that will stay with you. The temple, built in 879, is dedicated to the ancestors of King Indravarman I and was originally surrounded by a wall and a moat. It is the only one of the temples to still have some of the original plaster covering the bricks. As in Lolei there are numerous niches with fine statues inside and there are also some delicate carvings on the lintels and columns. There are six brick towers on low platforms, the ones in the front being larger than those behind. The small towers were dedicated to the king's female ancestors and the large ones

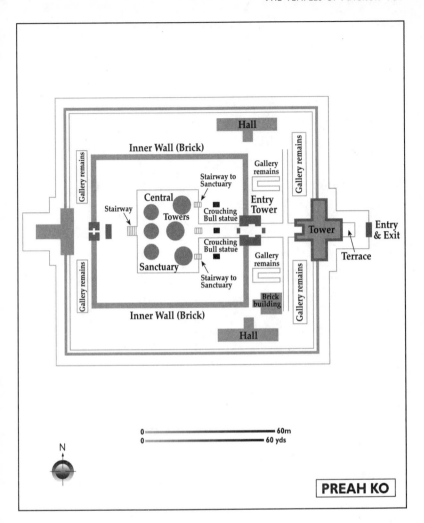

PREAH KO

to the male ancestors. Work is currently under way to renovate the temple, with funding from Germany, and a form of cement is being mixed to put between the rows of bricks made from palm sugar, lime, clay and crushed brick. This is the nearest to the original cement used although the exact method is still not clear, as on first inspection there appears to be nothing holding the structure together.

Bakhon

To the south of Preah Ko is Bakhon, the largest of the three Roluos temples and the most impressive. Built in 881 and dedicated to Siva, it has five levels with a central tower surrounded by eight brick towers representing Mount Meru. The corners of each level are mounted with statues of elephants. The whole of the temple complex is surrounded by a laterite wall enclosing a

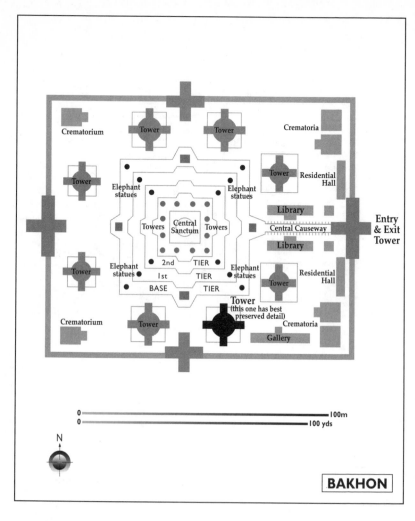

now dry moat and a causeway on the east and west sides crossing the moat. The causeway has balustrades on either side made of *nagas*. The eight towers each have four doors but three of them are false with fine decorations. In common with the other two temples there are niches on the tower walls containing small statues. A rather incongruous Buddhist temple has been built inside the complex with a busy community of monks.

Phnom Krom

Located near to where the boats arrive from Phnom Penh, this 9th/10th century temple with a hilltop setting has stunning views over Tonle Sap Lake and offers a perfect view of the sunrise or sunset. The temple has three sandstone towers in a line dedicated to Siva, Vishnu and Brahma which are enclosed by a laterite wall with an entrance on each side. Parts of the towers have collapsed and much

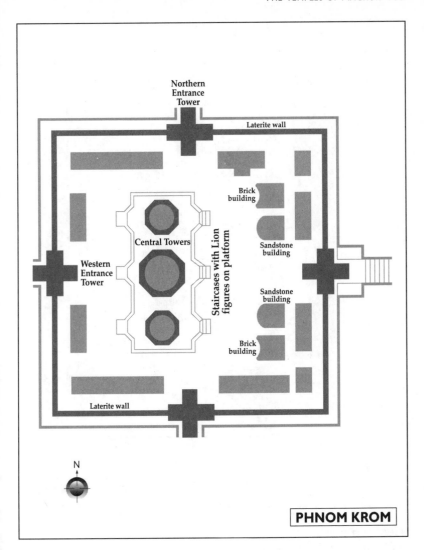

PHNOM KROM

of the decoration on their walls has been eroded. Also within the enclosing wall are four buildings which may have been used for cremation purposes.

Banteay Samre

Like Banteay Srei this is another remote temple which was built by Suryavarman II in the middle of the 12th century. This little-visited Hindu temple, dedicated to Vishnu, contains some well-preserved bas-reliefs although a number have been damaged by thieves. The temple, similar in style to Angkor Wat, is enclosed by a laterite wall inside which is a moat. There are entrances on each side of the wall, but the one on the east side leads you to the central sanctuary. Interestingly, the bas-reliefs on the upper levels of the central tower depict Buddhist scenes.

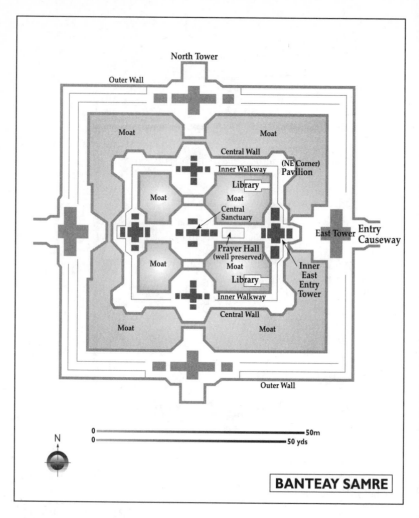

BANTEAY SAMRE

Western Baray

This is out past the airport to the west of Siem Reap. It is the largest artificial lake in the Angkor region and in the middle of it are the ruins of the temple of **West Mebon**. It is believed to have been built in the second half of the 11th century and dedicated to Vishnu. A magnificent bronze statue of Vishnu was found in the temple and this is now on display in the National Museum in Phnom Penh.

BATTAMBANG

Battambang is one of the most charming towns in Cambodia, with faded colonial buildings including the wonderful old Governor's House, the first building of note you see on entering the city from Phnom Penh. The road by the river is pleasant to walk along, particularly at night when there are numerous food stalls to choose from. Open to visitors only in the past couple of years, the relaxed ambience of the town belies its recent past as a government stronghold, frequently attacked by the Khmer Rouge. Although it is Cambodia's second city it is fairly compact and quite manageable on foot. Many of the shops are along Street 1 bordering the river. The province of Battambang is actually home to more temples than at Angkor, but many are inaccessible.

The province of Battambang is known as Cambodia's rice bowl as rice paddies stretch unbroken into the distance. The province is a relatively wealthy one because of the rice, particularly as it has a small export market to Thailand. In fact the province's links with Thailand go back a long way as Battambang has had a rather chequered history. Battambang province together with Siem Reap and Sisophon was long claimed by the Siamese. In 1863 King Norodom decided to make Cambodia a French Protectorate, which he felt would stop the country being carved up between the Siamese and the Vietnamese. However, he was unprepared for the fact that the French would recognise the claims of the Siamese. The three provinces came under the control of Siam but at the end of the 19th century French troops tried to regain them, succeeding only in 1907. Battambang was once again ceded to Thailand in 1941 (Siam changed its name to Thailand in 1939) following the occupation of Cambodia by the Japanese during World War II. However, this lasted only until 1946 when the province was once again returned to Cambodia.

Getting there and away
By air
The three domestic airlines offer flights between Phnom Penh and Battambang and the journey time is approximately 45 minutes. One airline advertised flights between Battambang and Siem Reap but they weren't running when I was there. The published timetables change regularly so do check days of operation and do not fail to reconfirm your booking two to three days before departure. It is also advisable to contact the airline again the day before departure to check that the flight time has not changed. There is a domestic departure tax of US$4 from Battambang.

Phnom Penh Airways 72 St 3,Battambang; tel: 012 894782 (mobile). Phnom Penh Airways operates four flights per week on Monday, Wednesday, Friday and Saturday from Phnom Penh. Booking office open daily 07.00–17.00. Fares from Phnom Penh US$40 single and US$80 return.

President Airlines 225 St 3, Sangkat Ekpheap Srok Svay Por, Battambang; tel: 053 952915. This airline has an early morning flight every day except Sundays from Phnom Penh. Booking office open daily 07.00–11.00 and 14.00–17.00. Fares from Phnom Penh US$45 single and US$85 return.

Royal Air Cambodge Plauv Kapko, Battambang; tel: 053 952794. RAC fly daily from Phnom Penh to Battambang with all flights in the early morning. Booking office open daily 08.00–12.00 and 13.00–17.00 but closed Sunday afternoons. Fares from Phnom Penh US$45 single and US$90 return.

By boat

There is a daily speedboat service between Battambang and Siem Reap. It departs from close to the bridge near Battambang hospital at 07.00. The service from Siem Reap also departs at 07.00 from the dock approximately 13km from Siem Reap (or possibly further away during the dry season). The boat takes 60 people and the one-way fare is US$15 with a journey time of 3.5 hours. However, during the dry season tiny speedboats have to be used which take around 12 people. These frequently break down but there is an engineer on board who sits on the engines at the back ready to undertake running repairs or clear vegetation from the propeller blades. It is not the most comfortable journey on the small boats but it is a lovely way to see life on the river especially when passing through the many floating villages en route.

By train

There is a daily train service between Battambang and Phnom Penh which takes around 12–14 hours leaving at 06.00 in both directions. If you want to travel overland, you're faced with a tough decision between being uncomfortable in the train or in a taxi.

By road

Long-distance taxis travel the route between Battambang and Phnom Penh. Taxis depart from the market in Battambang and the Central Market in Phnom Penh. The fare is 20,000 riels for a seat in a pickup truck or 15,000 riels if you are prepared to sit on the back. The journey along Route 5 varies from good to appalling: several places have enormous craters in the road, often with trucks jammed in them, causing absolute chaos but a form of entertainment for the locals. Be prepared to be jiggled about for around eight hours.

The route from Battambang to Siem Reap is equally as bad along Route 5 and Route 6. The journey time is between six and eight hours and the fare US$7.

Getting around

Battambang is small enough to walk around comfortably but there are plenty of motos around town and a journey should cost no more than 1,000 riels. In order to get out of town to some of the interesting temples you should negotiate with a moto driver for a day rate of around US$10. Your guesthouse will probably be able to arrange a car for the day, if required, for around US$35 to take you to some of the more out-of-the-way sites.

Accommodation

For a town that has seen little tourism in recent years it has some surprisingly good hotels. The main reason for this is that many were built for UN personnel in the early 1990s and a large number have survived because there is a lot of NGO activity in the area. Fortunately prices are good throughout the town.

Angkor Hotel St 1 Sangkat Svay Por, Battambang; tel: 053 952310. Located on the main street facing the river with many of the 27 rooms having a small balcony

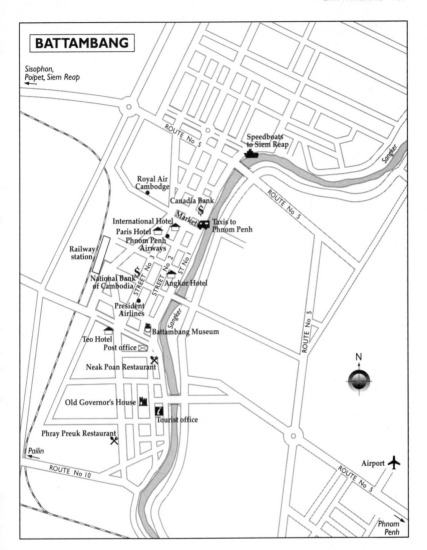

BATTAMBANG

Sisophon,
Poipet, Siem Reap

ROUTE No 5

Speedboats
to Siem Reap

Songker

Royal Air
Cambodge

ROUTE No 5

Canadia Bank

Market

International Hotel

Taxis to
Phnom Penh

Paris Hotel

Phnom Penh
Airways

Railway
station

STREET No 3

ST No 2

ST No 1

National Bank
of Cambodia

Angkor Hotel

President
Airlines

ROUTE No 5

Songker

Teo Hotel

Battambang Museum

Post office

N

Neak Poan Restaurant

Old Governor's House

Tourist office

Phray Preuk Restaurant

Pailin

ROUTE No 10

Airport

ROUTE No 5

Phnom
Penh

overlooking the river. Rooms are good and clean with air conditioning, satellite TV
and private bathroom, some with hot water. There is no restaurant. Rooms cost
US$10 and US$12 with hot water.

Paris Hotel 30 St 3, Battambang. Acceptable standard hotel but can be rather noisy at
night. Twenty-seven rooms with either fan or air conditioning, satellite TV and private
bathroom (only air-conditioned rooms have hot water). No restaurant. Rooms with fan
cost US$5 and those with air conditioning cost US$8 single and US$10 twin.

International Hotel Battambang. Not as good as the Angkor or Paris but still quite
reasonable. Well located opposite the market, but this could be rather noisy,
particularly in the early morning. It has 26 rooms with air conditioning, satellite TV
and private bathroom with hot water. No restaurant. Rooms cost US$10.

Teo Hotel St 3 Khum Svay Por, Battambang; tel: 053 952288. The best and possibly the largest hotel in Battambang with 81 rooms and very friendly service. This is popular with the NGOs visiting the province and the rooms are bright and well finished with air conditioning, satellite TV and private bathroom with hot water. Has a restaurant with quite an extensive menu and good breakfasts. Rooms cost US$10 single, US$12 twin and US$15 for a suite.

Restaurants

The restaurants in town are good value for money and popular with both visitors and locals, which is always a good recommendation. The food stalls which appear by the river in the evening are also worth a try.

The **Chipsreng** is rather a scruffy restaurant but excellent food, particularly the hotpots. Excellent prices and always busy with locals and foreign NGOs.

The **Neak Poan** is a large outdoor restaurant serving good Khmer food but rather spoilt by the appalling singers on stage during the evenings.

The **Phray Preuk Restaurant** is close to the Teo Hotel. It is open all day serving hearty breakfasts and tasty Khmer food. Very good value for money and definitely the best place in town.

Practical information
Currency exchange

The National Bank of Cambodia and Canadia Bank in Battambang can exchange travellers' cheques and there is a 2% commission charge. For exchanging cash the jewellery stalls in the market have a better exchange rate. The National Bank is open Monday to Friday 07.30–11.00 and 13.00–15.00 and the Canadia Bank 08.00–15.30 Monday to Friday and 08.00–11.00 on Saturday. The Canadia Bank is planning to introduce credit card transactions at the end of 2000. The proximity of Battambang to Thailand means that Thai baht is legal tender here.

Post office

The staff in this office speak a little English and are very willing to help. It is possible to make phone calls within Cambodia from the post office, but not overseas. The post is sent to Phnom Penh on Tuesday, Thursday and Sunday for onward delivery. It is open Monday to Saturday 06.00–18.00 and Sunday 08.00–11.00 and 14.00–17.00.

Phone/fax/internet/email

There are numerous interphone shops around Battambang, particularly along Street 1. Here it is possible to make international phone calls and send faxes and the charge for one minute is US$1.50 to Europe, Australia and the USA. Some of the shops even have internet/email facilities where the charge is US$2 per minute.

There are Camintel street phones throughout the town using the phonecards which are on sale close to the location of each phone.

What to see

The colonial area of the city and the area by the river are particularly pleasant to explore. One place worth a visit in town is the **Battambang Museum** which has a collection of artefacts from the many temples in the surrounding area. At one stage every town in Cambodia had its own museum, but now only this one and the National Museum in Phnom Penh survive. The museum has a rather hefty entrance fee of US$5 and is open Monday to Friday 08.00–15.00. Next door to the museum is a permanent cultural exhibition with hundreds of photos, displayed in no particular order. Photos show typical scenes from the present day and the French period, national dress, traditional dancers, mine victims and even photos of the temples of Angkor dating from 1921 which show that, even then, many of the heads of the statues had already been stolen.

The area around Battambang is rich in temples although many are still inaccessible. Around 20km south of Battambang is **Wat Banan**, a 10th-century temple. The smaller roads leading to the area in which the temple is located are kept in good order by a World Food Programme project where local people work for food. The project ensures that the road is kept open and maintained by the locals. The countryside is very peaceful with miles of rice paddies and large citrus plantations. Wat Banan is on top of a small hill reached by a flight of stairs that were, at one time, guarded by a number of lion statues. Many of these have sadly been stolen or damaged. Five laterite and sandstones towers top the hillside, although one has collapsed completely and the whole area is rather overgrown and neglected. Many of the delicate bas-reliefs decorating each tower have been vandalised and the faces of *apsaras* and elephants have been hacked off. It is widely believed that the theft of artefacts is paid for by Thai collectors. To one side of the temples is an abandoned Vietnamese gun which was used during fighting with the Khmer Rouge during the 1980s when the whole area was a battlefield. Many of the houses in the village below are quite new as many families feel that it is now safe to return to the area.

From a distance **Phnom Sampeau** is truly spectacular as the temple sits atop a soaring rocky outcrop visible from miles around. It is located about 25km from Battambang. There are over 600 steps to reach the top so take the opportunity to drink some refreshing coconut milk from the food stalls at the bottom before attempting the climb. However, the steps divide into a few different paths so there are a number of stops to be made on the way up. Children hang around offering to be your guide and they are to be recommended as paths criss-cross the hilltop and it would be easy to get lost. A series of caves is used as a temple with a small community of monks and nuns living there, one of whom lives inside a small cave made cosy by many candles. A rocky path leads to a killing field where victims were thrown down into a cave below. The skulls and bones are housed in a large cabinet with the victims' tatty clothing hanging up to one side. There are also two large Vietnamese guns hidden on the hill. The wat itself at the top of the hill is rather disappointing as it is very plain and modern-looking.

After visiting Phnom Sampeau a short ride takes you to **Kamping Poy**, the site of a long dyke which was part of an irrigation project built by slave workers of the Khmer Rouge. This was one of many similar projects carried out around the country during that period. Thousands of Cambodians are believed to have died during the construction. Now it is a very peaceful area where people come to swim, fish or take boat trips on the lake.

Wat Ek Phnom, 15km north of Battambang is a tumbledown 11th-century temple which looks as though a set of massive building blocks has been thrown on the floor. It is quite amazing that some of the walls are still standing as they teeter at strange angles. It is quite beautiful in its present, tragic position. A lot of the damage was caused by the Khmer Rouge who smashed up the stones to build irrigation canals.

PAILIN

Pailin must be one of the strangest towns I visited in Cambodia. The economy of the town exists on the income from the nearby gem mines and its proximity to the Thai border 30km away gives it a definite frontier feel. At the moment the border is only officially open to Thai and Cambodian nationals. The town is interesting in that it is under the control of Ieng Sary, a former Khmer Rouge minister who changed sides, together with all his men, in 1996. The change was hardly noticeable as all the characters remained the same but they now represent the government instead of the Khmer Rouge. Officials in the town are quite open about the fact that they are the Khmer Rouge with a new image. Prior to this the Khmer Rouge had regularly launched attacks from Pailin on the government soldiers in and around Battambang.

The gem-rich town benefits greatly from business with Thailand, although the money does not seem to reach the town itself as it is rather scruffy. Every other stall in the market deals in gems, and jewellery is hand-made on the spot. However, it is important that you know what you are doing before handing over vast amounts of cash as the quality of gems varies enormously. Pailin was the only town I entered where there was an official-looking military post, supposedly checking for smuggled items. However, the search was very cursory and the obligatory cash 'donation' was passed over.

Getting there and away

Pailin is reached on a very poor road from Battambang, 83km away, and it takes anything between two and four hours depending on the season. The area was heavily mined during the civil war so it is important never to stray from roads and paths around town and en route there from Battambang. Demining is still in progress and the road to Pailin passes a big base belonging to one of the mine-clearing organisations. There are also huge billboards at regular intervals graphically showing the consequences of standing on or picking up landmines. Despite this problem many people are moving into the area and a number of new villages are appearing. Long-distance taxis are the

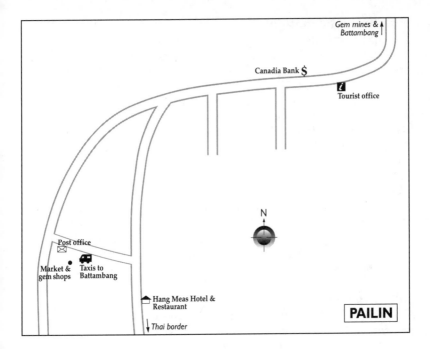

only way to travel between the two towns and these can be found by the markets in Pailin and the Psah Leu on the outskirts of Battambang. The fare is 20,000 riels inside and 15,000 riels on the back of the pickup.

There are plans to open the border with Thailand at some stage and the road from Pailin will be upgraded in 2001.

Accommodation
Pailin has only one main hotel in town although there are a number of unnamed guesthouses. The situation may change once the border is open and when tourists feel happy to stay in the town.

Hang Meas Hotel Pailin; tel: 016 820675 (mobile). Although only opened in June 1999 it already looks rather shabby. However, the staff are very friendly and the accommodation is fine with 50 rooms with air conditioning, satellite TV and bathrooms with hot water. There is a huge restaurant with a karaoke system which is probably very popular at weekends. Rooms cost US$11 single and US$17 twin with breakfast included.

Restaurants
There are numerous unnamed small restaurants and food stalls around town, especially in the market area and on the road to Battambang.

Hang Meas Pailin Restaurant Pailin; tel: 016 820675 (mobile). Located in the grounds of the Hang Meas Hotel and serves very good Khmer food at excellent prices.

Practical information
Currency exchange
The number of jewellery stalls in the market makes visitors spoilt for choice when it comes to exchanging money. The keen competition means that the exchange rate is good. Travellers' cheques can be exchanged at the Canadia Bank and the commission charge is 2%. At the moment credit cards are not accepted. The bank is open Monday to Friday 08.00–15.30 and Saturday 08.00–11.30. Because of Pailin's proximity to the Thai border the Thai baht is legal tender here so it is common for prices to be quoted in baht and for baht to be given in change.

Post office
There is a tiny office by the market selling stamps. Post is sent to Phnom Penh on Mondays and Thursdays. There are no land lines in Pailin so only mobile phones are used. However, there is a Samart office (a Thai phone company) in town from where overseas calls can be made. There are plans to introduce street phones in 2001.

What to see
The main reason to visit Pailin is to go to the gem-mining areas which are close to town and stretch into the distance. The mines are quite different from those in Rattanakiri province. Here the soil is deposited in ponds to be washed and panned in a similar way to gold whereas in Rattanakiri the soil is brought up from deep circular holes and the dry earth is sifted for gems. The prospectors search through the damp soil looking for sapphires and rubies, although to the unpractised eye it is a mystery how they ever spot the gems when everything is covered in mud. A few of them even have a generator to pump water to wash away the mud. The workers are quite relaxed about handing over a bag of gems for you to inspect. The stones are sold to the merchants in town who polish them by hand and then sell them loose or set them in jewellery. The small shops in the market and around town are happy to show you hundreds of loose gems varying in value from a few dollars to hundreds of dollars.

SISOPHON
Most people will only find themselves in Sisophon if travelling overland from Thailand to Siem Reap. Even then they are unlikely to stay there unless the going on the road is so slow and it is getting too late in the day to continue the journey. Because of the poor state of the road it is often easier to drive off-road than on. Once Route 6 linking Thailand to Siem Reap is upgraded the situation could change dramatically and the formal go-ahead was given for this in May 2000 with work to begin very shortly. Naturally more tourists will pass through and the town could benefit from an increase in trade. Alternatively people may literally drive through without stopping. The town is located at an intersection of roads – Route 5 from Battambang and Phnom Penh, Route 6 from Siem Reap and Phnom Penh, the road to Poipet and Thailand and the road to Banteay Chhmar and the Dangrek Mountains.

If you find yourself having to overnight in town there are numerous guesthouses on the main road which offer basic facilities for around US$3. Rooms for around US$10 with air conditioning and bathrooms with hot water can be found at the **Phnom Svay Hotel** and the **Proum Meanchey Hotel**.

Getting there and away

Shared pickup taxis travel between Sisophon and Poipet on the Thai border for around US$2, Siem Reap for US$4 and Battambang for US$2. The journey time to either Siem Reap or Battambang can be around 6–8 hours. There is a daily train service between Sisophon and Battambang taking around 3–4 hours.

What to see

Sixty kilometres north of Sisophon is a little-visited Angkorian temple, **Banteay Chhmar**. The road to the temple is quite appalling and the security situation should be checked with the NGOs in Sisophon before setting out. Because of its remote location, and its closeness to Thailand, the temple has been plundered several times with the most recent major robbery taking place in 1998.

POIPET

The border between Thailand and Cambodia at Poipet has been open to foreigners for a few years now and is well used. The town is very scruffy, probably because it was often the scene of battles between the Khmer Rouge and government troops until 1997. The town looks as though it has been thrown up and the streets turn to a quagmire in the rainy season. The border itself is a hive of activity with a steady flow of consumer goods, both legal and smuggled, crossing over.

It is very unlikely that you will need to overnight in Poipet and better if you don't as many guesthouses quote room rates by the hour! Better to stop in Aranyaprathet on the Thai side or, if time, continue to Sisophon.

KOMPONG THOM

Until fairly recently Kompong Thom was a no-go area because it was under the control of the Khmer Rouge led by the infamous Ta Mok. Now a trickle of visitors are finding their way to the town to visit the nearby ruins of Sambor Prei Kuk (see page 195). Kompong Thom itself is a little dull but, as in any town, there is a bustling market which is always worth a visit.

Getting there and away
By road
The only way to reach Kompong Thom is by road as there is no airport nor is there a speedboat service. Shared long-distance taxis travel from Kompong Thom to Phnom Penh and Siem Reap. Taxis depart from the Central

Market in Phnom Penh and by the market Psah Leu in Siem Reap. The taxi station in Kompong Thom is near to the Post Office and Neak Meas Hotel. The 4WD taxis on the Siem Reap route cost 20,000 riels per person. The journey from Siem Reap starts well but after around 1.5 hours the road deteriorates and has numerous potholes. Old women make a show of filling the potholes with dirt in the hope of securing a few riels from passing vehicles and then shake their fists when no money is forthcoming. The journey time is around five hours. The road is good from Phnom Penh to Kompong Thom so 4WD is not necessary. Cars cost 7,000 riels per person for up to seven people and a seat in a minibus costs 5,000 riels for up to 19 passengers.

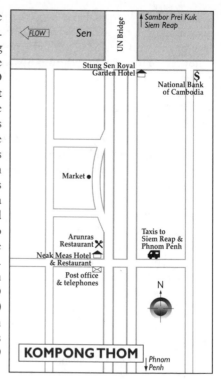

Accommodation

Stung Sen Royal Garden Hotel Kompong Thom; tel: 062 961228. Quiet location close to the Sen River and the modern metal bridge over the river built by the UN. Good-sized rooms, 33 in total, with air conditioning, satellite TV and private bathroom with hot water. There was no restaurant at the time of my stay but there will be one added during 2000. Singles cost US$20 and twins US$25.

Neak Meas Hotel Kompong Thom; tel: 062 961294. Rather dingy hotel but the rooms themselves are fine, particularly those on the first and second floors which have private bathrooms with hot water. All 37 rooms have satellite TV, air conditioning and private bathrooms. The disadvantage is that there is a noisy nightclub/karaoke bar which doubles as a restaurant on the ground floor. First- and second-floor rooms cost US$12 and third-floor rooms US$8.

Restaurants

There are numerous unnamed local restaurants and food stalls around town, particularly in the market area, but most people go to the Arunras Restaurant which is close to the Neak Meas Hotel and just down the road from the Stung Sen Hotel. It is open from early morning for breakfast, when it is very busy, and the Khmer-only meals are very good with excellent prices. There is a restaurant attached to the Neak Meas Hotel which is also always busy but very noisy.

Practical information
Currency exchange
Money can be exchanged in the market. There is a National Bank of Cambodia in town but it does not currently accept travellers' cheques or credit cards.

Post office
Friendly office run by a French-speaking gentleman. Post goes to Phnom Penh every day from Monday to Friday. Office is open 07.30–11.30 and 14.00–17.00 and closed on Saturday and Sunday.

In the grounds of the post office is a Camintel office for international phone calls. Mobitel also plan to introduce an IDD service next to the post office.

Shopping
A lively local market dominates the town selling fruit, vegetables, meat and household items. The meat stalls are not for the squeamish as all parts of the slaughtered animals are on display and it is not uncommon to come face to face with a pig's head as it is carried away by the purchaser.

SAMBOR PREI KUK
This little-visited site predates Angkor by a few hundred years, and was established by King Isnavarman I at the beginning of the 7th century as the capital of the kingdom of Chenla. He probably chose this site in the valley of the Sen River for the fertility of the plain which is partially flooded in the rainy season. The journey to Sambor Prei Kuk takes around 1.5 hours from Kompong Thom along a very bad road and a local guide is absolutely necessary to find the site. However, it was announced in May 2000 that approval had been given to upgrade the road to the temples and this project should be completed by the end of 2001. Compared with those of Angkor the ruins are rather disappointing, but bearing in mind the age of the temples the site is quite remarkable. There were originally over 200 temples but only 107 remain with 17 of these being in good condition.

The temples are divided into three groups, built at different times throughout the 7th century, and dotted around the forest which was cleared by UNESCO between 1993 and 1995. It was impossible to visit the temples before then. Local residents now receive food from the World Food Programme in return for keeping the forest clear. The temples are shaped like square or octagonal towers built from brick, many with highly decorated sandstone lintels and bas-reliefs on the outer walls. The inside of each tower is quite impressive as the bricks rise to a narrow shaft. Scattered around the towers are the remains of pedestals for lingum. The temples were Hindu, dedicated to Siva, and some Sanskrit inscriptions have been found.

The northern and southern groups are believed to have been built by Isnavarman I but the central group was built at a later date by his son. Remains of the laterite surrounding wall can still be seen as well as the remnants of the east gate which is held together by tree roots. A few pillars from a causeway still survive in the southern group.

The site is open daily and there is an entrance fee of US$2 per person. Allow a full day to reach the site and to explore it properly.

PREAH VIHEAR

Although it is located in Cambodia, the best and really the only way to reach the temple of Preah Vihear is from Thailand. In fact, until 1963, it was claimed by the Thais. Perched dramatically on a hilltop in the Dangrek Mountains the temple has a commanding view over northern Cambodia and for this reason it is strategically well-positioned militarily. Thus from time to time it has been in the hands of the Khmer Rouge and off-limits to visitors. The temple has been accessible since 1998 and this time it is hoped that this will be a permanent state of affairs.

The 11th-century temple is once again open to visitors, and very popular too, although care must be taken never to stray from paths as the danger from land mines is significant. You should also be prepared to climb many steps because of its hilltop location. Access is from Ubon Ratchatani province in Thailand and the site is open daily from 08.00 to 16.00. When you leave Thailand and enter Cambodian territory the Thai authorities keep hold of your passport until you return. Make sure you take a picnic lunch with you as there are currently no foodstalls, which is strange as most temples are jam packed with them.

KOMPONG CHHNANG

The fast boats between Phnom Penh and Siem Reap stop at Kompong Chhnang and the view of the town from the docks is not a pleasant one. However, travellers passing through on Route 5 from Phnom Penh to Battambang will see an attractive town with some delightful colonial architecture. There are no particular sights in town so there's no need to break your boat journey for an overnight stop, but visitors travelling by car may wish to have a break here. Alternatively it is a pleasant day trip by Ho Wah Genting bus from Phnom Penh. Buses leave from near the Central Market throughout the day but day-trippers should look at taking one of the buses leaving at 06.40, 08.00 or 09.00. In the afternoon buses return to Phnom Penh at 14.00, 15.30 and 16.30. The fare is 4,500 riels each way.

Appendix 1

LANGUAGE

The Khmer language has 33 consonants and, amazingly, 26 vowels. Unlike Chinese and Vietnamese, it is not a tonal language, which makes it easier.

Ai	is pronounced as in high	Bp	takes the p sound
Ay	as in pay	Oo	as in look
Dt	takes the t sound	Ao	as in cow

Useful terms

English	Khmer pronunciation
Hello	*jum-reap soo-a*
Goodbye	*jum-reap leah*
Good morning	*arun suor sdei*
Good evening	*sa-yoanh suor sdei*
Good night	*reah-trey suor sdei*
How are you?	*tau neak sok sabbay jeu tay*
My name is	*kínyom tch muoh*
What is your name?	*neak ch'muah ei*
Yes	*baat*
No	*dteh*
Please	*sohm mehta*
Thank you	*or-koon*
See you later	*juab kanea tangay kray*
How much?	*tílay bponmane*
It is too expensive	*tílay na*
Where is…?	*noev eah nah*
Excuse me	*sohm dtoh*
Help me	*neak aa-it juay knyom*
Call a doctor	*juay hav kruu paet mao*
Call the police	*juay hav polih mao*
I don't understand	*kínyom men yoo-ul the*
I want	*kínyom jang baan*
Turn right	*bot dtov kahng s'dum*
Turn left	*bot dtov kahng ch'wayng*
Straight on	*dtov dtrong*

Useful words and phrases

airport	*wial yaun hawh*	tea	*dtae*
bus station	*kuhnlaing laan*	water	*dteuk*
	ch'nual	meat	*saich*
railway station	*ra dteah plerng*	vegetables	*ponlae*
post office	*bprai sa nee*	fish	*dt'ray*
restaurant	*haang bai*	bread	*num bpung*
toilet	*bawn gooun*	salad	*salat*
beer	*bia*	doctor	*krou paet*
coffee	*cafe*	hospital	*monthii paet*

Days of the week

Monday	*t-ngai jan*	Friday	*t-ngai sok*
Tuesday	*t-ngai ong-gee-a*	Saturday	*t-ngai sao*
Wednesday	*t-ngai bpoot*	Sunday	*t-ngai aa-dteut*
Thursday	*t-ngai bpran-hoa-a*		

Months of the year

January	*ma ga raa*	July	*ka kada*
February	*komphreal*	August	*say haa*
March	*meenah*	September	*kan'ya*
April	*meh sah*	October	*dto laa*
May	*oo so phea*	November	*wech a gaa*
June	*mi thok nah*	December	*t'noo*

Numbers

1	*moo ay*	30	*saam seup*
2	*bpee*	40	*seah seup*
3	*bey*	50	*haa seup*
4	*buon*	60	*hok seup*
5	*bpram*	70	*jeht seup*
6	*bpram moo ay*	80	*bpait seup*
7	*bprm bpee*	90	*gao seup*
8	*bpram bey*	100	*moo-ay roy*
9	*bpram buon*	1,000	*moo-ay bpoan*
10	*dahp*	10,000	*moo-ay meun*
11	*dahp moo ay*	100,000	*moo-ay sain*
20	*m'phey*	1,000,000	*moo-ay lee-un*

Appendix 2

GLOSSARY

Apsara	Heavenly dancer
ASEAN	Association of Southeast Asian Nations
Baray	Man-made water reservoir
Bas-relief	Wall carvings which project slightly from the background
Buddha	A person who has reached enlightenment
CGDK	Coalition Government of Democratic Kampuchea
Cham	Muslim people originally from central Vietnam
Chenla	A state which existed in Cambodia from the 6th to 8th centuries
Chunchiet	Hill tribes
CPP	Cambodian People's Party
Democratic Republic of Kampuchea	Khmer Rouge period of Cambodian history
Devaraja	Cult of the god king initiated by Jayavarman II
FUNCINPEC	National Front for an Independent, Neutral, Peaceful and Cooperative Cambodia
Funan	A state which existed in Cambodia from the 3rd to the 7th centuries
Garuda	Half man and half bird
HALO Trust	Mine-clearing charity
Ho Chi Minh Trail	Supply route for the north Vietnamese troops
Khmer Republic	Period of government under pro-Western Lon Nol
Khmer Rouge	Revolutionary soldiers who seized power in 1975 and instigated a reign of terror
Khmers	Indigenous people of Cambodia
Kingdom of Cambodia	Period from independence in 1953 until 1970 and once again from 1993
KPNLF	Khmer People's National Liberation Front
Krama	Scarf worn by many Cambodians
Laterite	Red, porous soil used in road building and in temple construction in ancient times
Linga	Symbol of the male sexual organ
MAG	Mines Advisory Group
Moto	Motorbike taxi

Naga	Mythical multi-headed serpent
New people	City residents prior to the Khmer Rouge period
NGO	Non-governmental organisation
Old people	Peasants prior to the Khmer Rouge period
People's Republic of Kampuchea	Period when Cambodia was run by a government installed by the Vietnamese
Phnom	Hill or mountain
Psah	Market
Ramayana	Hindu epic
State of Cambodia	Period following the withdrawal of the Vietnamese and prior to Sihanouk being crowned as king once again
Tonle Sap	Largest freshwater lake in Cambodia
UNDP	United Nations Development Programme
UNTAC	United Nations Transitional Authority in Cambodia
Wat	Word originating from Thailand meaning 'temple'
WRI	World Resources Institute
WWF	Worldwide Fund for Nature
Year Zero	The advent of the Khmer Rouge period in 1975

Appendix 3

FURTHER INFORMATION
Further reading
History
Brown, Ian *Oxfam Country Profiles: Cambodia*, Oxfam Educational 1999. Profiles Cambodia as it goes through a period of rapid change

Chandler, David *A History of Cambodia*, Silkworm Books, Thailand 1996. An in-depth study of the last one thousand years in the history of Cambodia

Chandler, David *Brother Number One* – A political biography of Pol Pot, Allen & Unwin, 1993

Kiernan, Ben *How Pol Pot came to Power*, Verso, London 1985. A history of events in Cambodia prior to 1975

Ngor, Haing S *Surviving the Killing Fields*, Chatto & Windus, London 1985

Ponchaud, Francois *Cambodia Year Zero*, An analysis of Cambodia 1975–9 originally published in French

Shawcross, William *Sideshow: Kissinger, Nixon and the Destruction of Cambodia*, Simon & Schuster, New York 1979. A critical examination of US policies

Shawcross, William *The Quality of Mercy: Cambodia, Holocaust and the Modern Conscience*, Fontana 1984. A study of the period immediately after the liberation from the Khmer Rouge

Szymusiak, Molyda *The Stones Cry Out: A Cambodian Childhood 1975–80*, New York 1986. An account of life under the Khmer Rouge, originally published in French

Temples of Angkor
Dagens, Bruno *Angkor Heart of an Asian Empire*, Thames & Hudson. Fascinating accounts of various explorers who encountered Angkor.

Jacques, Claude *Angkor*, Konemann, Cologne 1996. English version of a coffee-table book which takes an in-depth look at all aspects of Angkor

Jacques, Claude and Freeman, Michael *Ancient Angkor*, Thames & Hudson, 2000. A paperback handbook of the ancient temples

Rooney, Dawn Angkor *An Introduction to the Temples*, Odyssey Guides, Hong Kong 1997. The recommended book for visitors to the temples at Angkor

Zephir, Thierry *Khmer Lost Empire of Cambodia*, Thames & Hudson. The story of Angkor when it was at its most powerful.

Non fiction

Children of Cambodia's Killing Fields – Memoirs by Survivors, compiled by Dith Pran, Silkworm Books, Thailand 1997

Anderson, Liz *Red Lights and Green Lizards: a Cambodian Adventure*, Wayfarer 1999

Downie, Sue *Down Highway One*, Allen & Unwin 1993. A journey through Vietnam and Cambodia.

Lewis, Norman *A Dragon Apparent – Travels in Cambodia, Laos and Vietnam*, Eland Books, reprinted 1982. A classic tale of Lewis' journey in 1950.

Livingstone, Carol *Gecko Tails*, Weidenfeld & Nicolson, London 1996. A fascinating tale of a young stringer working in Cambodia during the UNTAC period.

Osborne, Milton *Sihanouk: Prince of Light, Prince of Darkness*, Allen & Unwin 1996. A biography of King Sihanouk.

Swain, Jon *River of Time*, Minerva, 1996. An account of his time in Vietnam and Cambodia between 1970 and 1975.

Yathay, Pin *Stay Alive, My Son*, Bloomsbury, London 1987. A compelling tale of individual survival during the Khmer Rouge period.

Websites

There are numerous sites on Cambodia and many have excellent links to related sites.

www.cambodia-web.net Official website of the Kingdom of Cambodia with maps, tourist information, online business directory with links to websites for hotels, travel agencies etc and events calendar. Is not updated regularly but gives useful general information.

www.tourismcambodia.com Informative site in conjunction with the Ministry of Tourism.

www.cambodia.org Good site with some links to informative pages.

www.embassy.org/cambodia Official website for the Cambodian embassy in Washington DC. Contains visa information, help with the language, tourist information and some useful tourism statistics.

www.bigpond.com.kh/kids/Phnom_Penh/preface.htm Everything the visitor needs to know about Phnom Penh.

www.bigpond.com.kh/kids/Siem_Reap/preface.htm Everything the visitor needs to know about Siem Reap.

www.bigpond.com.kh/kids/Sihanoukville/preface.htm Everything the visitor needs to know about Sihanoukville.

www.datacomm.ch/pmgeiser/cambodia Internet travel pages but rather sketchy and not always updated.

www.newspapers.com.kh Site for the *Phnom Penh Post*. To see the full version of the paper it is necessary to be a subscriber.

www.principal-city.com Site for the *Principal* magazine which has a small selection of its articles but was rather incomplete at the time of checking.

www.phnompenhdaily.com Series of articles from back issues, but partly still under construction.

www.itisnet.com Internet Travel Information Service which has detailed information on countries worldwide including Cambodia. Not always up to date.

www.krousar-thmey.org Charity which assists and protects the street children of Cambodia. Can help their work by sponsoring.

www.members.aol.com/cambodia/index.htm Good site with links to interesting background information sites but rather out of date.

www.oanda.com/converter/classic Gives the daily exchange rate for the riel and other worldwide currencies.

www.thehungersite.com By clicking on a donate button two cups of food are donated free of charge to a developing country. The food is distributed by the United Nations World Food Programme and is paid for by the site's sponsors. The Hunger Site was founded in 1999 to use the internet in a creative way.

www.fco.gov.uk/travel The UK Foreign Office site to check for travel advice on Cambodia. For obvious reasons the information there, based on advice from the British Embassy in Cambodia, is understandably cautious. Fellow travellers are usually the best source of up-to-date information.

MEASUREMENTS AND CONVERSIONS

To convert	Multiply by
Inches to centimetres	2.54
Centimetres to inches	0.3937
Feet to metres	0.3048
Metres to feet	3.281
Yards to metres	0.9144
Metres to yards	1.094
Miles to kilometres	1.609
Kilometres to miles	0.6214
Acres to hectares	0.4047
Hectares to acres	2.471
Imperial gallons to litres	4.546
Litres to imperial gallons	0.22
US gallons to litres	3.785
Litres to US gallons	0.264
Ounces to grams	28.35
Grams to ounces	0.03527
Pounds to grams	453.6
Grams to pounds	0.002205
Pounds to kilograms	0.4536
Kilograms to pounds	2.205
British tons to kilograms	1016.0
Kilograms to British tons	0.0009812
US tons to kilograms	907.0
Kilograms to US tons	0.000907

5 imperial gallons are equal to 6 US gallons
A British ton is 2,240 lbs. A US ton is 2,000 lbs.

Temperature conversion table
The bold figures in the central columns can be read as either centigrade or fahrenheit.

°C		°F	°C		°F
−18	0	32	10	50	122
−15	5	41	13	55	131
−12	10	50	16	60	140
−9	15	59	18	65	149
−7	20	68	21	70	158
−4	25	77	24	75	167
−1	30	86	27	80	176
2	35	95	32	90	194
4	40	104	38	100	212
7	45	113	40	104	219

A stone effigy of Boddhisattva, AngkorThom

Index